Kant and Ph of Science Today

ROYAL INSTITUTE OF PHILOSOPHY SUPPLEMENT: 63

EDITED BY

Michela Massimi

CAMBRIDGE
UNIVERSITY PRESS

PUBLISHED BY THE PRESS SYNDICATE OF THE UNIVERSITY OF CAMBRIDGE
The Pitt Building, Trumpington Street, Cambridge, CB2 1RP,
United Kingdom

CAMBRIDGE UNIVERSITY PRESS
The Edinburgh Building, Cambridge CB2 8RU, United Kingdom
32 Avenue of the Americas, New York, NY 10013–2473, USA
477 Williamstown Road, Port Melbourne, VIC 3207, Australia
Ruiz de Alarcón 13, 28014 Madrid, Spain
Dock House, The Waterfront, Cape Town 8001, South Africa

Printed in the United Kingdom at the University Press, Cambridge
Typeset by Techset Composition Ltd, Salisbury, UK

A catalogue record for this book is available from the British Library

Library of Congress Cataloguing-in-Publication Data applied for

ISBN 978-0-521-73544-5
ISSN 1358-2461

Contents

Preface

This volume contains the proceedings of the Royal Institute of Philosophy Annual Conference *Kant and Philosophy of Science Today*, hosted and organised by the Dept. of Science and Technology Studies, University College London, 2–3 July 2007. The aim of the conference was to explore the far-reaching Kantian legacy in modern debates in philosophy of science. This is an area that has attracted increasing attention in the past two decades, and both the contributors and the articles in this volume testify to the presence of Kantian themes across a significant array of topics: scientific realism and antirealism; pragmatism; unification in physics; symmetries and invariance principles; and the foundations of mathematics. Most articles combine philosophical discussions with historical perspectives about the Kantian legacy in modern physics and mathematics (from Poincaré to Einstein; from Hilbert to Wigner; from Frege to Brouwer).

I would like to thank all the contributors to the volume for their lectures and articles. I am very grateful to my colleagues Hasok Chang and Marcus Giaquinto for sharing my Kantian interests and co-organising the conference. Special thanks are due to Anthony O'Hear and Steve Miller for their endorsement of the conference from the very start. Finally, I would like to acknowledge the generous support of the Royal Institute of Philosophy; the British Academy; the British Society for Philosophy of Science; the Institute of Philosophy, School of Advanced Studies; and the Mathematical and Physical Sciences (MAPS) Faculty at UCL, for having made this event possible.

Michela Massimi

List of Contributors

Michela Massimi, University College London

Margaret Morrison, University of Toronto

Thomas Ryckman, Stanford University

Roberto Torretti, University of Puerto Rico

Michael Friedman, Stanford University

Hasok Chang, University College London

Daniel Sutherland, University of Illinois at Chicago

Carl Posy, The Hebrew University of Jerusalem

Why There are No Ready-Made Phenomena: What Philosophers of Science Should Learn From Kant

MICHELA MASSIMI

1. Introduction: the problem of knowledge between scientific realism and constructive empiricism

The debate on scientific realism has raged among philosophers of science for decades. The scientific realist's claim that science aims to give us a literally *true* description of the way things are, has come under severe scrutiny and attack by Bas van Fraassen's constructive empiricism. All science aims at is to save the observable phenomena, according to van Fraassen. Scientific realists have faced since a main sceptical challenge: the burden is on them to prove that the entities postulated by our scientific theories are real and that science is still in the 'truth' business.

But how do we know that the entities, their properties and relations as described by our best scientific theories truly correspond to the way things are in nature? How is it possible to bridge the gap between what we *believe* there is (to the best of our scientific knowledge) and what there *is*? Let us call this the *problem of knowledge*. It is not a new problem, not one specifically concerning current debates in philosophy of science: it is indeed one of the oldest problems in the history of philosophy. I believe that this problem is the source of the ongoing controversy between scientific realists and constructive

I am very grateful to Mark Sprevak, Peter Lipton, Hasok Chang, Marcus Giaquinto, Bas van Fraassen, Eckart Förster for reading earlier drafts of this paper and for very helpful comments and suggestions. I owe a very special thank to both Roberto Torretti and Michael Friedman: I cannot detail the number of scholarly suggestions and comments they have both contributed. I have also benefited from discussions with Graciela De Pierris on some key aspects of this paper. Many thanks to John Norton, Don Howard, Ernan McMullin, John Worrall, and to the audiences of the Kant conference (UCL), BSPS seminar series 2007–8, and & HPS1 (Pittsburgh), where earlier versions of this paper were presented, for most thought-provoking comments and reactions.

doi:10.1017/S1358246108000027

Michela Massimi

empiricists today, who in different ways are trying to give answers to it.

Traditional realist answers to the problem of knowledge via the success of science have been challenged. Bas van Fraassen has reformulated the realist 'no miracle' argument as an argument for the survival of empirically adequate (as opposed to true) theories. Pessimistic meta-induction has questioned the alleged success of science. Underdetermination of theory by evidence has challenged the view that we may have objectively good reasons for believing in one theory over another. The quest for explanation as a royal road to truth has also been played down as unnecessary.

The antirealist's answer to the problem of knowledge, on the other hand, is not itself exempt from difficulties. Bas van Fraassen's solution to the problem of knowledge consists in confining it: science does not aim at bridging the gap between what we believe there is and what there is, *tout court*. We can only bridge this gap as far as observable phenomena are concerned. If a theory 'saves the observable phenomena' (i.e., if it is empirically adequate), then what it says about observable things and events in the world is true. But if a theory goes beyond the observable phenomena and involves unobservable entities, then we can no longer know that what the theory says about unobservable things and events in the world is true, and we should 'suspend' belief. The main problem for constructive empiricists—as their opponents have noted—is that there seems to be a clear gap between the sort of phenomena observable-to-us *qua* human beings with inherent perceptual limitations, and the far richer variety of phenomena scientists deal with in practice. No wonder, most of the debate surrounding van Fraassen's view has concentrated on the observable/unobservable distinction, trying to show how this distinction has less epistemological relevance than van Fraassen attaches to it, and that the limits of what we can know cannot be identified with our rough-and-ready perceptual limits.

It is not my aim in this paper to review this philosophical literature or to enter into the details of the various arguments and counterarguments offered on both sides. Instead, I want to draw attention to the fact that we have reached an intellectual stand-off: either we set great expectations for scientific knowledge, which are however vulnerable to antirealist's objections; or we confine our scientific expectations to observable phenomena at the cost of leaving behind a remarkable class of scientific practices. Both options seem to face some serious difficulties. I believe that one of the main causes (although arguably not the only one) for this intellectual stand-off can be traced back to

Why There are No Ready-Made Phenomena

a widespread and influential conception of phenomena, around which in my view most of the current debate seems to have revolved.

According to this widespread conception, phenomena are what 'appear' to us, and to our perceptual apparatus. It seems to me that—with some important distinctions, as clarified in footnotes 1 and 2—both scientific realists and constructive empiricists surreptitiously tend to subscribe to the view that phenomena are empirical manifestations (from the Greek *phainómena*) of what there is, while of course disagreeing about epistemic commitments. For scientific realists, science aims at inferring the hypothesis that best *explains* the phenomena, and hence that it is more likely to be true about what there is in nature.[1] For constructive empiricists, on the other hand, science aims at introducing hypotheses that do not claim to be true about what there is or the way things are in nature, but that can simply *save* the observable phenomena.[2]

---

[1]   The first important distinction to make is that not all scientific realists would subscribe to this view of phenomena. Some scientific realists, for instance, have a more robust and sophisticated conception of phenomena than mere empirical manifestations of what there is. For instance, Bogen and Woodward (1988) have famously introduced the distinction between data and phenomena and argued that while data must be observable records of occurrences, phenomena need not be empirically accessible in any relevant sense. The main worry for scientific realists is to show how our *inferential* practices can bridge the gap between the two: if we are justified in believing in unobservable phenomena on the basis of reliable data, we can similarly be justified in believing in unobservable entities. Although Bogen and Woodward's analysis is arguably unorthodox in the realist panorama, it is nonetheless worth a specific mention. In Massimi (2007), I latched onto Bogen and Woodward's distinction between data and phenomena and expanded on it by showing how unobservable phenomena may appear in data models. However, the aim of my paper was not to defend traditional scientific realism. I wanted to defend instead a mild form of Kantianism, according to which we 'construct' phenomena in data models in such a way that the gap between the phenomena and the underlying entities is not as wide as both empiricists and realists have typically portrayed it.

[2]   Another important distinction is in order here. Van Fraassen would not agree with my characterization of phenomena as empirical manifestations of what there is, and would maintain that phenomena are to all intents and purposes 'objects', observable and perceivable 'objects' (but not copies, or images, or empirical manifestations of objects). For instance, van Fraassen would argue that the phenomenon is the tree in front of my window, not the image of the tree reflected in a nearby pond: 'If you see a reflection of a tree in the water, you can also look at the tree and gather information about the geometric relations between the tree, the reflection, and your vantage

Michela Massimi

My original motivation for this paper was a sense of dissatisfaction with this widespread conception of phenomena. I believe that this picture is inadequate to capture the great variety of phenomena that scientists deal with: from particle physics to astrophysics, from geophysics to condensed matter physics, the phenomena scientists deal with are surely not just empirical manifestations of what there is.

---

point. The invariances in those relations are precisely what warrant the assertion that the reflection is a picture of the tree. (...) But now you are postulating that these relations hold, rather than gathering information about whether that is so' (2001), p. 160 (see on this point also van Fraassen 2008; I am very grateful to Carlo Gabbani for this quotation in his comments to Massimi (2007) at the seminar in Florence). Yet I think that there is some lingering ambiguity in this apparently very simple and intuitive characterization of phenomena. How can we say that we can look at the tree, and also look at the reflection of the tree in the water, without 'postulating that these relations hold'? Or, how can we say that we have the image of an amoeba in a microscope, but we should not really ask whether this is the image, or empirical manifestation of 'an amoeba'? Is not it tantamount to saying that we *do* have after all empirical manifestations of *things*—be they observable things, like a tree, or unobservable ones, like an amoeba—but that from an empirical point of view we should not ask *what* they are 'empirical manifestations' of? And why is the reflection of the tree in the water, or for that matter on my retina, any different from the reflection of the amoeba (through the microscope) on my retina? Once we start using these examples, I am not sure that we can consistently speak of phenomena as rough-and-ready observable/perceivable 'objects', as opposed to *empirical manifestations* of objects. But there is also another important distinction to be made. Constructive empiricists of course acknowledge that sometimes phenomena may manifest themselves in data models and hence that there may be an element of construction in the phenomena that science saves (see on this point the exchange between Teller (2001) and van Fraassen (2001)). However, constructive empiricists would maintain that despite this, we can still draw a distinction between observable phenomena, on the one hand, and whatever goes beyond the observable phenomena, on the other hand. As it will become clear later in this paper, the alternative Kantian conception of phenomena that I am going to propose, insofar as it stresses the non-ready made nature of phenomena, has the effect of blurring that very same distinction dear to constructive empiricists and realists alike. In other words, despite the fact that Kantians and constructive empiricists may share the idea that sometimes phenomena are something that we make (rather than ready-made in nature), nevertheless they draw very different epistemological lessons about what we should believe and how to bridge the gap between what we believe there is and what there is (which is precisely what the problem of knowledge is all about).

Why There are No Ready-Made Phenomena

The purpose of this paper is to show that phenomena are not ready-made for a scientific theory to either save them or give a literally true story of them. Hence, we need to redefine the very same philosophical conception of what a phenomenon is so as to make it more pertinent to scientific practice.

The alternative philosophical conception of phenomena that I am about to explore goes back to Immanuel Kant. As we shall see in section 2, from a Kantian point of view phenomena are *not* empirical manifestations of what there is. Kant developed a sophisticated conception of phenomena, which—in my opinion—does better justice to the complexity of phenomena we encounter in scientific practice while at the same time can help us overcome the current stand-off in the debate between scientific realism and constructive empiricism. But, first, let me say something about how the view of ready-made phenomena could become so widespread to still influence modern debates in philosophy of science.

If we want to understand the philosophical origins of this view of phenomena as empirical manifestations of what there is as well as the very same origins of van Fraassen's view on 'saving the phenomena', we have to go back to the empiricist tradition behind it. And no one, in my opinion, has better described those philosophical origins than the French philosopher and physicist Pierre Duhem in a short but illuminating series of historical essays called *To Save the Phenomena*. Duhem traced the philosophical tradition of saving the phenomena back to Plato. Plato introduced what Duhem calls the *method of the astronomer*, which influenced the development of astronomy for many centuries: the astronomer should be fully satisfied when the hypotheses he has introduced succeed in saving the phenomena. However, as ancient astronomers such as Hipparchus and Ptolemy were well aware of, different hypotheses may all render the same phenomena equally well: indeed we can use epicycles or eccentric circles to save the same phenomena, so that it is impossible for astronomy to discover the true hypothesis, the one that presumably corresponds to the nature of things. Saving the phenomena was the principal aim of astronomy, according to Duhem, who saw it as a natural consequence of Platonism and of the divide it imposed between heavenly things and earthly things, as is well captured in Proclus's commentary on Plato's *Timaeus*.[3] Duhem concludes with an insightful note that is worth quoting:

[3] 'Among these hypotheses there are some which save the phenomena by means of epicycles, others which do so by means of eccentrics, still others which save the phenomena by means of counterturning spheres

5

Astronomy cannot grasp the essence of heavenly things. It merely gives us an *image* of them. And even this image is far from exact: it merely comes close. Astronomy rests with 'the nearly so'. The geometric contrivances we use to save the phenomena are neither true nor likely. They are purely conceptual, and any effort to reify them must engender contradictions. (. . .) Very different hypotheses may yield identical conclusions, one saving the appearances as well as the other. Nor should we be surprised that astronomy has this character: it shows us that man's knowledge is limited and relative, that human science cannot vie with divine science. (. . .) In more than one respect, Proclus' doctrine can be likened to positivism. In the study of nature *it separates, as does positivism, the objects accessible to human knowledge from those that are essentially unknowable to man.* But the line of demarcation is not the same for Proclus as it is for John Stuart Mill. (. . .) By extending to all bodies what Proclus had reserved for the stars, by declaring that only the phenomenal effects of any material are accessible to human knowledge whereas the inner nature of this material eludes our understanding, modern positivism came into being.[4]

Whether or not Duhem gives in this passage a philosophically accurate depiction of Platonism is of course questionable, but for the purpose of this paper we should leave this question aside. What matters for the purpose of this paper is the fact that Duhem gives us a historical reconstruction of how the modern empiricist/positivist idea that our knowledge is confined to the 'phenomenal effects of any material' derives from the old adage of 'saving the phenomena' that for centuries, in his view, Platonism recommended as the only feasible aim of astronomy. Duhem places himself within this philosophical tradition. Indeed, after a detailed reconstruction of how this idea passed on from Medieval Christian Scholasticism to Osiander's Preface to Copernicus' *De revolutionibus*, Duhem takes a look at the turning point marked by Galileo's new sciences. According to Duhem, it is only with Galileo that the philosophical trend of 'saving the phenomena' stopped and

---

devoid of planets. Surely, the gods' judgment is more certain. But as for us, we must be satisfied to "come close" to those things, for we are men, who speak according to what is likely, and whose lectures resemble fables' Proclus *In Platonis Timaeum commentaria.* Quotation from Duhem (1908), English translation (1969), p. 21.

[4]   Duhem (1908), English translation (1969), pp. 21–2. Emphasis added.

reversed. Galileo wanted the foundations of astronomy to conform to reality, he believed that the Copernican system was not just a system of 'mere contrivances for the calculation of astronomical tables but propositions that conform to the nature of things. He wanted them established on the ground of physics. (...) and since he did not think that a truth could contradict Scripture (whose divine inspiration he recognised), he was bound to attempt to reconcile his assertions with biblical texts'.[5] Galileo's attempt to reconcile heavenly things with earthly ones, and to raise the status of astronomy from a system of mere contrivances to a system of physical truths cost him a condemnation by the Inquisition. Duhem concludes with a pessimistic note: 'Despite Kepler and Galileo, we believe today, with Osiander and Bellarmini, that the hypotheses of physics are mere mathematical contrivances devised for the purpose of saving the phenomena. But thanks to Kepler and Galileo, we now require that they save *all the phenomena* of the inanimate universe *together*'.[6]

Are we really the heirs of Bellarmini, rather than of Galileo? Surely, there is a kernel of truth in Duhem's surprising remark. Current philosophers of science defending the view of saving the phenomena are indeed on the same conceptual path that from Duhem's take on Platonism arrives at Osiander, Bellarmini, and modern empiricism in claiming that there are some intrinsic limitations to human knowledge and that we should refrain from taking our physical hypotheses as truths about nature. They believe that a gap inevitably remains between what we *believe* there is and what there *is* (which is precisely what the problem of knowledge is about). Consider, for instance, van Fraassen's analysis of Galileo's mathematization of nature, in a recent article devoted to the philosophical origins of structuralism:

> Perhaps, Galileo's contemporaries might have said, the scientific image represents only some aspects of the real and manifest world, leaving many other real aspects out of account. (...) We are reminded here of Cardinal Bellarmini's advice to Galileo of how to view the Copernican system. One imagines that Bellarmini would wish Galileo to think no better of his 'new sciences' in general. Galileo himself, and the mechanical philosophers generally [Descartes's followers] were more radical. They rejected any such moderate structuralism in favour of *reification* of their world image. They said, *No, THIS* is all there is to it. (...) Galileo's discipline was to determine beforehand a small set

5   *Ibid.*, p. 105.
6   *Ibid.*, p. 117.

of properties and restrict scientific descriptions to those. Not coincidentally, of course, they were the properties representable by geometry and arithmetic: number, size, shape...(...) Modern science began with Galileo's and Descartes' evangelical reification of the scientific image of the world.[7]

In the light of these remarks, we can now see how Galileo's mathematization of nature is historically at the crossroad of two rival philosophical traditions about the aims of science. For scientific realists, Galileo was one of the fathers of the scientific revolution by fighting for the view that science gives us a true story about nature. For Duhem and van Fraassen, on the other hand, Galileo marks the end of the tradition of saving the phenomena and the beginning of the 'evangelical reification of the scientific image', in van Fraassen's words.

In this paper, I want to go back to Galileo, and take Galileo's mathematization of nature as a springboard for illustrating a Kantian answer to the problem of knowledge, alternative to both scientific realism and constructive empiricism. This Kantian answer is based on a new conception of phenomena that goes against the widespread view of phenomena sketched above. Most importantly, the Kantian conception of phenomena is strictly intertwined with Galileo's mathematization of nature, as I shall discuss at length in this paper. Kant's new conception of phenomena is indeed patterned upon Galileo's in believing that the scientific investigation of nature can reveal its inner lawfulness, and therefore that the gap between what we *believe* there is and what there *is*, is not as big as Bellarmine and his followers claimed. Insofar as it goes back to Galileo, Kant's conception of phenomena is old. But, at the same time, there is a revolutionary new element in it. Kant believed that phenomena are not ready-made in nature: 'experience cannot be received as a representation which comes to us, but must be made'.[8] This fragment taken from Kant's 'Transition from the Metaphysical Foundations of Natural Science to Physics', of which we have to talk more in this paper, expresses precisely this revolutionary new idea that phenomena are something that—in a way that has to be clarified in this paper—we *make*, rather than something that comes to us as ready-made in nature. Hence the title of my paper.[9] It is now time to spell out the slogan.

[7] Van Fraassen (2006), pp. 281, 287.

[8] Kant (1936, 1938), English translation (1993), 22: 322.

[9] The adjective 'ready-made' has been intentionally chosen to echo Goodman (1978) and Putnam (1982). This paper is indeed Goodmanian–Putnamian in spirit, in urging to abandon traditional realist views in

2. Kant's solution to the problem of knowledge: a new conception of phenomena

The Kantian solution to the problem of knowledge can be found in Kant's Copernican turn, according to which 'our representation of things as they are given to us does not conform to these things as they are in themselves but rather these objects as appearances conform to our way of representing'.[10] Traditionally, the problem of knowledge has been set in the following terms: how can our representations ever conform to things as they are in nature? In other words, how can we bridge the gap between what we believe there is (to the best of our scientific knowledge) and what there is? In terms of the ongoing debate in philosophy of science, how can we bridge the gap between the scientific hypotheses that we form about nature and nature itself? Do these hypotheses give us a true story about the way things are in nature, or do they simply save the observable phenomena? Kant's Copernican revolution turned this traditional way of posing the problem of knowledge topsy-turvy. Kant realised that the above questions are ill-posed, and as such bound to remain unanswered (despite strenuous and ongoing attempts to try to explain how science can represent nature). According to Kant, we should instead ask a different type of question: namely, how objects as they appear to us (as *appearances*) can conform to *our way of representing* (and not the other way around). It is only by turning topsy-turvy the traditional way of posing the problem of knowledge that knowledge ceases to be a problem. We are no longer faced with the aforementioned dilemma of either being unable to answer the problem (with scientific realists) or confining it at the cost of sacrificing scientific practice (with constructive empiricists). Kant's solution to the problem of knowledge is a truly revolutionary one, and, as with all revolutionary solutions, it side-steps the traditional terms of the debate altogether.

We should immediately avoid a possible misunderstanding at this point. When Kant speaks of appearances that have to conform to our way of representing, 'appearances' should not be confused with sense data, i.e. with things as they *appear to our senses* as phenomenalism would have it. For Kant, appearances are not perceptual states;

---

favour of a Kantian one (although I am not going to subscribe to either Goodman's 'worldmaking' view or Putnam's 'internal realist' one).

[10]   Kant (1781, 1787). English translation (1997), Preface to the second edition, Bxx.

Michela Massimi

rather, the possibility of perception is defined in terms of conformity to a set of a priori conditions of sensibility, such as space and time. What is then given to us as appearances, for Kant, are *spatiotemporal objects* as given to the mind in intuition. It is at this point that we have to mark an important distinction between appearances and phenomena that is pivotal to the rest of my analysis.

At the outset of the Transcendental Aesthetic Kant defined an appearance as 'the undetermined object of an empirical intuition' (A20/B34). Appearance refers then to an object as merely given in sensibility and conceptually still 'undetermined', not brought yet under the categories of the faculty of understanding. A phenomenon, on the other hand, is a *conceptually determined appearance*, namely an appearance that has been brought under the categories of the understanding. Kant gives a detailed analysis of this distinction in the Third Chapter of the Analytic of Principles 'On the ground of the distinction of all objects in general into phenomena and noumena', where he speaks of the 'empirical use of a concept', which consists in its being related 'to **appearances**, i.e. objects of a **possible experience**' (B298/A239). The concepts of the faculty of understanding have to be related to 'empirical intuitions, i.e., to data for possible experience. Without this they have no objective validity at all'. For instance, in mathematics, concepts such as space has three dimensions or between two points there can be only one straight line, although a priori, 'would still not signify anything at all if we could not always exhibit their significance in appearances', by which Kant means the construction of a figure 'which is an appearance present to the senses (even though brought about a priori)' (B299/A240). That is why he concludes that the pure concepts of the understanding should always be of empirical use, in the specific sense that they must be related to empirical intuitions. And he clarifies that 'appearances, to the extent that as objects they are thought in accordance with the unity of the categories, are called phenomena' (A249). Thus, while appearances are the spatiotemporal objects of empirical intuitions, the *data for possible experience*, phenomena are appearances brought under the concepts of the faculty of understanding so as to make experience finally possible:

> If, therefore, we say: The senses represent objects to us **as they appear**, but the understanding, **as they are**, then the latter is not to be taken in a transcendental but in a merely empirical way, signifying, namely, how they must be represented as objects of experience, in the thoroughgoing connection of appearances, and not how they might be outside of the relation

10

to possible experience and consequently to sense in general, thus as objects of pure understanding. For this will always remain unknown to us. (. . . .) With us **understanding** and **sensibility** can determine an object **only in combination**. If we separate them, then we have intuitions without concepts, or concepts without intuitions, but in either case representations that we cannot relate to any determinate object. (A258/B314)

Going then back to the Copernican turn and to the problem of knowledge, we have now found the answer in the revolutionary conception of phenomena that Kant proposes. From a Kantian perspective, the problem of knowledge disappears. We gain scientific knowledge of nature by subsuming appearances (i.e. spatiotemporal objects as given to our mind in empirical intuition) under a priori concepts of the understanding (via schemata). Our scientific knowledge of nature is then confined to phenomena intended as *objects of experience*, i.e. as *conceptually determined appearances*. Phenomena are not empirical manifestations of what there is. Kant's solution to the problem of knowledge can be found in the revolutionary new conception of phenomena that he put forward in opposition to both the empiricist and realist tradition. And in the Preface to the second edition of the *Critique of Pure Reason* (1787), as a paradigmatic example of his Copernican turn, Kant chose Galileo (together with Torricelli and Stahl), and his famous experiment with the inclined plane:

When Galileo rolled balls of a weight chosen by himself down an inclined plane, (. . .) a light dawned on all those who study nature. They comprehended that reason has insight only into what it itself produces according to its own design; that it must take the lead with principles for its judgements according to constant laws and compel nature to answer its questions, rather than letting nature guide its movements by keeping reason, as it were, in leading-strings; for otherwise accidental observations (. . .) can never connect up into a necessary law, which is yet what reason seeks and requires. Reason, in order to be taught by nature, must approach nature with its **principles** in one hand, (. . .) and, in the other hand, the **experiments** thought out in accordance with these principles—yet in order to be instructed by nature not like a pupil, who has recited to him whatever the teacher wants to say, but like an appointed judge who compels witnesses to answer the questions he puts to them. (. . .) This is how natural science was first brought to the secure course of a science after groping about for so many centuries. (B xiii–xiv, emphases added)

Michela Massimi

Galileo is here portrayed as the scientist who paradigmatically accomplished the revolutionary shift that Kant was urging: namely, the shift from the deeply instilled view that our scientific knowledge proceeds from nature itself (i.e. that what we *believe* there is proceeds from what there *is*, which is the very source of the problem of knowledge) to the opposite revolutionary Kantian view, according to which 'we can cognize of things a priori only what we ourselves have put into them'.[11] The certainty and secure foundation achieved by natural science from the time of Galileo onwards is—to Kant's eyes—the paradigmatic expression of this shift. Reason must approach nature with its *principles* on the one hand, and with *experiments* thought out in accordance with these principles, on the other hand. We should therefore take a look at Kant's new conception of phenomena in close connection with his position on Galileo's mathematization of nature as outlined in the Preface.

3. Kant on Galileo's mathematization of nature: why there are no ready-made phenomena

3.1. From the Metaphysical Foundations of Natural Science *to the 'Transition from the Metaphysical Foundations of Natural Science to Physics': developing a new conception of phenomena*

In what follows, I want to clarify the particular stance Kant took on Galileo against the empiricist tradition exemplified by Duhem's and van Fraassen's aforementioned remarks. Kant too, like Duhem and van Fraassen, saw in Galileo a turning-point in the history of science, but for very different reasons. By asking how pure natural science is possible, Kant was trying to justify why we *can* have and indeed *do* have a new science of nature from the time of Galileo onwards, against the empiricist tradition that takes nature as a bunch of phenomena to be saved by introducing hypotheses that do not claim to be true. It is from this particular perspective—I want to suggest—that we can read the *Metaphysical Foundations of Natural Science* (1786, henceforth abbreviated as MAN) and, more in general, Kant's philosophical enterprise from MAN until his last incomplete work 'Transition from the Metaphysical Foundations of Natural Science to Physics' published in the *Opus postumum*. I shall in particular take a look at the Xth/XIth fascicles of the *Opus postumum* (presumably written between August 1799 and

[11]   *Ibid.*, Bxviii.

April 1800, almost ten years after the third critique and four years before Kant's death).[12] Indeed, it is in this last and incomplete work, which in Kant's intentions was meant to fill a gap that he felt was still open in his critical philosophy after the *Critique of Judgment*, that we find some interesting clues about Kant's new conception of phenomena and his view on Galileo's mathematization of nature.

In the *Metaphysical Foundations of Natural Science*, in the chapter called 'Metaphysical Foundations of Dynamics', Kant had defined the empirical concept of matter according to the category of quality as the *movable* that fills a space through a *particular moving force*. More precisely, he had introduced *attractive and repulsive forces* as two fundamental moving forces, through which matter can fill a space by either causing other bodies to approach it or to be removed from it. Kant derived these two fundamental moving forces a priori from two basic properties of matter, namely its ability to resist penetration (impenetrability) and, at the same time, its ability to strive to enlarge the space that it fills so as to counteract the opposite tendency expressed by the repulsive force.

In the 'Transition', almost fourteen years after the *Metaphysical Foundations*, Kant claimed that in order to complete the transition from the metaphysical foundations of natural science to physics, it was not enough to establish a priori attraction and repulsion as two fundamental moving forces in nature. It was not enough because there remains a gap between postulating these two fundamental moving forces in nature from a metaphysical point of view, on the one hand, and accounting for the more specific empirical properties of matter that the chemical revolution was discovering at the end of eighteenth century, on the other hand:[13]

[12] These fascicles are published under the title 'How is physics possible? How is the transition to physics possible?' (Ak 22: 282–452) in the English translation of the *Opus postumum* by Eckart Förster and Michael Rosen (1993). All citations are taken from this English translation.

[13] Friedman (1992a), chapter 5, has illuminatingly pointed out how Lavoiser's chemical revolution, and the recent discoveries of pneumatic chemistry underlie and prompted the 'Transition', whose specific aim was to bridge the gap between the *Metaphysical Foundations* on the one hand, and the vast realm of empirical forces recently discovered, on the other hand (e.g. forces responsible for the solidification, liquefaction, elasticity, and cohesion of objects, which could not be accounted for within the Newtonian paradigm of MAN). On this specific issue, see also Pecere (2006).

Michela Massimi

The transition to physics cannot lie in the metaphysical foundations (attractions and repulsion, etc). For these furnish no specifically determined, empirical properties, and one can imagine no specific forces of which one could know whether they exist in nature, or whether their existence be demonstrable; rather, they can only be feigned to explain phenomena empirically or hypothetically, in a certain respect (22:282).

The increasing number of empirical properties of matter revealed by the chemical revolution at the end of eighteenth century was simply too rich to be encompassed by the two fundamental forces of attraction and repulsion, established a priori in MAN. Hence the necessity to bridge the gap between the all-encompassing metaphysical framework canvassed in the *Metaphysical Foundations*, on the one hand, and the multifarious range of more specific empirical properties of matter that natural scientists were discovering, on the other hand. This is the specific task that Kant aimed to accomplish with the 'Transition to Physics', where by physics Kant meant 'the systematic investigation of nature as to empirically given forces of matter, insofar as they are combined among one another in one system' (22: 298). The main concern of the 'Transition' was then to justify and ground a *system of empirically given forces* in nature. The problem is that in nature we may observe objects moving in space and time, changing physical state (from solid to liquid to gaseous) or displaying some properties (e.g. being elastic). But these are only appearances [Erscheinungen]. Only when we introduce moving forces as the underlying *causes* that make the objects move in space, or change their physical state, or displaying some physical or chemical properties, do we have a conceptually determined appearance or *phenomenon* as the proper object of scientific knowledge.

I think this is the crucial, distinctively new feature that Kant introduced in the conception of phenomena: a physical phenomenon—intended as a conceptually determined appearance—has built in it from the very outset the *concept of a moving force* as the *cause* of the observed appearance. It is the causal concept of a moving force that distinguishes phenomena from appearances, or better, that transforms appearances into phenomena, i.e. objects of possible experience into *objects of experience*.

Kant had already made this point very clearly in chapter 4 of MAN. In that chapter, the empirical concept of matter as the movable in space is defined according to the category of modality, and Kant's aim is to show how to transform *appearance (Erscheinung)* into *experience (Erfahrung)*; more precisely, how to transform *apparent motions* into *true motions*. According to Friedman,[14] since Kant rejected Newton's view on absolute space and time, he needed to find a way of explaining true or absolute motions without resorting to absolute space as a privileged reference frame. Kant's strategy consisted in identifying the centre of mass of our solar system as a privileged reference frame. To this purpose, he needed Newton's law of universal gravitation, responsible for the planetary motions in the solar system, as a necessary and universal feature of matter as the movable in space. Only in this way could he show how to transform apparent motions into true or absolute motions, intended now as motions with respect to the privileged reference frame of our solar system. Kant starts then from observed relative motions of satellites with respect to their primary bodies: the orbits of the moons of Jupiter, the orbits of the planets around the sun as described by Kepler's laws are all examples of apparent or relative motions that can be subsumed under the category of *possibility*. The next step consists in assuming that relative motions approximate to true motions: the reference frame defined by apparent motions is meant to approximate to the inertial reference frame, which in Newton's theory would be identified with absolute space but which Kant identified with the centre of mass of the solar system, following Friedman's interpretation. At this point Kant's second law of mechanics[15] (which is meant to encompass Newton's I and II law) can be applied. And it is on the basis of Kant's second law of mechanics—previously introduced and justified in ch. 3 of MAN—that Kant concludes that there must be an external cause for the relative accelerations of orbiting bodies. This external cause must be an impressed force, and—Friedman concludes—it follows mathematically from Kepler's laws (in particular from Kepler's first law) that this force must satisfy the inverse-square

---

[14]   Friedman (1992a), ch. 4.

[15]   Kant's second law of mechanics states that 'Every change in matter has an external cause. (Every body persists in its state of rest or motion, in the same direction, and with the same speed, if it is not compelled by an external cause to leave this state)', MAN, chapter 3, Proposition 3, *ibid.*, p. 82. This law seems to encompass both Newton's I law (i.e. a body persists in its state of rest or uniform motion) and Newton's II law ($F = ma$) in requiring an impressed force F as the *cause* of any change of uniform motion into accelerated motion. But this is in fact questionable because it would require to show that Kant's second law entails Newton's second law; and, this is not evident, given Kant's vague assertion about the existence of an external cause of change of motion (I thank Roberto Torretti for raising this point).

Michela Massimi

law. In this way, the true or absolute motions (inverse-square accelerations) are subsumed under the modal category of *actuality*. Without going any further into this discussion, the point I want to stress is that following Friedman's reading here, already in MAN Kant delineates a procedure to transform appearances into phenomena, or better to transform *appearance* (*Erscheinung*) into *experience* (*Erfahrung*). Most importantly, this procedure hinges on the concept of cause embodied in Kant's second law of mechanics and in its transcendental counterpart, namely the second analogy of experience.

If this analysis is correct, we can begin to catch a glimpse of the radically new conception of phenomena that Kant was introducing. Physical phenomena as conceptually determined appearances have already built in them the concept of, say, a *dynamic cause* responsible for the observed appearances and their kinematical (spatiotemporal) properties. But how do we know that we are not feigning gravitational attraction as a hypothesis to save appearances? How could Kant claim to know that the moving forces, as the dynamic causes of the observed appearances, are *real*?

In order to answer the above questions, the top-down approach typical of the *Metaphysical Foundations of Natural Science*—whereby the empirical concept of matter is schematized according to the four transcendental categories of quantity, quality, relation and modality, and ascribed a priori a series of fundamental properties (including attraction and repulsion)—cannot be of much help. And Kant's dissatisfaction with this top-down approach is testified by his search for an alternative, complementary approach from the time of the *Critique of Judgment* to the 'Transition' of the *Opus postumum*. We need a bottom-up approach that starts from appearances and empirically given forces, in order to show that those forces are not feigned to save appearances, i.e. they are not introduced as hypotheses to fit empirical regularities. In addition, we need to show that the increasing number of empirically given forces do not just form an aggregate, but a system instead. If physics is defined as 'the systematic investigation of nature as to empirically given forces of matter, insofar as they are combined among one another in one system', the key for the 'Transition' project was to show *how* such a system is possible.

Thus, I take that the crucial question Kant was trying to answer in the 'Transition' was the same question that concerns philosophers of science today: how do we know that we are not just and simply feigning hypotheses to save phenomena (in Duhem's and van Fraassen's sense)? Moreover, how do we know that our science does not reduce to a mere aggregate of empirical regularities, and that there is in fact some lawfulness in the empirical regularities we see in nature? In other words, how do we know that

1)   the alleged moving forces are the *true causes* of appearances;
2)   they form a *system* conferring lawfulness to what would otherwise be only an aggregate of empirical regularities?

In the next section 3.2, I take a look at Kant's answer to question 1). We shall see in section 3.3 his reply to question 2), and how it is related to his answer to 1). Once we clarify Kant's answer to point 1), we can get a better understanding of his radically new conception of phenomena, and why he believed that there are no ready-made phenomena in nature.

3.2. How do we know that the alleged moving forces are the true causes *of appearances? The Galileo case*

I want to suggest that Kant's reply to question 1) can be found in the passage of the Preface on Galileo that I quoted above, where Galileo is presented as someone that interrogated nature 'through principles of reason, on the one hand, and through experiments thought out in accordance with these principles, on the other hand' (Bxiv). Let us take a look at these two aspects of Galileo's case, starting with the role of observation and experiment.

Galileo's experiment with the inclined plane is instructive to illustrate Kant's view of phenomena as not ready-made in nature, and no wonder Kant mentioned it not only in the Preface to the second edition of the first *Critique* but also in the *Opus postumum*. Galileo started indeed with appearances, namely with observed relative motions of heavy bodies, whose kinematics he carefully studied. For the sake of experience, he inserted something a priori into these appearances: namely he took those relative motions as approximating to uniformly accelerated motions due to a moving force. Finally, with the experiment of the inclined plane, he extracted and demonstrated what he had previously inserted into appearances for the sake of possible experience, namely uniform acceleration due to a force. Of course, Galileo's focus was kinematics, not dynamics: he did not identify the moving force *causally* responsible for uniformly accelerated motions with gravitational attraction. This was Newton's achievement, building up on Galileo's kinematical studies. Galileo simply inferred a priori to a force causally responsible for the uniformly accelerated motion of free-falling bodies. It was only later with Newton that the force was identified and a full dynamical analysis given. But the very idea of a moving force as the *true cause* ('vera causa', in Galileo's language) of uniformly accelerated motion is already in Galileo's kinematics and in his opposition to Aristotelian physics. To Kant's eyes, Galileo paved the way to Newton by anticipating a concept of moving force that Newton filled in with gravitational attraction:

> The laws of motion were sufficiently established by Kepler's three analogies. They were entirely mechanical. Huygens knew also of composite yet derivative motion. . . .But no matter how close they both [came to postulating universal gravitation]–for Galileo had long before that given the law of the gravity of falling bodies at heights which led to an approximately equal moment in their fall—all that which had been achieved *remained empiricism in the doctrine of motion,* and there was as yet no universal principle properly so-called, that is, a *concept of reason,* from which it would be possible to infer a priori to a law for the determination of forces, as *from a cause to its effect.* This solution was given by Newton, inasmuch as he gave the moving force the name attraction, by which he made apparent that this cause was effected by the body itself immediately, not by communication of the motion to other bodies—thus, not mechanically, but purely dynamically ('Transition' 22: 528. Emphases added).

In this important passage, Kant claims that before Newton there was only *empiricism in the doctrine of motion,* and no concept of reason yet from which one could infer a priori—*as from a cause to its effect*—to a law for the determination of forces. To Kant's eyes, this was achieved by Newton, who championed a 'metaphysical-dynamical' approach, while scientists before Newton, such as Kepler for instance (but also Huygens and Descartes) defended a 'mathematical-mechanical' approach that tried to give an explanation of nature in terms of extended matter and geometrico-mathematical motions. It is only with Newton that fundamental moving forces were introduced and a *dynamical analysis* of nature became finally available, something that Kant regarded as crucial for the advancement of science.[16]

---

[16]   Indeed, already in the General Observation to Chapter 2 of MAN, Kant had stressed the inadequacy of Cartesian physics and the superiority of the Newtonian 'dynamical explanatory scheme', not least because it avoids feigning hypotheses by contrast with the mathematical-mechanical scheme that 'gives the imagination far too much freedom to make up by fabrication for the lack of any inner knowledge of nature' Kant (1786), English translation

Of course, from a historical point of view, Kant's take on Kepler here is questionable, because in his own ways Kepler too may be said to have provided a dynamical analysis of planetary motions in terms of his mystical doctrine of the *anima motrix* of the sun.[17] However, for the purpose of our analysis, what matters is the fact that Kant locates in Newton the crucial passage from the observation of relative motions with their kinematical properties to a proper dynamical analysis of nature:

> *Motion* can be treated entirely mathematically, for it is nothing but concepts of space and time, which can be presented *a priori* in pure intuition; the understanding *makes* them. Moving forces, however, as efficient *causes* of these motions, such as are required by physics and its laws, need philosophical principles. All mathematics then brings one not the least bit nearer to philosophical knowledge unless a causal combination, such as that of attraction and repulsion of matter by its moving forces, is first brought onto the scene and postulated for the sake of appearances. As soon as the latter occurs, the transition to physics has taken place, and there can be *philosophiae naturalis principia mathematica*. This step was taken by Newton in the role of a philosopher who bring new forces onto the scene.... Once Kepler's three analogies had grounded all the mathematically determined laws of motion of the planets by sufficient observation, there yet remained the question for physics regarding the *efficient cause of this appearance;* Newton, in order to find a way out of this difficulty, built a bridge from mathematics to physics, namely the principle of an attractive force.... according to the law of the

---

(2004), p. 71. On the difference between the mathematical-mechanical scheme and the metaphysical-dynamical one, see again Friedman (1992a), pp. 180–3.

[17] Indeed Kepler called his *Astronomia nova* 'aitiologetos' (I thank Roberto Torretti for pointing this out). However, to Kant's eyes, Kepler's view fell short of introducing the *right* sort of dynamic causes, namely those that could bridge the gap between kinematics and dynamics and pave the way to a *mathematical physics* of Newton's type, those same *dynamic causes* that could led us to infer a priori to a law such as Newton's law of gravitation. In other words, according to Kant, what Kepler did not have is the notion that external force does not cause just motion but change in motion (acceleration); whereas Galileo's description of free fall as uniformly accelerated motion (under a presumably constant force) contributed decisively to Newton's discovery, as we shall see below. On the Kepler–Newton relationship as Kant portrayed it in the 'Transition', see Caygill (2005).

inverse square of the distance. He did not, thus, rest content with appearances, but brought into play a primordially moving force ('Transition', 22:516. Emphasis added)

The fundamental role that Kant assigned to moving forces, in particular to Newton's gravitational force in the 'Transition' as the *efficient cause* of *appearances*, e.g. of relative motions of planets kinematically described by Kepler as well as of relative motions of free-falling objects described by Galileo, sits squarely with the interpretive line I have been suggesting about Kant's view of phenomena as conceptually determined appearances. Let us then take a closer look at this passage from kinematics to dynamics in the Galileo–Newton case.

The experiment Kant refers to is the famous experiment of the inclined plane that Galileo discussed in the Third Day of his *Discourses and Mathematical Demonstrations concerning Two New Sciences* (henceforth abbreviated as *Two New Sciences*, 1638). Galileo's aim was to prove that Aristotelians were wrong in claiming that free-falling bodies were moving towards a natural place. Galileo starts by describing an alternative possible type of motion, called uniformly accelerated that 'starting from rest, it acquires, during equal time-intervals, equal increments of speed [temporibus aequalibus aequalia celeritatis momenta sibi superaddit]'.[18] In other words, a uniformly accelerated motion is such that the ratio between Δv (i.e. the equal increments of speed or *celeritatis momenta*) and Δt (i.e. equal time-intervals) is constant. But this is only a definition, and—as Sagredo, one of the characters of Galileo's *Two New Sciences*, points out—as with any definition, one may doubt whether this definition is verified in the kind of accelerated motion that heavy bodies in fact employ in free fall. Salviati, who in the *Two New Sciences* speaks for Galileo himself, replies

> The present does not seem to be the proper time to investigate the cause of the acceleration of natural motion concerning which various opinions have been expressed by various philosophers, some explaining it by attraction to the center ['avvicinamento al centro', i.e. getting closer to the center—note no mention of 'attraction' in the Italian original text, MM], others to repulsion between the very small parts of the body ['restar successivamente manco parti del mezo da fendersi'] while still others attribute it to a certain stress in the surrounding medium which closes in behind the falling body and drives it from one of its position to

[18]   Galileo (1638), English translation (1914), p. 162.

another. Now, all these fantasies, and others too, ought to be examined; but it is not really worth while. At the present it is the purpose of our Author merely to investigate and to demonstrate some of the properties ['passioni'] of accelerated motion *whatever the cause of this acceleration may be.*[19]

The refusal to investigate the causes of uniformly accelerated motion in the quotation above should be understood—I want to suggest—as a stance against the tradition that takes phenomena as ready-made and reduces science to introducing a series of hypotheses that can save them (i.e. the same tradition that Duhem saw exemplified in what he called the *method of the astronomer*). Galileo seems to be taking the distance from this tradition in declaring himself not interested in speculating about the causal hypotheses that can save the phenomenon of uniformly accelerated motion. Instead, he is interested in demonstrating some of the properties of accelerated motions. But how could Galileo prove that free-falling bodies do indeed have uniformly accelerated motions?

It is at this point that Salviati introduced a key assumption or as he calls it *supposition:* 'This definition established, the Author makes a single assumption, namely: the speeds acquired by one and the same body moving down planes of different inclinations are equal when the heights of these planes are equal'.[20] This is the key assumption that is supposed to be true, and from which Galileo's demonstration of the law of free fall follows. Despite Galileo knew of the law of free fall as early as 1604 as originally announced in a letter to Paolo Sarpi on 16 October following a long period of experimenting with inclined planes in Padua, at the time he did not have what he called a natural principle from which to deduce the law. And the fact that thirty-four years later in *Two New Sciences*, when almost blind and under house-arrest in Arcetri, he felt the need to spell out the key assumption or supposition behind the mathematical demonstration of the law of free fall testifies to the central role that this supposition plays in Galileo's mathematization of nature.[21]

[19]   *Ibid.*, pp. 166–7. Emphases added.
[20]   *Ibid.*, p. 169.
[21]   As Domenico Bertoloni Meli (2008) has pointed out, in the second and third day of *Two New Sciences* Galileo's main concern was with establishing an axiomatic science of motion on the example of Archimedes. Despite a voluminous historical literature in recent times on Galileo's experiments and machines, 'his foundational efforts have attracted less attention, yet they constitute a major episode in the history of science.' It was precisely in his life-long strive to achieve a formal axiomatic presentation of the new

Michela Massimi

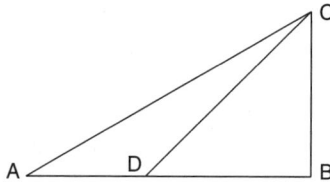

Figure 1.

The supposition says that the speeds acquired by the same body descending along say the inclined planes CA and CD, respectively, are equal since the heights of theses planes are equal, namely CB [see Figure 1].

More in general, this is the same speed that would also be acquired by the body falling vertically from C to B. In order 'to increase the probability [of this assumption] to an extent which shall be little short of a rigid demonstration', Salviati presents the following thought experiment ('esperienza').[22] Imagine a vertical wall with a nail driven into it, and from the nail let us suspend a fine vertical thread with a lead bullet from A to B [see Fig. 2].

Then consider the horizontal line DC, at right angles to the vertical thread AB. If we now bring the thread with the bullet into the position AC and we set it free, we can observe it to descend along the arc CBD, until it almost reaches the horizontal DC. From this we infer that the bullet in its descent through the arc CB acquired a momentum ['impeto'] on reaching B which was sufficient to carry it through a similar arc BD to the same height. The same applies to all other arcs BG and BI (starting from points E and F, respectively). Salviati then concludes:

> this experiment leaves no room for doubt as to the truth of our **supposition**; (. . .) in general, every momentum acquired by

---

science of motion that in *Two New Sciences* Galileo was looking for a natural and self-evident principle from which to deduce his law of free fall (already found on experimental grounds in 1604).

22   The Italian 'esperienza' is translated in Crew and de Salvio as 'experiment'. I translate it as 'thought experiment' instead because there is an element of idealisation as indicated by the verb 'imagine' in the following discussion about arcs reaching the horizontal plane (we are assuming that there is no air resistance, or friction, etc.).

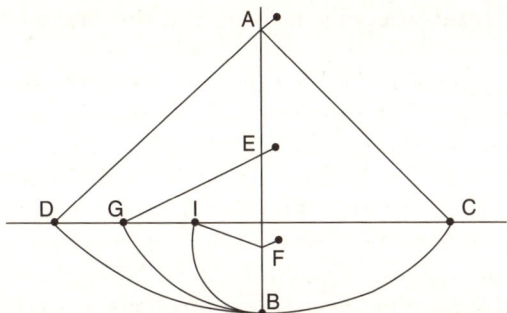

Figure 2.

> fall through an arc is equal to that which can lift the same body
> through the same arc. (…) Therefore all the momenta gained
> by fall through the arcs DB, GB, IB are equal.[23]

This is further generalised and taken to be valid not just for arcs but
also for the chords subtended to these arcs, and hence for inclined
planes as required by the supposition. There is however an obvious
inferential leap in this procedure and Salviati concedes that 'we are
not able, by similar means, to show that the event would be identical
in the case of a perfectly round ball descending along planes whose
inclinations are respectively the same as the chords of these arcs.'
This difficulty notwithstanding, Salviati concludes 'but this obstacle,
which interferes with the experiment, once removed, it is clear that
the momentum [impeto] (which gains in strength with descent)
will be able to carry the body to the same height. Let us then, for
the present, take this as a **postulate**, the absolute truth of which
will be established when we find that the inferences from it correspond to and agree perfectly with experiment'.[24] In other words,
Galileo's quasi-demonstration for the supposition depends on
accepting the postulate; but the postulate is not self-evident and in
fact it goes against intuitive experience. This supposition, and the
postulate on which it relies, incorporates what I take to be the a
priori element in Galileo's procedure, namely that the moving force
causally responsible for the observed appearances must be such that
the rate of acceleration must be constant (i.e. equal increments of

---

[23]   *Ibid.*, p. 171–2.
[24]   *Ibid.*, p. 172.

Michela Massimi

speed in equal time-intervals, as is indeed the case with gravitational acceleration).

From the supposition Galileo then derives two theorems, in particular '[Theorem II] If a moveable descend from rest in uniformly accelerated motion, the spaces run through in any times whatever are to each other as the duplicate ratio of their times; that is, are as the squares of those times'. The demonstration of this theorem is very ingenious indeed: Galileo could not in fact avail himself of calculus to calculate instantaneous velocities. Nevertheless, he was able to prove that the ratio between space intervals was equal to the ratio between the *squares of the time intervals* required to traverse those spaces.[25] But Simplicius, who represents the naïve Aristotelian in *Two New Sciences*, at this point intervenes in the discussion to cast doubt on this entire procedure and to ask for some experimental evidence to prove that these mathematical conclusions are indeed true. To which Salviati replies by describing the famous experiments with the inclined planes that Kant refers to.

Consider a bronze ball descending along a groove in a wooden beam tilted by elevating one end of it above the horizontal plane at will, and measure with precision the time it takes for the ball to descend along the entire groove. By repeating the experiment with the same ball descending this time only one-quarter the length of

[25]   He imagines the flow of time between any initial and final instant A and B as a vertical line AB, in which we can identify some time intervals AD and AE. He then represented space with another vertical line going from H to I, such that the space interval HL is run through in the first time interval AD and the space interval HM in the time interval AE. How can he prove that $HM:HL = AE^2:AD^2$? He imagined another time line AC drawn from A at any angle whatever with AB. Suppose we now draw parallel lines that from points D and E intersect the new time line AC in O and P, respectively. The parallel line DO now represents the maximum degree of speed acquired at instant D of time AD, and EP the maximum degree of speed acquired at instant E of time AE. In the previous Theorem I, the so-called mean speed theorem, Galileo had proved that the time in which a certain space is traversed by a moveable in uniformly accelerated motion from rest is equal to the time in which the same space would be traversed by the same moveable carried in uniform motion whose degree of speed is one-half the maximum and final degree of speed of the uniformly accelerated motion. Then, he can now conclude that the spaces HM and HL are the same spaces that would be traversed in times AE and AD by a moveable in uniform motion whose degree of speed is one-half EP and DO (which represent the maximum degree of speed at instant E and D respectively). Therefore, the spaces HM and HL are in duplicate ratio of the times AE and AD. QED.

the groove, Galileo found out that the time it takes to descend one-quarter of the groove is precisely one-half of the time it takes to descend the entire groove. By repeating the experiment for other lengths (two-thirds, or one-half) many times, it was always found that spaces were to one another as the squares of the times (and this held for all possible inclinations of the plane). Thus, despite the fact that Galileo could not measure instantaneous velocity, but only space intervals and time intervals, he was able to derive relations between space, time, velocity, and hence acceleration that allowed him to demonstrate the uniformly accelerated motion of bodies descending through an inclined plane. Galileo did not give any numerical value for the acceleration of the rolling ball; nevertheless the result he found about $s = at^2$ (when the initial velocity is 0) smoothed the path to Newton, who identified the moving force causally responsible for those accelerated motions with gravitational acceleration (a was replaced by the gravitational constant g) which is indeed at work both in the case of balls rolling down an inclined place and in the case of free-falling bodies.

For the purpose of my Kantian analysis, I want to draw attention to Galileo's deductive procedure of starting with a supposition and a postulate and deriving a series of theorems from them. This procedure has nothing to do with and should not be confused with hypothetico-deductivism, as also the Galilean scholar W. L. Wisan has rightly noted.[26] From a Kantian perspective, the goal of the inclined plane experiment was to extract from the appearance (motion of a bronze ball along an inclined plane) the property of uniform acceleration that Galileo had himself a priori inserted in the appearance for the sake of possible experience. Hence, from a Kantian point of view, we should not think that what we observe, say, a free-falling object, is the rough-and-ready observable phenomenon (in van Fraassen's terms) to be saved by introducing hypotheses that do not give us a literally true description of the way things are (since there may well be alternative hypotheses that save the same phenomenon equally well). If we stick to the level of observable phenomena (again in van Fraassen's terms), then Galileo may seem no more right than Aristotle. What appears to us as a free-falling object can well be accounted for either by the hypothesis of motion towards a natural place, with Aristotle, or by the hypothesis

---

[26] 'The method of the *Two New Sciences* is clearly not that of hypothesis, deduction and experiment in the modern sense. In fact, Galileo was quite unable to treat the principles of a demonstrative science as hypothetical for they must be true and evident' Wisan (1978), p. 43.

Michela Massimi

of uniformly accelerated motion, with Galileo. And the role of Galileo's experiment would simply reduce to testing these alternative hypotheses, according to some sort of hypothetico-deductive procedure.

No wonder then many philosophers of science—including Feyerabend's famous analysis of Galileo's tower argument[27]—have concluded that there was an element of propaganda in Galileo. In the end, Galileo was inventing new auxiliary dynamic hypotheses (be it circular inertia for the tower argument, or the aforementioned one about uniformly accelerated motion), and there was no intrinsic reason for the scientific community to shift to Galileo's new science, apart from the propaganda that finally gathered scientists' consensus around Galileo. I think that Feyerabend captured very nicely the theory-ladeness of observation in Galileo's strategy, but went astray in concluding that Galileo 'invented' a new conceptual system and used propaganda to defend it. This conclusion follows—I believe—from a widespread scepticism among philosophers of science about the possibility of choosing between alternative hypotheses that can both accommodate the available evidence. And this scepticism is of course nothing but a consequence of the empiricist tradition about 'saving the phenomena'.

By contrast with this tradition, I want to suggest that the particular use Galileo made of the postulate in backing up the supposition, from which the law of free fall follows, incorporates what I take to be the a priori[28] element that Kant might have rightly seen in Galileo's procedure. Namely, for the sake of experiencing uniformly accelerated motion, we must *constitute* the kinematical properties of free-falling bodies according to the aforementioned supposition (no matter how counterintuitive the postulate necessary to back it up). But Galileo not only *constituted* the kinematical properties of free-falling bodies according to this supposition, he tried also to subsume these kinematical properties under the causal concept of a moving force that he called *momentum gravitatis* or 'impeto'.[29] And no matter the fact that

27 Feyerabend (1975).
28 I intend here 'a priori' in the sense of being *constitutive of the object of experience*, which as Michael Friedman (2001a) has illuminatingly pointed out, is the relevant Kantian meaning of 'a priori' that still applies after Kant.
29 It is worth noting in the demonstration above Galileo's interchangeable use of 'momento' and 'impeto', where by 'impeto' Galileo does not mean the Medieval *impetus* of Oresme and Buridan (i.e. an internal force keeping the projectile in motion). In Galileo, 'impeto' is almost synonymous with 'momento', and it is the product of a body's weight and speed. Already in the Pisan work *Le meccaniche* in 1597, working on balances, Galileo had

Galileo's notion of impeto (as weight times speed) was still reminiscent of the Archimedean science of weight and was not the exact causal story about free-falling bodies. What matters is that for the very first time, physics was not regarded as introducing hypotheses to save the phenomena, but instead as a science whose secure foundations depended on the specific mathematical–physical way in which phenomena were constituted. This is the central contribution Galileo's mathematization of nature made to the scientific revolution. This is the central role Galileo occupies in the transition from Aristotelian to Newtonian physics, as Kant saw it.

To sum up, Kant suggested a radically new conception of phenomena, according to which a phenomenon, say the phenomenon of a uniformly accelerated free-falling object, is something that from the very outset we have mathematically–geometrically *constituted* as an object having certain *spatiotemporal properties* (for instance, the property of acquiring the same speeds over different inclined planes with the same height), and, most importantly, subsumed under a *causal concept* by tracing those spatiotemporal properties back to some moving force, such as Galileo's *momentum gravitatis* or 'impeto'. Only in this way, can we transform kinematical appearances into physical phenomena that become the actual objects of scientific inquiry.[30]

---

defined the 'momento' as the propensity of a body to move downwards because of its weight and its position on the balance. In Koyré's words, 'the *impetus* of the moving body is nothing other than the dynamic impulse given to it by its gravity' Koyré (1939), English translation (1978), p. 185. As Hooper (1998), pp. 159–160, has illuminatingly pointed out 'In motion on inclined planes, the *momenta gravitatis*, which are due to the angle of descent, are shown to be congruent to the *momenta velocitatis* given by the rules of speed, and are taken as the explanation and cause of the latter'.

[30] This Kantian moves is still vulnerable to the following objection: once we build causes *in* the phenomena (via suitable dynamic forces), we can eschew the underdetermination problem at the cost of facing another problem, namely that of explaining how we know what the phenomena are (I thank Peter Lipton for pointing this out). Of course, this is not much of a problem for Kant himself: his task was to justify *retrospectively* the universal and necessary validity of Newtonian physics. He *knew* (or, at least, he believed to know) what the phenomena were. But the problem remains for us, after the scientific revolutions of twentieth century physics and after Kuhn. From Newton to Einstein, the dynamical analysis of free falling bodies has changed; Newton's gravitation is not quite Einstein's gravitation, and quantum gravity may in turn be different from both. This raises of course very serious issues for any Kantian philosopher of

In this specific sense, Galileo exemplified Kant's Copernican turn by showing how the phenomena that scientists investigate are not ready-made for us to either save them or give a literally true story of them, but instead they have built in them some a priori elements that we have then to extract and prove through experiment. We can now understand why, according to Kant, Galileo marks the beginning of modern physics by displaying a unique and distinctive scientific methodology: we can gain scientific knowledge of nature only through principles of reason, on the one hand, and through experiments thought out in accordance with these principles, on the other hand. In other words, we can gain scientific knowledge of nature only by making appearances conform to *our way of representing*, rather than trying hard to make our hypotheses conform to nature. And this is why, as I hope to have clarified, Galileo's method inspired Kant's Copernican turn, and as such it is all the more relevant to address the problem of knowledge that still troubles us today. In this way and in this way only, could Kant answer positively the aforementioned question about how we know that 1) the alleged moving forces are the *true causes* of appearances (as opposed to hypotheses feigned to save them).

3.3. How do we know that moving forces form a system conferring lawfulness to empirical regularities? The Newton case

An obvious question arises at this point. What has the concept of cause—which, if the above analysis is correct, Kant saw as inserted in the Galilean phenomenon of free-falling bodies from the ground up—got to do with principles of reason? Is not causation a principle of the faculty of understanding, namely the second analogy of experience, rather than a principle of the faculty of reason? A propos of this specific point, Michael Friedman has pointed out how 'the dynamical

---

science, and no wonder it has been a debated topic in the most recent literature. How to reconcile Kant with Kuhn (see Friedman 2001a for a possible answer to this question)? And was Kuhn himself right in 'relativising' Kantianism to paradigms or scientific lexicons? Can we really say with Kuhn that whenever a scientific revolution occurs, scientists 'live in a different world', presumably populated by different phenomena? I intend to investigate this further issue and the problems it raises in future research. I have intentionally left it out of this paper, because the aim of this paper was to analyse Kant's conception of phenomena itself, rather than its implications for scientific revolutions.

principles of the understanding—in particular, the analogies of experience—are regulative rather than constitutive'[31] because they provide us with a regulative ideal. For instance, causation (the second analogy of experience) is instantiated in Kant's II law of mechanics (which, recall, is a combination of Newton's I and II law); in particular, it is instantiated in Newton's $F = ma$ and hence in Kant's II law that requires an impressed force F as the *cause* of any change of uniform motion into accelerated motion. But Kant's II law of mechanics, with its a priori nature and transcendental backing in the second analogy of experience, *per se* cannot guarantee that there are phenomena in nature that instantiate such an impressed force as the causal factor responsible for their change of motion. We can only infer their actual existence a posteriori, namely via observation and experiments. Yet the second analogy of experience provides us with a rule for seeking after such phenomena: without it, we would not even be able to identify some empirical regularities as instantiating accelerated motion (as opposed to uniform motion), and hence as instantiating an impressed force causally responsible for it. It is in virtue of this *regulative* function—which in the first *Critique* Kant deemed to be distinctive of the faculty of reason—that I think we can legitimately regard causation as one of the 'principles of reason' Kant refers to a propos of Galileo in the Preface. Galileo transformed the appearance of free-falling bodies into a physical phenomenon to study by inserting from the ground up the concept of cause via a moving force, whose nature nonetheless he did not investigate. It was Newton who completed the work that Galileo begun, by investigating the properties of this moving force that Galileo had simply hinted at, as a regulative ideal of scientific inquiry.

While the analogies of experience, in particular causation, can be regarded as having a regulative function (despite being principles of the faculty of understanding), on the other hand, there is one principle of the faculty of reason that Kant repeatedly presented as the regulative principle *par excellence*: this is the principle of systematic unity or systematicity. In the Appendix to the Transcendental Dialectic, Kant spoke of systematicity as a regulative ideal of scientific inquiry 'bringing unity into particular cognitions' and hence transforming a 'contingent aggregate' into a 'system interconnected in accordance with necessary laws'.[32] Despite this regulative function, Kant however did not regard systematicity only as a desirable feature of the faculty of reason in its striving towards the never

---

[31] Friedman (1992b), p. 182.
[32] Kant (1781, 1787), A645/B673 – A647/B 675.

Michela Massimi

fully attainable goal of a complete science of nature, but instead as a necessary requirement for a coherent use of the very same faculty of understanding, and even as a 'mark of empirical truth' (see A651/ B679).

I think we can foresee here an important link between systematicity and causation as having itself a regulative function. For the faculty of understanding to work properly, and hence for the second analogy of experience to apply, we need an overarching regulative principle of reason, namely systematicity, which can guide us to bring unity into particular cognitions and to transform a contingent aggregate into a system interconnected in accordance with necessary laws. In other words, we need to go beyond the specific causal judgments concerning, for instance, the causal factor responsible for uniformly accelerated motion, and seek after a broader *system* of moving forces causally responsible for the great variety of phenomena in nature (from cohesion, to liquefaction, to elasticity, etc.).

Kant assigned an increasingly important role to systematicity in the First (unpublished) Introduction to the *Critique of Judgment*, where systematicity is no longer assigned to the faculty of reason, but to the faculty of reflective judgment. The task of reflective judgment consists in arranging lower-level empirical regularities into a system of higher-level laws, which are nonetheless still empirical. In this respect, the faculty of reflective judgment too has a distinctively regulative function, with its own transcendental principle that postulates the systematic unity of empirical concepts and laws as a regulative ideal so that a system of empirical science becomes possible.[33] And systematicity as a regulative principle of reflective judgment becomes a key feature in the 'Transition' project.[34] No wonder there are

[33] See on this point Friedman (1991), pp. 74–5.

[34] Friedman (1992a), p. 245, gives a penetrating analysis of how the chemical revolution revealed a gap in Kant's critical philosophy, in particular a gap between the top-down approach typical of the *Metaphysical Foundations* (which moved from Kant's transcendental principles to metaphysical principles of natural science, from which the empirical law of universal gravitation could then be derived) and the bottom-up approach typical of systematicity as a regulative principle of reflective judgment, which embraces the variety of empirically given forces in nature and strives to subsume them under higher-order concepts. According to Friedman, the 'Transition' project tried to reconcile the top-down approach with the bottom-up one, i.e. it tried to reconcile the constitutive aspect inherent the *Metaphysical Foundations* with the regulative aspect championed in the *Critique of Judgment*, and to show that these two opposite paths intersect at some point, namely that the increasing empirical variety

Why There are No Ready-Made Phenomena

plenty of references to physics as a *system* or as a 'systematic investigation of nature' throughout the *Opus postumum*. There is a clear continuity between systematicity as advocated in the *Critique of Judgment* and in the 'Transition', whereby physics is defined as 'the systematic investigation of nature as to empirically given forces of matter, insofar as they are combined among one another in one system'. Kant's task in the 'Transition' was to endorse the bottom-up approach typical of the faculty of reflective judgment (with the regulative principle of systematicity) in order to show *whether*, and eventually *how* the wide range of empirically given forces in nature could form a system.

Thus, we can now go back and answer question 2) above, namely how we know that such forces form indeed a system conferring lawfulness to what would otherwise be only an aggregate of empirical regularities. It is only in virtue of a regulative principle such as systematicity that we can seek after a *system* of moving forces, through which and within which only one can claim that the alleged moving force *necessarily* causes the observed appearance (e.g. gravitational attraction *necessarily* causes free-falling bodies to move with uniformly accelerated motion). Systematicity is what confers *nomic necessity* upon an otherwise contingent aggregate of Humean empirical regularities. I want to suggest then that it is this regulative principle of reason that complements observation and experiment in Kant's analysis of Galileo's mathematization of nature.

Although with his experiment of the inclined plane, Galileo arrived at the law of free-falling bodies, he fell nonetheless short of investigating the properties of the force causally responsible for uniformly accelerated motion. In order to move from the identification of a moving force as the true cause (the Galilean *vera causa*) of those motions to a properly physical/dynamical analysis of those motions, is not enough to apply the concept of cause. It is not enough because Kant had already shown in MAN back in 1786 how the concept of cause (the second analogy of experience) underpinned phenomena

---

subsumed under the principle of reflective judgment eventually leads up to the two fundamental forces of attraction and repulsion envisaged in the *Metaphysical Foundations*. Eckart Förster (2000) compares and contrasts Friedman's interpretation with that of Mathieu and Tuschling, and offers an alternative analysis for the role of systematicity in the 'Transition' as rooted in Kant's principle of a formal purposiveness of nature disclosed solely by aesthetic judgments of natural beauty, in continuity with the *Critique of Judgment*.

Michela Massimi

via the metaphysical principles of pure natural science (namely, via Kant's II law of mechanics). In order to complete the *transition* from the metaphysical foundations of natural science to physics—the very same 'Transition' Kant was working on in the last decade of his life and that he felt was urgently needed to fill a gap in his transcendental philosophy—we need more than just the concept of cause: i.e., we must identify the moving force as a force due to gravity and we must study its nature and properties as Newton did. In order to ground Galileo's kinematics into a proper 'system' of nature, we must shift from what Kant calls the 'philosophical foundations' (with the concept of cause) to what he calls the 'mathematical principles of the philosophical doctrine of nature', namely Newton's *Philosophiae Naturalis Principia Mathematica*:[35]

> Transition from the metaphysical foundations to physics, according to a priori principles. Galileo, Kepler, Huyghens, and Newton. Huyghens's transition from the metaphysical foundations of

[35] See for details *Opus postumum*, 22:516. We reach at this point a controversial part of the 'Transition', where several passages suggest that Kant was actually taking the distance from Newton to the point of even rejecting the very same Newtonian expression 'natural philosophy' in favour of *scientia naturalis*. A propos of this, Caygill (2005), pp. 34–5 writes: 'Kant questioned not so much the *fact* of Newton's dynamic history of planetary motion as its philosophical or scientific character (...). The *Principia* performs the amphiboly of making philosophy and metaphysics into a branch of mathematics rather than recognising that philosophy "must set the philosophical foundations prior to mathematical ones".' First of all, let me note that Caygill's analysis of Kant's on Newton in the XIth fascicle of the *Opus postumum* fundamentally agrees with my interpretive line in this paper about how Kant saw the transition from kinematics to dynamics operated by Newton, and the pivotal role that in Kant's eyes Newton played towards a science of moving forces in nature. So, it is not the *fact* of Newton's dynamics that is at stake here. What is at stake instead is the 'philosophical' character of Newton's *Principia*, according to Caygill, and why Kant saw his 'Transition' as a fundamental challenge to Newton's *Principia*. Let me just briefly note that I agree with Caygill that according to Kant the philosophical foundations must be set prior to the mathematical ones; but this is precisely what Kant had already done with respect to Newton's *Principia* back to MAN in 1786. What is at stake in the 'Transition' is the specific search for a transition to 'physics' intended as a *system* of empirically given moving forces in nature, which starting with a bottom-up approach could possibly meet at some point the top-down approach laid out in MAN. And I do not see this as a challenge to Newton's *Principia*, but more as a way of complementing and expanding on Newton's project.

natural science to the mathematical ones, and that of Newton to physics—merely by means of the concept of gravitational attraction, which did not occur to Kepler ('Transition', 22:353).

To Kant's eyes, the passage from Galileo to Newton represents the historical instantiation of what the regulative principle of systematicity commends. Via Galileo and Newton, Kant saw historically realised the system that confers lawfulness to an otherwise contingent aggregate of Humean empirical regularities. In the case of the force of gravitation, we can properly speak of a system that unifies a great variety of phenomena under a single moving force/cause. And it is thanks to being part of this system that every phenomenon (from the planetary motions studied by Kepler to free-falling bodies studied by Galileo) is entrusted with nomic necessity. Nature's lawfulness is then a consequence of phenomena being systematized under a single common cause, under a single dynamical force such as gravitational attraction. To Kant's eyes, Galileo's experiments and Newton's systematization of phenomena under the single force of gravitation represented the two complementary poles of a sought-after 'Transition to physics'.

Despite what Kant portrays as a serendipitous transition from Galileo to Newton, this story does not have a happy ending. The more general question that Kant was trying to answer in the 'Transition' and that was bound to remain open was whether any similar system could be found for many other types of phenomena revealed by pneumatic chemistry and aether theories at the end of eighteenth century. Is there any similar system able to unify all moving forces in nature responsible for solidification, liquefaction, chemical combination of gases, transmission of light and sound, and even biological phenomena? Kant wondered whether it was possible to embed the Newtonian system into a much broader system providing a unified framework for the increasing variety of phenomena revealed by the physical sciences of his time. This was Kant's specific task in the 'Transition', a task that he could not fulfil. But we can catch a glimpse of Kant's heroic efforts from many passages of the *Opus postumum*. In vain did he attempt to identify Lavoisier's caloric (suitably reinterpreted as heat-matter [Wärmestoff] and even identified with aether) with an all-pervasive substance responsible both for the transmission of light and for states of aggregation of matter, and, hence, with a possible candidate for the sought-after unification of an increasing variety of phenomena.[36] While the

---

[36] On this point, see Friedman (1992a), pp. 290–341, and Pecere (2006). In a forthcoming paper of mine jointly authored with Silvia De

Michela Massimi

answer to this specific question could not be found and Kant's fragments leave us enough leeway to speculate about his views on aether, caloric and the more general project of the *Opus postumum*, the 'Transition' casts light on Kant's life-long stand on phenomena, which I have tried to spell out in this paper. We do not have ready-made phenomena, but somehow we *make* them. And we make them via observation and experiment on the one hand, and principles of reason, on the other hand:

> I cannot say I *have* this or that experience; rather, I *make* it for myself, and this system of perception is valid for everybody. *Observation and experiment* are ingredients [and] presuppose a principle in order to *make* experience (not experiences). The mathematical foundations of natural science precede a priori, as intuitions [with kinematical properties of appearances that we have to insert a priori for the sake of possible experience, as Galileo did—MM]; the philosophical [foundations] apply appearances to them [via the concept of a dynamical moving force as the *cause* of these appearances, as in MAN—MM]; the mathematical principles of the philosophical doctrine of nature [Newton's *Principia*, and hence the identification of the dynamical moving force with gravitational attraction— MM], however, fully ground the doctrinal system of the science of nature as physics ('Transition', 22: 444).

Bianchi, we investigate precisely the role that the aether played as a medium for the transmission of attractive and repulsive forces in an account of a variety of phenomena back in Kant's mid-1750s works (*On Fire, Universal Natural History and Theory of Heavens, Physical Monadology*, and *New Elucidation*). In particular, we reconstruct the tradition of mixed sciences (experimental physics and pneumatic chemistry with Boerhaave, Musschenbroek, s'Gravesande, Hales among others) as an important tradition somehow complementary to the Newtonian one (especially, the Newton of the II edition of *Principia* and of the *Optiks*), from which Kant's view of the aether as a medium of forces seems to have derived. There are some surprising analogies between some of Kant's early views on dynamics exposed in these 1750s works (in reference to specific chemical problems such as combustion, liquefaction, spirituous airs, etc.) and the views exposed at the end of his life in the 'Transition to physics', as if the late Kant felt the need to go back to some of the pressing physical problems which prompted his original philosophical investigations in the pre-critical period.

4. Conclusion

What good is Kant's conception of phenomena for today philosophy of science? Going back to the ongoing debate between scientific realists and constructive empiricists, I suggested that Kant's conception of phenomena should prompt philosophers of science to reconsider some traditional claims about science and its aims. In particular, it should prompt us to go beyond both scientific realism and constructive empiricism.

To scientific realists, who believe that science aims to give us a literally true description of the way things are in nature, Kant's conception of phenomena shows that we should believe, for instance, in gravitational attraction not because it provides the best explanation for the success of Newtonian mechanics in predicting the motion of free falling objects. Instead, we should believe in gravitational attraction because *without it, we would not have the very same kinematics* of uniformly accelerated free-falling objects that Galileo found, to start with.

To constructive empiricists, who believe that science aims to save the phenomena, Kant shows on the other hand that there are no ready-made phenomena as observable/perceivable 'objects' in nature. In a way, we have to *make* them. And, once we make them, we have to prove them right, namely we have to demonstrate that what we have inserted in the appearances for the sake of possible experience is *truly* there. Once we accept that we make phenomena in the specific Kantian sense clarified in this paper, the whole rationale for the epistemological dichotomy between, say, the observable phenomenon of a free-falling apple and gravitational attraction as an unobservable theoretical entity about which we should suspend belief, needs be carefully reconsidered.

Pace Duhem and his followers, we are not the heirs of Bellarmine. We are in fact the heirs of Galileo. Or better, we are the heirs of Kant's Galileo, the same Galileo that by approaching nature with experiments, on the one hand, and principles of reason, on the other hand, made a light dawn on all those who study nature.

Reduction, Unity and the Nature of Science: Kant's Legacy?

MARGARET MORRISON

1. Introduction: Kant, unification and modern physics

One of the hallmarks of Kantian philosophy, especially in connection with its characterization of scientific knowledge, is the importance of unity, a theme that is also the driving force behind a good deal of contemporary high energy physics. There are a variety of ways that unity figures in modern science—there is unity of method where the same kinds of mathematical techniques are used in different sciences, like physics and biology; the search for unified theories like the unification of electromagnetism and optics by Maxwell; and, more recently, the project of grand unification or the quest for a theory of everything which involves a reduction of the four fundamental forces (gravity, electromagnetism, weak and strong) under the umbrella of a single theory. In this latter case it is thought that when energies are high enough, the forces (interactions), while very different in strength, range and the types of particles on which they act, become one and the same force. The fact that these interactions are known to have many underlying mathematical features in common suggests that they can all be described by a unified field theory. Such a theory describes elementary particles in terms of force fields which further unifies all the interactions by treating particles and interactions in a technically and conceptually similar way. It is this theoretical framework that allows for the prediction that measurements made at a certain energy level will supposedly indicate that there is only one type of force. In other words, not only is there an ontological reduction of the forces themselves but the mathematical framework used to describe the fields associated with these forces facilitates their description in a unified theory. Specific types of symmetries serve an important function in establishing these kinds of unity, not only in the construction of quantum field theories but also in the classification of particles; classifications that can lead to new predictions and new ways of understanding properties like quantum numbers. Hence, in order to address issues about

doi:10.1017/S1358246108000039
Royal Institute of Philosophy Supplement **63** 2008

unification and reduction in contemporary physics we must also address the way that symmetries facilitate these processes.

But what does this have to do with Kant, aside from the fact that he too was interested in unity? Several commentators have stressed the different ways that unity functions in Kant's philosophy of science and how it emanates from both reason and the understanding.[1] Indeed there are several different notions or levels of unity at work in the Kantian system encompassing ontology, epistemology and methodology. Moreover, the unity of knowledge and experience acquired through intuition and understanding also requires a trans-cendental unity of consciousness, which in turn involves an act of synthesis. While the relation between synthesis and unity in the Kantian architectonic is important in its own right, its explication is less crucial for my project in this paper, which is to articulate what, if any, connection exists between the notion of unity embedded in modern physics and Kant's account of unity in his philosophy of science.

At a very basic level Kant's account of synthesis and unity can be summarized as follows: the imagination (via the synthesis of appre-hension) functions in a spontaneous way to produce a synthesis of the manifold of intuition and the a priori representations of space and time. The understanding and its categories secures the unity of the appearances represented in intuition under rules (A79/B105). In other words, the concepts of the understanding give unity to the synthesis of a manifold. Despite the crucial role played by the under-standing in the unifying process, it is reason that is predominant in achieving the type of unity we associate with scientific knowledge, knowledge that consists in a *system* connected according to necessary laws (A645/B673). In fact, Kant describes systematic unity as 'what first raises ordinary knowledge to the rank of science' or that which 'makes a system out of a mere aggregate' (A832/B860).[2]

There is however an apparent tension in Kant's presentation of the role of reason as a unifying faculty and in the description of what that unification consists in. Very often Kant seems to suggest that the requirement to seek unity is simply a subjective or logical principle rather than the embodiment of an objective fact about nature; especially since the notion of an 'all encompassing unity' is something that for us is a regulative idea (A647-8/B675-6). Other times Kant

---

[1]   Kitcher (1983), (1986); Buchdahl (1992); Guyer (1990); Morrison (1989).
[2]   I shall henceforth use Norman Kemp Smith's (1929) translation of the *Critique of Pure Reason* (New York: St. Martin's).

stresses the objective aspects of unity but when doing so seems to associate this objectivity with epistemic goals that involve what he calls the 'coherent employment of the understanding' (*ibid.*):

> Its function is to assist the understanding by means of ideas, in those cases in which the understanding cannot by itself establish rules, and at the same time to give to the numerous and diverse rules of the understanding unity of system under a single principle, and thus to secure coherence in every possible way (A648/B676).

Given that scientific knowledge involves the process of logical systematization (A832/B860) reason functions in a methodological way to urge us along in the process of constructing a unified system, something that we, nevertheless, typically find in nature when we go in search of it (A653-4/B681-2).[3]

Although this kind of unity can be seen as Kant's way of separating science from other 'non-scientific' knowledge, it seems to bear little resemblance to the goals of reductive unity constitutive of high energy physics. For that we need to go beyond the systematization of knowledge to embrace a full-blown reductionist *ontology*. In other words, the aim is a unification of *forces* under the framework of a single theory. Although Kant speaks of reducing different kinds of earths and the desire to find a common principle for the earths and salts, in these contexts he typically speaks about the *presupposition* that the unity of reason accords with nature. Even though this relationship between reason and nature is a presupposition, it is nevertheless a demand of reason rather than a convenient heuristic device (*ibid.*). But, the implication is that the source of the unity is first and foremost methodological rather than being grounded in the objects themselves.

However, remarks in *Metaphysical Foundations of Natural Science* (henceforth abbreviated as MAN, followed by the section number), *Opus postumum* (OP)[4] and other places in the *Critique of Pure*

---

[3]   I do not intend this claim as a resolution of the tension; in fact, as we shall see below the relation between the subjective and objective features of unity is a fundamental feature of Kant's transcendental program. The importance of this 'tension' and the role it plays will be discussed in section two.

[4]   Henceforth, I shall be using James Ellington's (1985) translation of the *Metaphysische Anfangsgründe der Naturwissenschaft* (Indianapolis: Hackett); and Förster and Rosen's (1993) translation of the *Opus postumum* (Cambridge: Cambridge University Press).

Margaret Morrison

Reason (KrV) suggest that Kant also embraced the importance of ontological reduction in the sciences. For example in MAN (534) Kant says that 'all natural philosophy consists in the reduction of given forces apparently diverse to a smaller number of forces and powers sufficient for the explication of the actions of the former. But this reduction continues only to fundamental forces, beyond which our reason cannot go.' This is now beginning to sound very similar to the program of reduction and unification that pervades contemporary particle physics. So, the question becomes how to square this approach to scientific ontology with the seeming anti-reductionist epistemology in the KrV. This is important for understanding whether Kant's account of unification bears any relation to the role of unification in contemporary physics. In other words, is there a Kantian legacy we can legitimately trace?

The key to answering this questions lies in explicating how the search for unity proceeds at the level of empirical science both for Kant and in modern physics, and the relation of those activities to the Kantian transcendental principles/conditions associated with reason and the understanding. That is, how did Kant see the relation between empirical science and reason and what, if any, bearing does that relation have on contemporary practice. Part of what is at stake here is the form that both physical explanation, and theories more generally, ought to take. For example, contemporary debates in philosophy of science frequently focus on whether we should be satisfied with a multiplicity of levels as exemplified by effective field theories, making the goal of a theory of everything simply a metaphysical hope; or is there reason to think that this latter kind of unity is attainable in practice.[5] In other words, what is the relation here between physics and metaphysics? These kinds of questions focus on what the limits of unity are for empirical science and what kind of evidence we have for that unity, issues Kant was especially concerned about. In other words, there are three different questions here that we need to address: (1) What is the relation between the empirical and transcendental in Kant's theory of science?; (2) What is the relation between

---

[5]   These are not just questions that preoccupy philosophers of science, they are very much a part of the scientific discussions that address the nature of fundamental physics. Many contemporary physicists are concerned with issues surrounding reduction and emergence and whether the search for a theory of everything is simply a metaphysical hope. See, for example, recent articles by Laughlin and Pines (2000) as well as Weinberg (1993) and Anderson (1972).

physics and metaphysics in contemporary science?; (3) Does the answer to (1) have any impact on (2)?

The relevance of Kant's answers to these questions for modern physics is far from straightforward. While his characterization of unity seems to bear a close relationship to many of the issues surrounding contemporary unification, a closer analysis reveals that that these connections may, in fact, be rather superficial. This is traceable, ultimately, to the relation between the transcendental and empirical, in particular the links between unification and reduction expressed in KrV and MAN. So, while the Kantian legacy in contemporary physics might appear to be rather strong, this is due to the fact that some of his ideas are adopted piecemeal into modern contexts with little or no attention paid to the underlying philosophical framework that legitimates them. But does this really matter? At the object level where science is practiced, perhaps it is enough that the use of symmetry principles, for example, can be interpreted along the lines of logical maxims or transcendental ideas of reason. We simply do not need the entire Kantian architectonic in order to locate his influence in contemporary science. While this might be a tempting line of argument I am doubtful about such a conclusion and in what follows I want to outline the reasons why.

In order to flesh out the story, I begin with a brief discussion of the *non-reductive* character of Kant's epistemology and go on to discuss how this feature relates to his ideas about unity and reduction in science. From there, I examine the extent to which these views find a place in contemporary physics and whether the reduction and unification present there can be seen as reflecting Kantian principles. I conclude by arguing that because contemporary science has more or less ignored Kant's Copernican revolution, many features the unification project it is engaged in embody the kind of transcendental realism Kant was at pains to avoid.

2. Kant's anti-reductionist epistemology

Rationalists like Descartes and Leibniz, as well as empiricists like Hume were all concerned with establishing the proper foundations for human knowledge. Part of that project involved reducing certain features of knowledge to its elementary constituents. Descartes, for example, attempted to derive physical laws from metaphysical principles and claimed in the *Principles of Philosophy* (section 203) that all of physics follows from the self-evident (clear and distinct) proposition that matter is extension. The latter followed from the *cogito*, together with the existence of God, and was guaranteed by reason. In fact, in the preface to the *Principles* Descartes remarks that one can derive knowledge of all things in the world from the basic principles of philosophy. A similar type of project, although much different in detail, was envisioned by the monadic metaphysics of Leibniz, who also espoused the reduction of mathematics to logic. While empiricists do not attempt to establish deductive relations founded on the certainty of reason, they nevertheless embrace a reduction of all knowledge to impressions/ideas. Even the Newtonian program of 'deduction from phenomena' embodies reductionist goals as is evident from *Optics* (Query XXXI) where Newton claims that ' . . . .to derive two or three general principles of motion from phenomena and . . . .to tell us how the properties and activities of all empirical things follow from these manifest principles would be a very great step in philosophy . . . '.

What differentiates Kant from this methodological picture is that his goal is not to seek the ultimate justification for the existence of the objects of physics or human knowledge more generally, or to ask *whether* knowledge of objects is possible, but to ask what makes possible the experience that we do have of objects in the physical world. Transcendental idealism is not concerned with locating the source of knowledge either outside ourselves or in our reason, but rather with denying the dichotomous nature of the reductionist project and in doing so establishing the dual source of knowledge in both experience and the understanding. As Kant argues in the Refutation of idealism, the existence of objects in space outside us is simply not in question. But, because these objects are conditioned, they do not play the same foundational role as the empiricist's impressions. In that sense then Kant is not wedded to the idea that knowledge is based on reduction to a fundamental level involving either reason or the ultimate constituents of experience (whatever they may be).

One might want to claim that the importance of the synthetic a priori as the ground of necessity and universality hints at a kind of reductionism to the extent that these principles function as the foundations that make knowledge possible. However, it is important to note that while synthetic a priori principles certainly structure our experience there is no accompanying deduction of any empirical laws from them; so in that sense their role is very different from the metaphysical truths of Descartes and Leibniz or the foundational project of the empiricists. There is no derivation of scientific laws from transcendental principles. Empirical laws are simply special determinations of the pure laws of the understanding. The latter make the former possible and it is through them that appearances take on an orderly character (A127-8; B165).

But what about the Newtonian version of reductionism? Newton's goal was to derive explanations of physical phenomena from *physical* principles, a practice that still very much defines the methodology of contemporary physics. So, the question is to what extent Kant adopted this kind of reductionism within empirical science itself. In order to answer that, we need to look more closely at Kant's views on unity in the context of empirical investigation. This is important for the issue I raised in the introduction, namely whether we can articulate some kind of Kantian legacy in the way science is actually practiced, even if we are unable to extend that legacy to its philosophical foundations. Because of the close relation between unity and reduction in contemporary physics the question is whether Kant's views on unity embody a similar relation. So, there are two issues/questions here: (1) To what extent do Kant's views on unity and reduction go together?; (2) Do Kant's views on the empirical nature of science in any way resemble contemporary practice?

As I noted above, there are various kinds of unity described by Kant, one of which is the province of the understanding and another, the domain of reason. The former involves a synthetic unity, the ground of which is contained 'a priori in the original sources of knowledge in our mind' (A125). But these 'subjective conditions' must also be 'objectively valid, being the possibility of knowing any object at all' (*ibid.*). The order and regularity we experience in nature consists in a connection of appearances and this connection is the unity produced by the understanding in the activity of thinking. As Kant notes in the transcendental deduction, *we* introduce order and regularity and hence unity to experience. Although this unity makes the practice of science possible there is another kind of unity that constitutes, if you will, the *doing* or *practice* of science itself; that is, the organization and systematization of empirical knowledge into a coherent system of laws. The latter is the task of reason but in directing us to search for the 'absolute totality of the conditions of all appearances' (A416/B384), we must recognize that these conditions are not given as objects of experience and hence the unity that we seek— the 'whole of all appearances' (A328)—is an unattainable ideal. Hence, the requirement that we 'find for the conditioned knowledge of the understanding the unconditioned whereby its unity is brought to completion' (B364), is a process that is itself uncompletable.

The search for something that is not a possible object of experience involves what Kant calls the hypothetical employment of reason; it is not constitutive and hence the unity it prescribes is grounded in what Kant terms a 'logical' principle concerned with knowledge in its unified form (A648/B676). Although the term 'principle' denotes a universal proposition obtained solely from concepts, the principles of reason depend on thought alone (A302) and are associated with problematic concepts for which there is no corresponding object. This is in contrast to the principles of the understanding which are grounded in the synthetic a priori features of knowledge. As a logical principle, the demand to seek unity is intended to secure the coherent employment of the understanding. Hence, this 'logical' employment of reason concerns itself with the attempt to reduce the knowledge obtained through the understanding to 'the smallest number of principles (universal conditions) and thereby achieve the highest possible unity' (A305), as in the construction of a logical system.

However, nothing follows from the logical demands of reason concerning a unified nature per se. Yet Kant claims that the principle requiring us to seek unity is a necessary principle, not because we achieve unity through the observation of objects in nature, but because it is only through the coherent employment of the understanding that an empirical criterion of truth is possible. In other words, empirical truth is not possible without the systematic employment of the understanding, something that is in turn made possible by the demand of reason. As Kant indicates in the discussion at B84-5/A60, the only access we have to empirical truth is via a negative condition, namely the agreement of knowledge with the general and formal laws of the understanding. But the understanding cannot function unless it can unify its various laws into a coherent system. Hence, the degree to which we can achieve this is what makes possible the *ability to judge* the truth or falsity of the knowledge acquired through the understanding. In other words, coherence allows for the *possibility* of a judgment about truth—it is not equated with truth; it provides an epistemic condition, not a semantic mark, or an ontological correspondence. Although reason's demand for systematic unity is a regulative constraint designed to secure a measure of coherence, this coherence is necessary to systematize knowledge of objects acquired through the understanding, a crucial component for characterizing science:

> ...to say that the constitution of the objects or the nature of the understanding which knows them as such, is in itself determined

to systematic unity, and that we can in a certain measure postulate this unity a priori, without reference to any such special interest of reason, and that we are therefore in a position to maintain that knowledge of the understanding in all its possible modes (including empirical knowledge) has the unity required by reason, and stands under common principles from which all its various modes can, in spite of their diversity, be deduced—that would be to assert a transcendental principle of reason, and would make the systematic unity necessary, not only subjectively and logically, as method, but objectively also (A648/B676).

What the above quote suggests is that the objectivity that we ascribe to the idea of unity is one that is mirrored in our knowledge of the empirical world. Although Kant does discuss various examples of the kind of reduction and unification we experience when doing empirical science, this endeavour while made possible by reason, is not, he claims, the justification of the principle. In the discussion of the chemist engaged in reducing different kinds of earths, the hypothesis of a common principle for earths and salts, if successful, imparts probability to the explanation that they are indeed unified. But this Kant refers to as a 'selfish purpose' that must be dinstinguished from the *idea* of reason which does not here 'beg but command' (A653/B681).

What this means is that these two activities are clearly distinct. More specifically, the empirical hypothesis of unity and the search for unity among scientific entities is not to be *identified* with the idea of reason, which is a transcendental principle. The latter, however, makes possible the former; and in that sense they are inextricably linked. Consequently, the objectivity Kant refers to in the quote above has to do with the fact that the understanding could not engage in the search for unity, were it not for the demands of reason. The relation between the subjective, methodological aims and 'objective' features are explicit in Kant's claim that if the logical principle of genera is to be applied to nature (objects that are given to us), then it presupposes a transcendental principle. And 'in accordance with this latter principle, homogeneity is necessarily presupposed in the manifold of possible experience (although we are not in a position to determine in an a priori fashion its degree); for in the absence of homogeneity, no empirical concepts, and therefore no experience, would be possible' (A654/B682). This suggests that although the kind of unity we seek in physics and other sciences is an empirical unity grounded in a logical principle or maxim, it is nevertheless a unity whose justification lies ultimately in a transcendental principle of reason.[6] And, it is a unity we seek not as a result of inductive success but because it is necessary for experience and 'constitutes' the activity of acquiring knowledge and doing science. In other words, it is objective because it is linked via the understanding to objects of experience.

That this kind of unity involves a type of reduction is further evident from Kant's remarks at (A663/B691) about the discovery of the elliptical nature of planetary orbits and ultimately a unity in the cause of all the laws of planetary motion, namely, gravitation. In extending these notions and by making use of the specific logical principles of affinity (continuity), unity (homogeneity) and manifoldness (specificity or variety), we further explain things that experience can never confirm, such as the paths of comets and the uniting of distant parts of the universe, a universe that is held together by one and the same moving force. These principles recommend: 1) in the case of homogeneity, to seek unity in variety; 2) in the case of manifoldness, to seek variety under unity; and 3) with respect to affinity or continuity, to seek similarities between things that recognize both unity and variety, as in the classification of entities into natural kinds. The principle of continuity is especially important because it arises from a union of the other two. It is only in ascending to the higher genera and descending to the lower species that we obtain the idea of 'systematic connection in its completeness' (A658/B686). In other words, we are able to see how differences in phenomena are nevertheless related to each other in so far as they 'one and all spring from one highest genus' (*ibid.*). For example, in noticing that the comets deviate from true circular orbits we draw inferences about their hyperbolic paths. The principle of continuity permits the kind of speculation that is necessary for the formulation of inductive hypotheses that take us beyond the immediate consequences of empirical experience, but not beyond possible experience.

Kant goes on to claim that this logical principle of *continuum specierum* (*formarum logicarum*) must presuppose a transcendental law (*lex continui in natura*) because otherwise the understanding might follow a path that is contrary to that prescribed by nature. Initially, this seems to suggest that nature itself (i.e. objects of experience) exhibits this type of continuity and as a result determines the way we ought to proceed in our investigations. But this interpretation

---

[6]   Because scientific knowledge constitutes a logical system the practice of constructing such a system involves logical principles. But, as Kant insists, these logical principles only have methodological force because they are grounded in transcendental principles.

is quickly dispelled by Kant's claim that the law must not rest on empirical grounds because, if it did it, would 'come later than the systems, whereas in actual fact it has itself given rise to all that is systematic in our knowledge of nature' (A660/B688). In other words, if the law were empirical, we would derive claims about systematization from our observations, making the process purely contingent. The formulation of the laws is not due to any hidden experimental design or by putting them forward in a hypothetical manner. However, when their content is confirmed empirically, this yields evidence for the hypothesis that the presupposed unity is well grounded and that the laws of parsimony of causes, manifoldness of effects, and affinity of the parts of nature, are in accordance with both reason and nature itself.[7]

But how should we understand this 'accordance'? Is it only sometimes that these laws lead us to the right conclusions? Apparently not, because even though these principles contain 'mere ideas' for the guidance of the empirical employment of reason Kant claims that they nevertheless posses, as synthetic a priori propositions, objective but indeterminate validity and, as such, serve as rules for possible experience (A663/B691). This means that they function as rules for possible experience insofar as they apply directly to the understanding, and hence indirectly to objects. Without them we would not have, for example, a concept of genus, or any other universal concepts that belong to the understanding. Indeed the understanding itself (and hence experience) would be non-existent (A654/B682). This is because the application of the logical principle of genera to nature presupposes a transcendental principle whereby homogeneity is necessarily presupposed in the manifold of possible experience (even though we cannot determine, in an a priori fashion, the degree to which this takes place). In the absence of this, no empirical concepts would be possible. So, although the transcendental principles can be employed as heuristic devices in the 'elaboration of experience' (A 663/B691), they also 'carry their recommendation directly in themselves and not merely as methodological devices' (A661/B689). While

---

[7] Similarly, in the case of specification, empirical inquiry soon comes to a stop in the distinction of the manifold, if it is not guided by the antecedent transcendental law of specification, which not only leads us to always seek further differentiation but suspects these differences even where the senses are unable to disclose them (A657/B685). Such discoveries are possible, Kant claims, only under the guidance of an antecedent rule of reason. We assume the presence of differences before we prescribe the understanding the task of searching for them.

we each may attend to different logical maxims/principles in different contexts, taken as a set they are necessary for the empirical employment of the understanding and experience in general. However, the method of looking for order in nature in accordance with transcendental principles, and the maxims that require us to regard such order as grounded in nature, leave undetermined where and to what extent that order will be found (A668/B696).[8]

What we have seen here is Kant's attempt to resolve the tension between the subjective logical employment of maxims and the objectivity that their relation to transcendental principles allegedly guarantees. The epistemology of transcendental idealism requires that we locate the source of unity in both reason and nature in the same way that knowledge in general has a dual source in experience and the understanding. Hence to ask whether nature constitutes a unified whole, independent of the requirement that we must seek unity in nature, is simply the wrong kind of question to ask. As we have seen above, we must presuppose a unified world if we are to have a coherent employment of the understanding and hence experience at all. But, the necessity of the presupposition should not be equated with a necessity in nature, which is why the maxims we employ at the level of empirical investigation have the status of logical principles, whose ultimate justification comes via their transcendental counterparts.

At the beginning I mentioned similarities between Kant's use of transcendental and logical principles in his argument for unity, the role of reduction in his account of empirical science, and the way that these ideas might be instantiated in modern physics via symmetry principles. And, as we saw above, Kant's logical and transcendental principles function as heuristic devices that guide our search for knowledge, knowledge that accords with both reason and nature itself. However, as heuristics they are more than just useful tools, not only because experience is limited in its ability to point us in new directions, but because, according to Kant, the discovery that absorbent earths are different kinds was possible *only* under the guidance of an antecedent rule of reason. In these kinds of situations reason is 'proceeding on the assumption that nature is so richly diversified that we may presume the presence of such differences and therefore prescribe to the understanding the task of searching for them' (A657/B686). In other words, reason points us in certain directions even when our senses are unable to do so. This way of

---

[8]   The important point is that the methodology is grounded, ultimately, in transcendental principles.

approaching empirical/theoretical investigation bears certain similarities to the way symmetries are used in particle physics, especially in cases where they function in the construction of theories that would not have been possible on phenomenological grounds alone (e.g. the electroweak theory).[9] In order to explore some of these parallels, let me now turn to a brief discussion of symmetries to see how closely the comparisons can be made.[10]

3. Symmetries as transcendental principles?

Symmetries function in the extension of our theoretical knowledge via the prediction and classification of elementary particles, as well as in the development of theories themselves, a situation analogous to Kant's principle of continuity. The notion of symmetry that is especially relevant here is the group theoretic one which defines symmetry as invariance under a specified group of transformations and applies not only to spatial figures but also to more abstract objects like mathematical (dynamical) equations. This feature makes the group theoretical apparatus especially useful in constructing physical theories. Essentially one can proceed in two ways, either by examining the symmetry properties of equations that one is interested in; or, starting with symmetries we assume have physical significance, and using those to search for dynamical equations that have certain properties. For example, the classification of hadrons through the representations of the SU(3) group suggested that these particles had certain similarities which led, eventually, to the quark hypothesis. Similarly, the Glashow–Weinberg–Salam (GWS) electroweak theory developed out of a synthesis of the SU(2) and U(1) symmetry groups that was spontaneously broken by the Higgs mechanism. The standard model adds to this combination the SU(3) group governing the strong interactions, which is now associated with the color quantum number of quarks. In both cases, and

---

[9] My remark about the impossibility of theory construction on the basis of phenomenology is simply meant to indicate that there were no reasons to assume that electromagnetism bore any relation to the weak force. In the former case the particle carrying the force is the massless photon, while in the latter much heavier massive bosons were required. No indication that two such theories could be unified emerged from the physical phenomenology.

[10] There have been some suggestions in the literature about interpreting symmetry principles (and their role in physics) as Kantian transcendental principles, see Falkenburg (1988) and Mainzer (1996). While this initially appears as an attractive approach, my claim is that it is ultimately unsuccessful, for the reasons I discuss below.

indeed in quantum field theory in general, theoretical development proceeds in a top-down way using symmetries and the mathematics of group theory rather than physical phenomenology.

The internal symmetries of particles are related to quantized properties like isospin, charm and other quantum numbers. These symmetries are identified with invariances under phase changes of the quantum states, and are especially important because if the classification includes all the quantum numbers for characterizing a particular particle, then it is possible to define the particles in terms of their transformation properties. In other words, a particle can be defined as a unitary transformation of, say, the inhomogeneous Lorentz group. Symmetry classifications are also used in the prediction of new particles, like the omega minus in connection with hadron classification, where the prediction was made on the basis of surplus structure in the mathematics.[11] Symmetry arguments that led to the development of the GWS theory in turn predicted the existence of the $W^{\pm}$ and Z^0 vector bosons.

We can see then how these symmetries function in a way analogous to Kant's principle of continuity, allowing us to group phenomena together according to certain classificatory schemes which highlight similarities and differences that can in turn be used to form the basis for theoretical hypotheses. Symmetries also lead to restrictions on theory development because quantum field theories (QFTs) are typically characterized by the symmetries of the fields and interactions, i.e. the requirement of invariance with respect to a transformation group results in restrictions to the form of the theory, its equations and the kinds of quantities that appear in it. For example, a constraint on modern QFTs is that they be gauge invariant in order to be renormalizable. Kant's principle of continuity operates in a similar way: it constrains our theorizing in that it assumes a continuity of kinds of motion under a common principle. Although these hypotheses and classifications are subject to empirical confirmation, it is the *postulated* similarity/continuity implicit in the symmetry principles/groups (and for Kant in the principle of continuity) that forms the foundation for the inferences we make.

In addition to sanctioning these kinds of inferences, symmetries also play a unifying role in physics.[12] Grand Unified Theories (GUT) unify what are considered the three fundamental gauge symmetries:

---

[11]   For an interesting account of the omega minus case, see Bangu (2008).

[12]   The very notion of symmetry itself is related to unity in the sense that the symmetry transformations of a group relate the elements to each other and to the whole. See Morrison (2000).

hypercharge, the weak force, and quantum chromodynamics (QCD). They are based on the idea that at extremely high energies all symmetries have the same gauge coupling strength, which is consistent with the notion that they are really different manifestations of a single overarching gauge symmetry. From a 'physical' point of view, this means that at energies 10^{14} GeV the weak, strong and electromagnetic forces are unified into a single field. But what exactly is the relation between these symmetries and the objects they supposedly govern? Are the symmetries simply mathematical heuristic devices? Or are they themselves features of the physical world that in turn explain other features? One might be tempted to say that the enormous success of symmetries in the prediction, explanation and unification of phenomena is a reason to assign them ontological status. In other words, they function so successfully because they constitute the structure of the physical world.[13]

More persuasive, however, are the arguments for the epistemic status of symmetries and it is here where parallels with Kant become especially relevant. In his famous 1967 work entitled *Symmetries and Reflections*, Eugene Wigner characterizes symmetries as properties of theories or natural laws that describe phenomena, rather than properties of the phenomena themselves. We can claim that they are indirectly related to objects because the requirement that certain laws be invariant under certain symmetries further constrains the kinds of events that are physically possible. In fact, for Wigner the symmetries of space and time are pre-requisites for discovering laws of nature. He claims that if the correlations between events changed from day to day, and were different for different points of space, it would be impossible to discover any laws. Symmetry principles provide the epistemological (and heuristic) guide required to uncover what otherwise might remain unknown to us. It is this meta-theoretical status that makes them especially important in theory construction and in our ability to know the physical world.

These remarks echo those made by Kant regarding the role of transcendental principles (specification) in the discovery of different kinds of absorbent earths, and in the extension of our knowledge using the principle of continuity. Indeed if we adopt Wigner's interpretation of symmetries the parallels are quite remarkable. As with transcendental principles, symmetries relate only indirectly

---

[13]   Two further arguments for the ontological status of symmetries are given on the basis of the geometrical symmetries of spacetime and the relation between symmetries and conservation laws as shown by Noether's theorem. For details of these arguments, see Brading and Brown (2003).

Margaret Morrison

to objects, yet they provide the conditions under which those objects can be known or discovered (as part of a system of knowledge). In speaking of symmetries Wigner claims that there is a structure in the events around us and it is this structure, i.e. the correlations between events, that science wishes to discover. And, in a rather striking resemblance to Kantian epistemology, he remarks that we would not live in the same sense we do, if events around us had no structure, making symmetries appear as conditions for the possibility of experience.

Yet, there is an ambiguity in Wigner's account that also mirrors the tension in Kant's discussion of homogeneity, specificity and continuity as both maxims/principles and as characteristics of objects and properties in nature. Wigner claims that without the symmetries of space-time we would have no 'stability' that could ground our investigation into the laws of nature. But, this seems to imply that while these symmetries must be reflected in our laws, they must also be features of space-time itself. More precisely, they must be identified with the geometrical structure of the physical world, which in turn must be interpreted ontologically, if we are to guarantee the kind of stability Wigner refers to. In other words, it is the ontological aspect of the symmetries that produces the stability required for laws of nature to exist. So, even though we employ symmetries in a kind of meta-theoretical way, the justification for doing so is ultimately ontological.

As we saw above, Kant's remarks sometimes suggest an ontological reading of the transcendental principles via the logical maxims; however, the epistemological program of KrV clarifies the way in which this needs to be understood. The following quote encapsulates the relationship between the epistemic and ontological aspects of the transcendental principles, a relationship that is only possible from within the framework of transcendental idealism:

> Now since every principle which prescribes a priori to the understanding thoroughgoing unity in its employment, also holds, although only indirectly, of the object of experience, the principles of pure reason must also have objective reality in respect of that object, not, however, in order to *determine* anything in it, but only in order to indicate the procedure whereby the empirical and determinate employment of the understanding can be brought into complete harmony with itself (A694/B666).

The point here harkens back to the discussion at the beginning about the non-reductive aspects of Kant's critical program. Because of the interactive relationship between the understanding and the objects of experience, we do not isolate foundational features of knowledge in either objects themselves or our conceptual framework. While Wigner's account of symmetries bears a *prima facie* similarity to Kant's discussion of transcendental principles, the need to 'specify' a location for symmetries, or 'identify' them as part of the physical world, undermines any attempt to strengthen the analogy. A brief reflection on Kant's epistemology reveals why.

The use of symmetries in modern physics raises philosophical questions about their status. Are they ontological features of the world, mathematical objects that function as heuristic devices, epistemic conditions imposed on laws, or perhaps all three? If we opt for the epistemic reading, the most easily defendable of the three, we can simply say that the equations in our theories must obey certain invariances in order for the calculations to give physically meaningful results, i.e. for our theories to be renormalizable. Similarly, Noether's theorem says that for every symmetry of a Lagrangian a corresponding conservation law can be derived. The symmetry here is actually the covariance of the form that the physical law takes with respect to a one-dimensional Lie group of transformations; so, in that sense, it is really a mathematical notion. Although it is associated with an invariance which is the conserved physical, measurable quantity, nothing follows from this about the physical status of the *symmetry*. In other words, questions still arise as to why symmetries should have epistemic importance over and above their mathematical function in theory construction. My point here is that in order to characterize symmetry principles as transcendental, we must have some principled epistemological reason for doing so. But none emerges outside of the Kantian framework, nor can we embed the practice of modern physics into that framework. We could, of course, simply say that symmetries have the status of logical maxims and function in a heuristic way as constraints on theorizing. But this is not necessarily Kantian in spirit, and as Kant is quick to point out, logical maxims require corresponding transcendental principles for their legitimation.

In her discussion of symmetry principles, Falkenburg suggests that Kant's concept of a systematic unity of Nature provides an interpretation for the unifying function and frequent empirical success of symmetry principles. Elementary particles that are unified through an internal symmetry represent a Kantian system, and the symmetry principles that enable us to discover this structure function as regulative principles. These symmetry principles, like Lorentz invariance, are 'presupposed in the general assumption that there is a systematic unity of Nature, and can be subsumed under the regulative principles which guide the acquisition of knowledge', something Kant derives

Margaret Morrison

from the rational idea of unity.[14] When our employment of symmetries is successful at the phenomenological level, they 'point to a systematic unity of fundamental structures in Nature'. It is the mathematical structure of symmetry groups that makes it possible to search for phenomena that are part of these structures. Mainzer makes a stronger statement for the role of symmetries by claiming that the way they function to determine the characteristics of a physical system (e.g. the form of the interactions) aligns them with what Kant would call 'the conditions for the possibility of an object at all'.[15] In Falkenburg's case the symmetries are part of the presupposition that Nature is unified, but given the necessity of this assumption in Kant's system the symmetries take on a more substantive role than simply regulative heuristics. The problem with this stronger reading and with Mainzer's account is that they elevate symmetry principles to a role that outstrips their function in modern physical theory. In order to associate them with Kant's account of the transcendental necessity and objectivity of ideas of reason, they must have universal applicability. However, as we know, symmetries in physics simply do not enjoy this type of universality.

Before proceeding any further, it is important to note that the Kantian account of a scientific theory involves more than simply the systematization of knowledge. The system must be capable of yielding law-like connections between its parts, connections that require the use of mathematics for their explication. In fact, in MAN (470) Kant explicitly identifies science with the application of mathematics. Given this remark, one option is to embed symmetries into the Kantian program as mathematical objects and account for their relation to physical entities via the strategy for the mathematization of nature described in KrV and MAN. The specific textual details of that strategy are complicated and controversial, and ultimately not necessary for my argument here. Instead let me simply address some of the broader claims made by Kant about mathematization to see whether a role for symmetries might be located within this framework.

3.1 Symmetries as mathematical objects

Some of Kant's remarks about the relationship between mathematics and experience are initially promising; remarks that resemble those made about the principle of continuity: 'Mathematics provides the

---

[14]   Falkenburg (1988), p. 134.
[15]   Mainzer (1996), p. 287.

most splendid example of the successful extension of pure reason by itself without the assistance of experience' (A712/B740). This ability to extend knowledge via inferences derived from a priori constructions is what makes mathematics indispensable for physics in the formulation of laws that have both predictive power and certainty. But, because mathematics is concerned not with existence but with the possibility of the relations of things in time and space, we also need metaphysics which deals with what belongs to the existence of things (substance, cause, etc.). As Kant remarks, in 'natural science metaphysics and the art of measurement (the application of mathematics to the measurement of objects in experience) shake hands' (A726/B754).

For our purposes here, the important issue is how this 'shaking hands' actually proceeds. In the case of knowledge extension described above, Kant's reference is to synthetic a priori judgments arrived at through a process of construction in intuition. In his discussion of the axioms of intuition, Kant claims that 'all intuitions have extensive magnitude' is a transcendental principle of the mathematics of appearances and greatly enhances our a priori knowledge. Indeed, it is 'this principle alone that makes mathematics, in its full precision applicable to objects of experience...' (A165/B206). This kind of mathematization of nature has its foundation in the synthesis of space and time, forms of pure intuition, which make possible the apprehension of appearance and every outer experience of objects. Hence, 'whatever pure mathematics establishes in regard to the synthesis of the form of apprehension is also necessarily valid of the objects of apprehension' (A166/B207). In other words, all appearances are given a priori as extensive and intensive magnitudes and consequently subject to mathematization. This, however, is a general claim about the possibility of objects of experience, and their relations to each other in space and time. As Kant points out, ' ... in mathematical problems ....existence is not the question, but only the (mathematical) properties of objects in themselves' (A719/B747). The full integration of metaphysics and mathematics requires that we are able to show *how* mathematics applies to the kinds of specific objects that physics deals with, i.e. motion, forces etc.; the kinds of objects that are governed by the analogies of experience. This is crucial for natural science since a 'doctrine of nature will only contain as much science proper as there can be mathematics applied in it' (MAN 471). In other words, objects must be mathematizable if they are to be measurable.

In MAN 524-5, Kant stresses that we must start with a metaphysics that explicitly enables the applicability of mathematics to nature, rather than starting with mathematical principles alone (as in the Galilean tradition) and assuming, without proof, that they apply to physical objects. The project of spelling out the interaction between mathematics and metaphysics begins in KrV and extends through MAN and the OP. Questions about the very ability to apply mathematics to nature and the justification for doing so lay at the heart of Kant's critical program. But, as we shall see below and in the following section, this is a program that embodies marked dissimilarities with the relation between the mathematical and the physical embedded in contemporary physics and also in the physics of Kant's own time. Descartes, for example, professed to have reduced physics to the laws of mathematics (letter to Mersenne, 11 March 1640), and although he may have been less than successful the project of providing a mathematical account of nature was certainly extended by Newton and has become definitive of modern physics as well. Since the time of the Pythagoreans, mathematics and harmony have been the keys to revealing the laws of the universe and contemporary particle physics is a manifestation of this in its use of mathematical symmetry groups.

In modern physics, however, the Cartesian goal of reduction to mathematics seems to have found a new voice. In *Dreams of a Final Theory* Steven Weinberg, for example, remarks that at the fundamental level symmetries are all there is.[16] This is not an attempt to explain the *application* of mathematics to nature or to justify that relation but rather to simply reduce the physical to the mathematical. The group theoretical description of the purely kinematical properties like spin for quantum relativistic systems associates each relativistic wave function with some unitary representation of the Poincaré group, and as such one can say that an elementary particle is simply a unitary irreducible representation of the group.[17] Given that definition, an elementary particle can be characterised by its mass and spin where spin turns out to be simply a group invariant characterising the unitary representation of the relativity group associated with the wave equation. Consequently, one thinks of spin not as the physical rotation associated with a particle, but rather as a symmetry, a way of mathematically

---

[16] Weinberg (1993).

[17] An irreducible representation is one that cannot be split up into smaller pieces, each of which would transform under a smaller representation of the same group. All the basic fields of physics transform as irreducible representations of the Lorentz and Poincaré groups. The complete set of finite dimensional representations of the rotation group $O(2)$ or the orthogonal group comes in two classes, the tensors and spinors.

stating that a system can undergo a certain rotation. Even in the Dirac equation, spin appears as a consequence of the transformation law of the solutions under rotation. The tradition continues with modern attempts at unification such as string theory, which serves as a paradigmatic example of mathematics replacing the physical.

This kind of methodology bears certain similarities to what Kant calls the mathematico-mechanical mode of explication. Its advantage is that one can make quick progress when doing physics because one has the certainty of mathematics and can proceed synthetically because there are no constraints due to the concrete nature of physical existents.[18] However, too much freedom is given to the imagination because the method fails to pursue rigorous explanation which includes, for Kant, an investigation into the forces associated with matter. Hence, this kind of approach is tantamount to metaphysical speculation because the process of applying mathematics to the empirical world involves the unjustified assumption that the world has a mathematical character. By contrast, Kant's account of the justification for the mathematization of nature is bound up with our cognitive principles and with establishing a metaphysical foundation which facilitates the application of mathematics, a project that is markedly different from the mathematization characteristic of early modern and contemporary physics.[19] In that sense then, it would be a mistake to associate the unity achieved in contemporary mathematical physics with Kant's ideas regarding the relation between physics and mathematics. In attempting to assimilate Kant's ideas to a modern framework, there is one final possibility that merits consideration and that is whether Kant's account of forces bears any relation to modern accounts of unity via reduction to fundamental forces.

4. Unity and the reduction to fundamental forces

At the beginning I mentioned how GUTs and Theories of Everything involve the reduction of the four fundamental forces and how symmetry functions as the methodology that structures the mathematical foundations of field theories. I have tried to persuade you that despite their heuristic/methodological role we cannot associate symmetries

[18] Kant identifies this mode of explication with the atomistic or corpuscular philosophy (MAN 533).
[19] The specific details of that story have been systematically spelled out by Friedman (1992a), Plaass (1965) and others.

with Kant's view of systematic unity via transcendental principles. However, if we shift our focus from the transcendental to the empirical level, from the meta-methodology of physics to object level practice, perhaps we can identify reduction to fundamental forces as a unification strategy common to both Kant and modern physics.[20]

Leaving aside the various intricacies associated with reduction in contemporary physics (i.e. the way the symmetry groups determine the form of the theory) the goal is relatively straightforward and can be captured quite accurately in Kant's claim that all natural philosophy consists in the reduction of given forces apparently diverse to a smaller number of forces; a reduction that carries on to the level of fundamental forces (MAN 534). Kant's account of forces is bound up with his theory of matter and the explication of the dynamical approach to understanding material nature. In fact, Kant claims that the concept of matter (and varieties of matter) should be reduced to moving forces because in space no activity or change can occur apart from motion. In that sense, the possibility of matter is proved by reducing it to these forces which are an a posteriori fact of experience.[21] So far this picture accords quite well with how forces and particles are understood in modern quantum field theory. While each of the fundamental forces has a corresponding quantum or vector boson associated with it, many contemporary physicists view the force fields as primary.[22]

However, the perceived agreement is merely superficial because Kant complicates the matter by asking 'Who claims to comprehend the possibility of fundamental forces?' (MAN 524). And, the situation gets worse, because he further claims that these forces (attractive and repulsive forces *in general*) cannot be constructed (525) nor conceived (conceptualized) (534); they can only be assumed. Actual

---

[20] I realize, of course, that one cannot in principle separate the transcendental and empirical levels, but what I have in mind here is a claim about how Kant saw reduction and forces as essential features of the practice of physics.

[21] Kant claims that the concept of force supplies us with a 'datum' for a 'mechanical construction' (MAN 498), a requirement for proving the 'real possibility' of matter. Here again the details surrounding Kant's theory of matter rise important philosophical points of interpretation, see especially Friedman (2001b) and Carrier (2001).

[22] There is a good deal of philosophical debate about the nature of the field and the role of particles in QFT. While these debates are extremely interesting, the details are not really relevant for the issue I am addressing in the paper.

forces 'can only be given empirically', because the possibility of fundamental forces can never be made comprehensible (A207/B252).

Given the importance of forces in Kant's theory of physics we need to ask what exactly these claims might mean—how should we interpret them and what are the implications for empirical science? A physical concept that is inconceivable (MAN 513) is one that cannot be derived from another more basic concept, and fundamental forces are those that are not further derivable. The challenge then for Kant's dynamical picture is to connect these forces (and hence matter) with mathematics to produce a unified physics that is not grounded in contingency. In other words, the coherency required for systematization cannot come via reduction to fundamental forces alone because, given the remarks above, they lack the status required to underwrite the project. While we experience forces given in nature, fundamental forces in general appear to occupy a different role.

So, what exactly are fundamental forces and how do they function in the context of physical theory? Do they bear any resemblance to the fundamental forces prominent in contemporary physics? A return to KrV provides a clue. At A648-50/B676-78 Kant discusses what he calls the causality of a substance, a power or force (*Kraft*). Despite the appearances of many different forces we are required, by a logical maxim, to reduce the diversity of these forces and hence detect a hidden identity. Although logic is not capable of deciding whether a fundamental force exists, the idea of such a force is the 'problem involved in a systematic representation of the multiplicity of forces' (A649/B677). In other words, the notion of a fundamental force acts like a regulative idea of reason that guides our empirical inquiry. This enables us to compare the relatively fundamental forces in order to ascertain the similarities between them with the goal of bringing them nearer to a 'single radical . . . . absolutely fundamental force'.

While Kant does not claim that such a force (power) is necessarily realised, he claims we must seek it in the interests of reason, as part of the endeavour to bring systematic unity to our knowledge of experience. However, like the ideas of homogeneity, continuity and specification, when we pass to the transcendental employment of the understanding we find that the notion of a fundamental force is not understood simply as a problem for the hypothetical use of reason, but it is taken to have objective reality. This reality consists not only in virtue of the postulation of systematic unity of various forces of a substance, but also as giving expression to an apodictic principle of reason (A650/B678). But, says Kant, even if we fail in the reduction of diverse forces we still presuppose that such a unity exists, not only for the case we are considering, but for matter in general. 'In all such cases reason presupposes the systematic unity of the various forces, on the ground that special natural laws fall under more general laws, and that parsimony in principles is not only an economical requirement of reason, but is one of nature's own laws' (A651/B679). In fact, he goes on to say that the employment of a logical principle requires that we also presuppose a transcendental principle, whereby systematic unity is a priori assumed to be necessarily inherent in objects. Otherwise, reason cannot treat the diversity in nature as disguised unity and derive this unity from a fundamental force. If reason is free to admit that all forces are heterogeneous, then the search for such unity would be inconsistent with the constitution of nature. Hence, the law of reason that bids us to seek unity is necessary since without it we would have no reason, no coherent employment of the understanding and no criterion of empirical truth.

The claim, then, is that Kant's notion of a fundamental force has essentially the same status as the transcendental principles discussed above. The process of reducing given powers or forces to a smaller number, in accordance with the logical demands of reason, is part of the empirical process of doing physics and to that extent we need to presuppose that objects of experience conform to the demands placed on the understanding by reason. But, the idea that we could actually complete this reduction and discover a fundamental force is a transcendental principle, and, as such, the product is not to be met with in experience. Moreover, as in the case of the logical maxims, the very notion of a fundamental force or power functioning as a methodological rule only makes sense if it is grounded in a transcendental principle. We must, however, be cautioned against associating this with a *metaphysical* claim about how nature is constituted. The following quotation nicely encapsulates the subtlety of Kant's position:

> the investigation of metaphysics behind what lies at the basis of the empirical concept of matter is useful only for the purpose of leading natural philosophy as far as possible in the investigation of the dynamical grounds of explication, because these alone admit hope of determinate laws, and consequently of a true rational coherence of explanations. This is all that metaphysics can ever hope to accomplish . . . .and hence on behalf of the application of mathematics to natural science respecting the properties by which matter fills space . . . .to regard these properties as dynamical and not as unconditioned original

positions. ...as a merely mathematical treatment would postulate (MAN 534).

To assume we can reach this fundamental level as a product of empirical inquiry and to assume that we can apply, without prior justification and argument, mathematics to empirical objects is to adopt the metaphysics of transcendental realism Kant hoped to banish in the antinomies. So, while the *practice* of reduction and the quest for fundamental forces in modern physics has an exact analogue in Kant's theory of science, the justification of that practice and the product could not be more different. The reduction of forces in modern physics is grounded in the assumption that we can complete the project, a project that for Kant, cannot, even in principle, be completed. That is to say, embedded in the practice of modern physics is a metaphysics that is ultimately incoherent.

5. Conclusions

We have seen then that neither the current approach to unity via symmetries as the methodology of modern physics, nor the ontological project of reduction to fundamental forces can be given a Kantian interpretation or justification. Although some empirical similarities exist between the two frameworks, it would be a mistake to identify these too closely, since any Kantian construal will ultimately locate the justification for the practice of unification and reduction not in the physics itself but in human reason; a view that seems decidedly at odds with the metaphysical realism implicit in contemporary physics. In some places this difference seems less evident, as in Kant's remark about the status of laws within his notion of a system. For example, we presuppose the unity of various powers on the ground that special natural laws fall under more general ones and that 'parsimony in principles is not only an economical requirement of reason but one of nature's own laws' (A650/B678). Because for Kant this has the status of a presupposition, its justification is ultimately linked with what is necessary in order to have experience in the first place and what is necessary for a specific kind of scientific experience. At A657/B685 Kant claims that we have an understanding only on the assumption of varieties in nature and that nature's objects exhibit a certain homogeneity. This is because it is only through the diversity that is contained in a concept that its application can be sanctioned; and that use of concepts is nothing other than the activity of the understanding. In other words, the question of whether systematic unity is an objective fact about nature is simply the wrong question to ask; not only is it objective, it is necessary.

In the end Kant's necessity of systematicity finds its expression in the faculty of reflective judgment, as outlined in the First Introduction to the Third Critique (the *Critique of Judgment*) and in that *Critique* itself. That transition raises many questions about the status and justification of systematicity and whether Kant can successfully uphold the project he outlined in KrV. Answers to those questions require a separate work.[23] In closing I would like to simply draw attention to what I think is perhaps one of Kant's most ingenious remarks, one that embodies what I hope philosophy of physics has learned from Kant even if the practice of physics has not. The remark concerns what he calls the second advantage of metaphysics which is '...knowing what relation the question has to empirical concepts, upon which all our judgments must at all times be based' (Ak. 2:368).[24] Kant claims that this advantage is the least known and most important and is attained at a fairly late stage after long experience. Surely, this is one of if not the most important task(s) for philosophy of science, and it is here where Kant's legacy is most prominently felt. In attempting to trace a lineage from Kant's epistemological work and its relation to his theory of physics to the methodology of present-day science, we must be ever mindful of Kant's justification of the practice of mathematical physics. But that justification appears, in most respects, fundamentally at odds with the presuppositions motivating the contemporary search for unity and reduction to fundamental forces. Of course, this is not to say that contemporary physics would not benefit from a Kantian reconstruction, but only to point out that its practices do not reflect those philosophical leanings.

23 For a detailed discussion of these issues, see Guyer (1990).
24 Kant (1766), English translation (1992), p. 354.

Invariance Principles as Regulative Ideals: From Wigner to Hilbert

THOMAS RYCKMAN

Wigner

Eugene Wigner's several general discussions of symmetry and invariance principles are among the canonical texts of contemporary philosophy of physics. Wigner spoke from a position of authority, having pioneered (and won the Nobel prize in 1963) for recognition of the importance of symmetry principles from nuclear to molecular physics. But perhaps recent commentators have not sufficiently stressed that Wigner always took care to situate the notion of *invariance principles* with respect to two others, *initial conditions* (or *events*) and *laws of nature*. Wigner's first such general consideration of invariance principles, an address presented at Einstein's 70th birthday celebration, held in Princeton on 19 March 1949, began by laying out just this distinction, and in a way that seems to suggest that the three notions arise through abstraction in an analysis of the general problem of cognition in the natural sciences:

> The world is very complicated and it is clearly impossible for the human mind to understand it completely. Man has therefore devised an artifice which permits the complicated nature of the world to be blamed on something which is called accidental and thus permits him to abstract a domain in which simple laws can be found. The complications are called initial conditions; the domain of regularities, laws of nature. (...) the underlying abstraction is probably one of the most fruitful the human mind has made. It has made the natural sciences possible.[1]

That we are able to discover laws of nature at all, Wigner went on to argue, arises from the circumstance that many regularities are relatively insensitive to initial conditions; that is, given essentially the same initial conditions, the same regularities result without regard to displacements of the system in space and time. It is here that the

---

[1] 'Invariance in Physical Theory', *Proceedings of the American Philosophical Society* 93, 1949; as reprinted in Wigner (1995), pp. 283–93.

doi:10.1017/S1358246108000040 © The Royal Institute of Philosophy and the contributors 2008
Royal Institute of Philosophy Supplement **63** 2008

Thomas Ryckman

notion of an invariance principle arises in the first instance (to be sure, as a 'geometrical', not a 'dynamical', principle of invariance).

First an observation, and then a comment on Wigner's conceptual constellation of *initial conditions, laws of nature*, and *invariance principles*. An observation: the distinction between initial conditions and laws of nature, simply taken over from the employment of ordinary differential equations in classical mechanics, is long familiar in philosophy of science and is widely assumed, mistakenly perhaps, to be unproblematic. For example, it is presupposed in D-N accounts of scientific explanation and many discussions of laws of nature. Certainly, philosophical accounts widely diverge over the cognitive status of laws of nature, whether there are such, whether they need be universal, and whether they are to be analyzed in regularity or necessitarian terms. In short, the status of laws of nature remains an issue of lively contention in philosophy of science. On the other hand, philosophical examination of invariance principles is relatively recent, occurring mostly within philosophy of physics rather than philosophy of science more broadly, and has had surprisingly little impact in the debate over scientific realism.[2] This is all the more noteworthy since leading unification programs in current physics adopt the postulate that Nature at the fundamental level is *supersymmetric*, while pronouncements like 'The secret of Nature is symmetry' from highly regarded fundamental physicists have become part and parcel of even the wider intellectual culture.[3]

Secondly, a comment. It is worth emphasizing that Wigner described the tripartite distinction between *initial conditions, laws of nature*, and *invariance principles* as 'an artifice' devised by human thought when confronting the enormous complexity of natural phenomena with, he implies, only the finite capacities of the human mind. Nonetheless, this artifice is 'one of the most fruitful (abstractions) the human mind has made ... (since) it has made the natural sciences possible'. Anticipating a bit, these remarks do suggest something of a 'finitist' philosophical tendency, whose broader outlines are readily surmised from other of Wigner's essays. For one thing, it is quite clear that Wigner himself held a non-realist or antirealist attitude towards physical theories; e.g., he stated, echoing Bohr, that

> Physics doesn't describe nature. Physics describes regularities among events and *only* regularities among events.[4]

---

[2] van Fraassen (1990); Brading and Castellani (2003); and very recently, Debs and Redhead (2007).
[3] Gross (1995).
[4] 'Symmetry in Nature' (1973), in Wigner (1995), p. 382.

Moreover, Wigner evinced a rather pragmatic attitude towards invariance principles, e.g., once observing that the physicist's belief in CPT symmetry

> is not based on nature's innate preference for symmetry; it is based on the stubborn fact that we cannot formulate equations of motion in quantum field theory that lack this symmetry and still satisfy the postulates of Einstein's theory of special relativity.[5]

Still further evidence of Wigner's dissent from realism can be found in his somewhat infamous view that resolution of the quantum measurement problem requires reference to consciousness. But rather than linger over these details, I wish, above all, to call attention to his characterization of these conceptual abstractions or patterns of understanding (*initial conditions, laws of nature*, and *invariance principles*) as a presupposition of physical theory ('It has made the natural sciences possible'). Putting matters this way suggests another, far older, attempt, rather more well-known to philosophers, to explain the possibility of the natural sciences, one also resting on a tripartite analysis of the three sources of human cognition:

> All our cognition starts from the senses, goes from there to the understanding, and ends with reason, beyond which there is nothing higher to be found in us to work on the matter of intuition and bring it under the highest unity of thinking (A298–299/B355).

This programmatic statement, occurring at the introduction to the Transcendental Dialectic, is Kant's most concise statement of how cognition originates in the distinct contributions of intuitions, concepts, and ideas. It is repeated almost *verbatim*, presumably to underscore its significance, as a conclusion at the end of the Transcendental Dialectic

> Thus all human cognition begins with intuitions, goes from there to concepts, and ends with ideas. (A702/B730)

Though little commented upon, the latter passage, appears as the epigram of Hilbert's classic Gauss–Weber *Festschrift* essay, *Grundlagen der Geometrie* (1899). I would not want to make too much of the fact that Wigner served as Hilbert's assistant in Göttingen in 1927–28, tasked with bringing Hilbert up-to-speed on the applications of group theory to the new quantum mechanics that Wigner, with the assistance of John von Neumann, pioneered. Nonetheless, as hinted above, I think that there is something of a 'family resemblance'

---

[5] 'Violations of Symmetry in Physics' (1965), in Wigner (1995), p. 355.

Thomas Ryckman

between Wigner's discussion and Hilbert's own physical applications of what he termed the 'axiomatic method', a method that, in published articulation, first appeared as applied to Euclidean geometry in *Grundlagen der Geometrie*.

Hilbert

The axiomatic method

At least in the scant literature on Hilbert's work in physics, it is widely assumed that Hilbert's references to 'axiomatic method' signal a typically modern mathematical concern with the rigorous explicit statement of a theory. Just so, but the 'axiomatic method' for Hilbert also connoted a specifically *logical and epistemological* method of investigation for 'deepening the foundations' of the theory. By invoking the 'axiomatic method', Hilbert called attention to a specific epistemological method of investigation of mathematical theories (including those of physics) that he pioneered, and which he saw as closely tied to the nature of thought itself.[6]

In more general terms, and as Kant's directive prescribes, the axiomatic method is conceived as a logical analysis that begins with certain 'facts' presented to our finite intuition or experience. Both pure mathematics and natural science alike begin with 'facts', i.e., singular judgments about 'something ...already ... given to us in representation (*in der Vorstellung*): certain extra-logical discrete objects, that are intuitively present as an immediate experience prior to all thinking'.[7] Analysis next determines the concepts under which such given facts can be classified and arranged. Finally one attempts to formulate the most general relations among these concepts, a 'framework of concepts' (*Fachwerk von Begriffen*) based upon the fewest possible number of axioms. The axioms are, as far as possible, independent of the

---

[6] In the 1905 Summer Semester Lectures *Logische Principien des mathematischen Denkens*, Hilbert writes 'The general idea of [the axiomatic method] always lies behind any theoretical and practical thinking', as cited and translated in Michael Hallett, 'Hilbert's Axiomatic Method and the Laws of Thought', in George (1994), p. 162.

[7] David Hilbert, *Neubegründung der Mathematik. Erste Mitteilung*, Abhandlungen aus dem mathematischen Seminar der Hamburgischen Universität 1 (1922), as reprinted in Hilbert (1935), pp. 157–77, 161. For Hilbert, the basic objects of number theory, the positive integers or rather the signs that are their symbolic counterparts, are given in a quasi-spatial, but not in spatial or temporal intuition.

particular intuitions (and so, concrete facts) with which the analysis began. By subjecting intuitively given data to such an analysis, the axiomatic method is concerned to separate out and highlight the self-sufficiency of the mathematical subject matter (which may then be developed autonomously), quite apart from any particular reference associated with particular terms or relations. In this way, a separation is effected between logical/mathematical vs. intuitional/experiential thought, even as the latter has thus been arranged in deductive form. According to Hilbert, it is just

> the service of axiomatics to have stressed a separation into the things of thought (*die gedanklichen Dinge*) of the (axiomatic) framework and the real things of the actual world, and then to have carried this through.[8]

As applied to any theory covering a sufficiently known (i.e., mathematized) domain of facts, whether of mathematics or natural science, the axiomatic method is a procedure for finding, for any given proposition of the theory, the premises from which it follows. Indeed, it rigorously implements the more general epistemological approach of regressive or analytic methods for isolating and determining the most general basic propositions on which a given body of knowledge rests. In each case, the aim is not, at least in the first instance, the discovery or recognition of *new* laws or principles, but the conceptual and logical clarification or reconstruction of known ones. As its culmination, the axiomatic method is concerned to demonstrate that the axioms for the theory possess the three metalogical properties or relations of mutual consistency, independence, and completeness.[9] Combining all these aspects together, successful pursuit of the axiomatic method leads to a 'deepening of the foundations' (*Teiferlegung der Fundamente*), i.e., of the *mathematical foundations*, of any theory to which it is applied, and this, indeed, is the overall objective.[10]

---

[8]   David Hilbert, Winter Semester lectures 1922−3 *Wissen und mathematisches Denken*. Ausgearbeitet von Wilhelm Ackermann. Mathematische Institut Göttingen. Published in a limited edition, Göttingen, 1988.

[9]   Hilbert's 1905 Summer Semester Göttingen lectures, *op. cit.* note 6, already characterized the general idea of the axiomatic method as stressing the consistency, independence, and completeness of an axiom system.

[10]   Hilbert (1918) as reprinted in Hilbert (1935), pp. 146−56, 148: 'The procedure of the axiomatic method (...) amounts to a *deepening of the foundations* of the individual domains of knowledge, just as becomes necessary for every edifice that one wishes to extend and build higher while preserving its stability.'

Thomas Ryckman

Two further considerations require emphasis. First, a theory thus axiomatized satisfies, according to Hilbert, the criteria of existence and truth solely through a *consistency proof*, i.e., a demonstration of the mutual consistency of the axioms and all their consequences. Yet the axiomatic method requires that consistency obtain not only with respect to the various axioms, but also with respect to what Hilbert termed the 'conditions of possibility of all conceptual knowledge and all experience'. In other words, all appearance of conflict between the different contributions to scientific knowledge— intuitions, concepts, ideas—should be removed, yielding a 'complete agreement and most pleasant harmony' between the experiences of everyday life and 'the most demanding sciences'.[11] This emphasis on the compatibility between the different sources of knowledge is crucial to understanding Hilbert's project in relativistic physics in 1915–17.

Secondly, the mathematical axioms standing at the pinnacle of the *Fachwerk von Begriffen* are not only general but also *ideal*: as we shall see, Hilbert regarded them as *Ideen* in Kant's regulative sense, principles that have a guiding regulative significance but not a constitutive employment in cognition (however, Hilbert's revision of Kantian epistemology rejects a sharp *constitutive/regulative* distinction). In virtue of their ideality, and so severance from experience and intuition, axioms can play at best a hypothetical or heuristic role in cognition.

Hilbert's application of the axiomatic method in 1915–17

As many will know, in November 1915, Einstein and Hilbert were engaged in what might be described as a sprint to the finish.

---

[11] Lecturing in 1918 on the 'Basic Ideas of General Relativity', Hilbert stressed that the new conceptions of space, time and motion of Einstein's theory were still compatible with 'the traditional intuition' of 'everyday life, our practice and custom': 'Thus we have listed all the essential features of the old conception of space, time and motion. But (. . .) it is still absolutely necessary to bring to mind how excellent this conception of space-time has proved to be. As far as natural sciences and their applications are concerned, we find that everything is based on this conception. And in this construction everything fits together perfectly. Even the boldest speculations of physicists and astronomers are brilliantly confirmed in the minutest detail so that one can say that the experiences of everyday life, our practice and custom, the traditional intuition and the most demanding sciences were in complete agreement and most pleasant harmony with each other.' As cited and translated in Majer (1995), p. 274.

Many will also know that the 'priority question' regarding the generally covariant gravitational field equations recently has been revisited with an unequivocal decision in Einstein's favor. Moreover, Hilbert's two papers on generally invariant physics of 1915 and 1917, both then, and ever since, have been assessed solely in terms of the contributions they made, or failed to make, to general relativity. Now *our* view (here I am drawing on recent work carried out jointly with Katherine Brading)[12] is that Hilbert's work merits examination on its own terms, namely, as an explicit treatment of gravitation and electromagnetism within the framework of the 'axiomatic method' where the principle of general covariance (Hilbert: general invariance) is adopted as an *axiom*. The issue of 'priority' is here an enormous distraction, preventing any detailed internal examination.[13]

First, the facts. In November and December 1915, Hilbert made two presentations to the Göttingen Academy of Sciences under the common title *Die Grundlagen der Physik* but distinguished as 'First Contribution' and 'Second Contribution'. Two papers with these designations eventually appeared in the *Nachrichten* of that Academy, the latter not until January 1917. In his initial communication, on 21 November 1915, Hilbert sketched an elegant variational argument, first constructing what was subsequently termed the 'Hilbert–Einstein Action' based on the Riemann scalar, from which follow, under certain further assumptions, the generally covariant field equations of gravitation. As we know, in November, Einstein submitted four papers to the Berlin Academy: one to each weekly meeting. The last of these, on 25 November 1915, contained, for the first time, the generally covariant field equations of gravitation known to the world since as the Einstein Equations. However, there are *two* extant versions of Hilbert's first contribution: one eventually published in the *Nachrichten* on 31 March 1916 (the delay presumably due to a wartime paper shortage) as well as the printer's proofs stamped with the date 6 December 1915 that was found by Leo Corry in 1996 in archives at the Mathematical Institute in Göttingen. As was widely reported at the time, Corry's discovery

---

[12]   Brading and Ryckman (2008).
[13]   In our defense of this mode of proceeding, there is the assessment of Felix Klein, who noted, in 1921: 'There can be no talk of a question of priority, since both authors pursued entirely different trains of thought (and to be sure, to such an extent that the compatibility of the results did not at once seem assured)'. Klein (1917); as reprinted with additional remarks in Klein (1921), p. 566, fn 8.

Thomas Ryckman

of this document brought a 'belated decision' to the priority question.[14] For the Einstein field equations do not explicitly appear in the printer proofs of Hilbert's paper but only as Euler–Lagrange derivatives, whereas they do so explicitly appear in the published version. Einstein's 25 November 1915 presentation had been published long before, on 2 December 1915, in the *Sitzungsberichte* of the Berlin Academy.

These new developments obviously raise troubling questions regarding a seeming gap between Hilbert's claims and what he actually accomplished in November 1915. Katherine Brading and I believe we have shown that Hilbert's aims and his achievements only in part overlap with Einstein's, but above all must be seen as deeply embedded within the epistemological context of the 'axiomatic method'. The purpose of the remainder of this paper is to briefly present reasons why one might think this, while showing that Hilbert's far more explicit treatment of axioms of invariance in physical theory as 'regulative ideals' conceivably elaborates and amplifies Wigner's more guarded thoughts on the role and significance of invariance principles.

Notably, at the 1900 International Congress of Mathematicians in Paris, Hilbert had proposed 'the axiomatisation of physics' as the sixth of his famous twenty three 'mathematical problems'.[15] Both versions of his first contribution on 'Foundations of Physics' are Hilbert's attempt to solve that problem, subsuming all known physical interactions in 1915 (i.e., gravitation and electromagnetism) under two axioms that essentially present the fundamental laws of physics as solutions to a variational ('least action') problem, under the guiding condition of general invariance:

AXIOM I ('Mie's Axiom of the World Function'). Using the term 'world function', familiar from his lectures on axiomatizing physical theories since 1905, Hilbert formulated a variational argument for a 'world function' H, depending upon the 10 gravitational potentials $g_{\mu\nu}$, their first and second derivatives, as well as the 4 electromagnetic potentials q_s, and their first derivatives:

$$\delta \int H \sqrt{g} d\omega = 0 (g = \det|g_{\mu\nu}|, \, d\omega = dw^1 dw^2 dw^3 dw^4).$$

[14]   Corry, Renn, and Stachel (1997).
[15]   See Gray (2000) for discussion and an English translation of Hilbert's 1900 lecture.

AXIOM II ('Axiom of General Invariance'). The world function H is an invariant with respect to arbitrary transformations of the 'world parameters' w_s ($s = 1, 2, 3, 4$).[16] In both versions Hilbert affirms that this axiom is

> the simplest mathematical expression for the demand that the interconnection of the potentials $g_{\mu\nu}$ and q_s is ... completely independent of the way in which one designates the world points through world parameters.[17]

Hilbert next turns to the derivation of the Euler–Lagrange differential equations for gravitation and electromagnetism. The former arise from differentiation of H with respect to the gravitational potentials $g_{\mu\nu}$ and their first and second derivatives, yielding (using Hilbert's numbering) ten gravitational equations,

$$\frac{\partial \sqrt{g} H}{\partial g^{\mu\nu}} - \sum_k \frac{\partial}{\partial w_k} \frac{\partial \sqrt{g} H}{\partial g_k^{\mu\nu}} + \sum_{k,l} \frac{\partial^2}{\partial w_k \partial w_l} \frac{\partial \sqrt{g} H}{g_{kl}^{\mu\nu}} = 0,$$

or, in Hilbert's abbreviation, (4)

$$[\sqrt{g} H]_{\mu\nu} = 0 \left[\text{notation: } g_l^{\mu\nu} = \frac{\partial g^{\mu\nu}}{\partial w_l}; \ g_{lk}^{\mu\nu} = \frac{\partial^2 g^{\mu\nu}}{\partial w_l \partial w_k} \right].$$

The latter arise from differentiation of H with respect to the electromagnetic potentials q_s and their first derivatives, yielding four equations of electrodynamics, which, following Mie as Hilbert

[16]   Hilbert's use of the term 'world parameters' in place of the standard locution 'space-time coordinates' is instructive. As expressly stated in his (1917), and as Mie also observed, it is intended to highlight the analogy Hilbert sought to draw between the arbitrariness of parameter representations of curves in the calculus of variations, and the arbitrariness of coordinates on a space-time manifold. Hilbert was, of course, a grand master of the calculus of variations, as this communication will demonstrate. In both cases, objective significance will accrue only to objects invariant under arbitrary transformation of the parameters, respectively, coordinates. As Hilbert used precisely the same language of 'world parameters' also in the Proofs, this is *prima facie* evidence that his views regarding the lack of physical meaningfulness accruing to space-time coordinates were already in place.

[17]   Hilbert (1915a). Also (1915b), p. 396.

71

Thomas Ryckman

indeed did, is the basis of Mie's theory of matter:

$$\frac{\partial \sqrt{g} H}{\partial q_h} - \sum_\sigma \frac{\partial}{\partial w_k} \frac{\partial \sqrt{g} H}{\partial q_{hk}} = 0,$$ (5)

or, $[\sqrt{g} H]_h = 0$ [notation: $q_{hk} = \frac{\partial q_h}{\partial w_k} (h, k = 1, 2, 3, 4)$].[18]

The fourteen equations 4 and 5 are termed respectively, 'the basic equations of gravitation' and 'the basic equations of electrodynamics or generalized Maxwell equations'. On the assumption that the Mie electromagnetic theory of matter was viable, these equations encompassed the entirety of known fundamental physics in 1915.

Before proceeding further Hilbert then stated, without proof, a theorem described as the '*Leitmotiv* of my theory', whose content may be more briefly stated thus:

THEOREM I ('*Leitmotiv*'). In the system of n Euler–Lagrange differential equations in n variables obtained from a generally covariant variational integral such as in Axiom I, 4 of the n equations are always a consequence of the other $n-4$ in the sense that 4 linearly independent combinations of the n equations and their total derivatives are always identically satisfied.[19]

---

[18] The form of equations 4 and 5 is trivially algebraically different between (1915a) and (1915b). Here the published version (1915b) is followed. For ease of comparison with the text, Hilbert's non-standard designation of the electromagnetic potential as well as his practice of using roman letters as indices for that potential and for the 'world parameters' is followed.

[19] Hilbert (1915a), pp. 2–3; (1915b), p. 397. Hilbert regards the invariant H as the additive sum of *two* general invariants $H = K + L$, where K (the Riemann scalar) represents the source-free gravitational Lagrangian and L is the source term associated with the addition of matter fields (the electromagnetic field in Hilbert's theory). As Klein (1917), p. 481, first pointed out, there are therefore eight identities available; four associated with K and four with L. According to Klein, the identities associated with L reveal that the conservation laws of the matter field equations are consequences of the gravitational field equations, and he concluded that they therefore 'have no physical significance'. This redundancy in the field equations, a feature of the generally invariant structure of the theory, prompted Hilbert's interpretation of the electromagnetic equations as a consequence of the gravitational equations.

Theorem I states very clearly, and for the first time, a property of general relativity that is now well known and is indeed associated with Noether's second theorem (1918). However in a passage appearing in the December Proofs, but removed in the published version, Hilbert explicitly spells out the implications of Theorem I for his system of fundamental equations of physics.

> Our mathematical theorem teaches that the above axioms I and II can yield for the 14 potentials only 10 equations essentially independent of one another. On the other hand, by upholding general invariance, no more than 10 essentially independent equations for the 14 potentials $g_{\mu\nu}$, q_s, are possible at all. Therefore, if we want to preserve the determinate character of the fundamental equations of physics according to Cauchy's theory of differential equations, the requirement of four additional non-invariant equations supplementing (4) and (5) is essential.[20]

As befits its preeminent concern with the *consistency* of all axioms and assumptions that underlie a theory, the axiomatic method has here revealed a seeming conflict between general covariance and causality in the sense of an apparent failure of univocal determination, a conflict characterized as whether *any* theory satisfying Axioms I and II admits of a well-posed Cauchy problem. Theorem I suggests that it is a property of any such theory that it does not. For a system of second order partial differential equations, the Cauchy problem is that of showing that, from given initial data assignments to the field functions and their first (time) derivatives in a bounded region, the initial data yield unique solutions to these equations as far as possible away from that region (the region's 'domain of dependence'). In field theories formulated on spacetime, the initial data are formulated on a given 3-dimensional spatial surface (a 'space-like hypersurface'), and the essential problem is that of showing that the field equations determine the evolution of the data off that surface according to the second time derivatives of the given field quantities. As Hilbert repeatedly emphasized in period lectures, in all physical theories prior to general relativity, Cauchy determination is satisfied in that there are precisely as many independent equations as there are independent functions to be determined. However, the situation is complicated in a generally covariant spacetime theory (as was notoriously shown by Einstein in the so-called 'Hole Argument' in 1913–5)[21] by the

[20] Hilbert (1915a), pp. 3–4.
[21] See e.g., Stachel, 'The Meaning of General Covariance: The Hole Story', in Earman *et al.* (eds) (1993), pp. 129–60.

Thomas Ryckman

freedom to make arbitrary coordinate transformations (equivalently, local diffeomorphic point transformations) of solutions to the field equations. In terms of Theorem I, this results from the fact that, on account of the axiom of general invariance, not all of the Euler–Lagrange equations obtained by variation of the integral invariant with respect to the field quantities and their derivatives are independent. More precisely, 4 of these are always the result of the remaining $n-4$ space-time equations. Thus, Theorem I is *a precise mathematical statement of the tension between the postulate of general covariance (or, general invariance) and the requirement of causality in the mathematical sense of univocal determination.*

Notice that univocal causal determination—in the sense of Cauchy determination (one equation for each independent variable)—is not an axiom in Hilbert's construction. Nevertheless, it is a requirement satisfied by previous physical theories, and so its seeming failure in the context of general covariance surely sparked Hilbert's interest. In short, a central outcome Hilbert reached by means of the axiomatic method is this: *any generally covariant spacetime theory raises deep questions about causality, in both the mathematical and the physical sense (and in the distinction between these).*

Accordingly, Hilbert set himself the task, in the December Proofs, to find the four missing equations required for a well-posed Cauchy problem. After the lengthy construction of an 'energy form', the requisite four equations are derived by imposing special coordinate restrictions on an 'energy vector', namely that it must satisfy the divergence equation, given again in Hilbert's numbering,

$$\sum_l \frac{\partial e_s^l}{\partial w_l} = 0, \text{ iff the four quantities } e_s = 0. \tag{15}$$

Here the w_i are now special spacetime coordinates adapted to this 'energy theorem', as stated in a third, and final axiom appearing only in the December Proofs:

AXIOM III: ('The Axiom of Space and Time'): 'The space-time coordinates are such particular world parameters for which the energy theorem (15) is valid.'

Elucidating this result, Hilbert clarified the main point, that these 4 non-covariant equations complete the system of fundamental equations of physics:

> On account of the same number of equations and of definite potentials, the causality principle for physical happenings (*Geschehen*) is also ensured, and with it is unveiled to us the

narrowest connection between the energy theorem and the principle of causality, in that each conditions the other.[22]

Now the idea that satisfaction of energy conservation (the energy theorem (15)) requires 4 non-covariant equations is almost certainly taken from the Einstein–Grossmann *Entwurf* theory of 1913–4, where four non-generally covariant equations ensure energy conservation by restricting the covariance class of the field equations.[23] But Hilbert's rather more complicated construction has, philosophically and motivationally, a different *raison d'être*. His four non-generally covariant equations ensuring energy conservation are used to *extract a Cauchy-determinate structure within an otherwise generally covariant theory*, (and *not* to abandon general invariance, which is, after all, an *axiom*).

The very complex mathematical derivation in the Proofs leading to the four non-covariant energy equations was cut, together with *all* of its motivation, from the published version. The reason, surely, is that Einstein's 25 November 1915 paper contained an implicitly generally covariant treatment of energy conservation. So Hilbert recognized he had adopted the wrong approach for resolving the tension between general covariance and Cauchy-determination. In the published version, Hilbert derived a generally covariant 'energy equation' that anyway is consonant with the so-called 'trace' term in the gravitational field equations popping out through explicit calculation from their Lagrangian derivatives. But then, *also in the published version, all reference to the tension between general invariance and causality implied by Theorem I was deleted*!

Of course, the issue of causality in a generally covariant theory did not go away.[24] Hilbert's second contribution[25] indeed begins with a discussion of the problem of causal order, and contains a much revised, and lengthy, reconsideration of this issue. It is rightly understood as resolving the problems posed in the December Proofs.

Without going into much further detail, which is largely irrelevant here, the strategy in this second Hilbert paper is to adopt a criterion of physical meaningfulness and objective validity in terms of general

---

[22] Hilbert (1915a), 7.
[23] Renn and Stachel (1999), p. 32, note Einstein's conviction '(e)ven before Einstein developed the hole argument', that energy–momentum conservation requires such a restriction.
[24] The topic of energy–momentum in general relativity did not go away either: it was the subject of ongoing discussions between Hilbert, Einstein and Klein, and remains a delicate issue.
[25] Hilbert (1917).

Thomas Ryckman

invariance, while recognizing that human experience (measurement and observation) requires a restricted representation of space and time in which the causal relation is preserved.[26] To this end, he introduced what he called 'proper coordinate systems'.[27] In the case of a general Riemannian metric, these amount to so-called 'reality relations'[28] reflecting the physical requirement of metrical indefiniteness: that 3 of the coordinate axes are space-like, and 1 time-like. Moreover, since a time-like curve remains a time-like curve under a proper coordinate transformation, two world points along such a curve can never receive the same value of the time coordinate through a 'proper space-time coordinate transformation', ensuring that causal order between events along such a curve is always preserved. This reconciliation, set in the frame of the Cauchy problem, produced the four needed coordinate conditions to restore univocal determination of future states from present ones, and the requirement of causality is accordingly modified:

> So we see that the concepts of cause and effect lying at the basis of the principle of causality also in the new physics never leads to inner contradiction, as soon as we always take the inequalities (31) in addition to our fundamental equations; that is, we restrict ourselves to the use of *proper* space-time coordinates.[29]

---

[26]   In brief, general invariance (or, general covariance) allows for local diffeomorphic point-transformations among the solutions to the field equations; for causal (time-like) curves, this permits inversion of the ordering of space-time points on such curves. Obviously, this can lead to causal anomalies. Hilbert first recognized that the full invariance (or covariance) of a generally invariant theory must be broken in order to adequately establish causality (in terms of the initial value and Cauchy problems). On the other hand, Hilbert held that the fundamental equations of physics must be time-reversal invariant, and so favoring the causal ordering by adopting particular coordinate systems is but an 'anthropomorphic' epistemic condition.

[27]   'Proper coordinate systems' are defined by the satisfaction of 4 inequalities among the components of the metric tensor. Where x_4 is the time coordinate, using Hilbert's numbering (31),

$$\text{these are: } g_{11} > 0, \begin{vmatrix} g_{11} & g_{12} \\ g_{21} & g_{22} \end{vmatrix} > 0, \begin{vmatrix} g_{11} & g_{12} & g_{13} \\ g_{21} & g_{22} & g_{23} \\ g_{31} & g_{32} & g_{33} \end{vmatrix} > 0, g_{44} < 0.$$

[28]   Pauli termed them *'Wirklichkeitsverhältniße'* in Pauli (1921), English translation (1958), §22.

[29]   Hilbert (1917), p. 58. For a definition of the aforementioned inequalities (31), see footnote 27.

Hilbert is essentially stating here that it is the structure of our cognitive experience (in Kantian terms, that imposed by our sensibility and understanding) that leads to the requirement that we use proper coordinate systems—this restriction has to do *not* with the ideal generally invariant objects of physics, but with the possible objects of experience (physical facts as determined by 'measure threads' and 'light clocks') as these are represented standing in causal relations within spatiotemporal empirical intuition.

With this conception of the causality principle in hand, the necessary and sufficient conditions for a proposition to be physically meaningful are now these:

(a)   The proposition must have a generally covariant formulation.

(b)   When the proposition is expressed with respect to a proper coordinate system, the truth value of that description must be *uniquely* determined by an appropriate space-like past hypersurface, abiding the human epistemic interest in causal relations.

From Hilbert's point of view, the physical principle of causality, as preserved by the coordinate conditions of a well-posed Cauchy problem, is a lingering but ineliminable constraint upon human cognition ('physical meaningfulness'), a necessary condition imposed by the mind in structuring experience. Like the subjectivity of the sense qualities, the requirement of physical causality is *anthropomorphic*, having to do not with the objective world of physics but rather with our experience of that world.

It might be said that Hilbert, through the axiomatic method, was the first to put a finger on where exactly the general theory of relativity required a modification of the traditional Kantian transcendental framework that expressly binds considerations of objectivity to conditions of possible experience. According to Kant, for a cognition to be *objectively valid* (i.e., to be a representation pertaining to a possible object *for us*, hence to be *meaningful*) is for it to invoke *our* specifically human type of finite, receptive spatiotemporal sensory intuition of objects. Hilbert essentially argued that this is no longer the case once the requirement of general invariance is adopted in fundamental physical theory. While retaining part of Kant's tie of conditions of physical *meaningfulness* to *sensibility*, Hilbert placed invariance as the *superordinate* criterion of physical objectivity, attributing this development expressly to the influence of Einstein's gravitational theory.

The 'axiomatic method' is ideally suited to show this, for it is the instrument for working up a domain of intuitively presented physical facts into a purely logical-formal system of relations, crowned in

Thomas Ryckman

Hilbert's papers of 1915 and 1917 by an axiom positing a generally invariant spacetime integral. However, space, time, (and causality, which presupposes both) are necessary moments of human cognition, required also as conditions of the possibility of observation and measurement in science. Thus, though they remain conditions of the possibility of experience, representation in space and time reflects merely the subjective origin of cognition in sensible experience; in the new physics, such representation is no longer a necessary criterion of *being a possible object of physics*. There, Hilbert made it clear, the pull of objectivity leads *away* from intuition, away from physical observation and measurement, and indeed from everything *anthropomorphic*. This, of course, is just the direction of cognition captured within the axiomatic method. While the goal of physical science remains that of a completely objective description of nature, a systematically unified, observer-free cognition of nature requires a (never fully attainable) emancipation of our view of the processes of nature from all the subjective elements pertaining to human sensibility. The principal step along this new path is Einstein's requirement of general covariance:

> Hitherto, the objectification of our view of the processes of nature took place by emancipation from the subjectivity of human sensations. But a more far-reaching objectification is necessary, to be obtained by emancipating ourselves from the *subjective* moments of human *intuition* with respect to space and time. This emancipation, which is at the same time the high-point of scientific objectification, is achieved in Einstein's theory, it means a radical elimination of *anthropomorphic* slag (*Schlacke*), and leads us to that kind of description of nature which is *independent* of our senses and intuition and is directed purely to the goals of objectivity and systematic unity.[30]

Fundamental physical theory, in accordance with the axiom of general invariance aspires to a *non-anthropomorphic* account of physical objectivity, that is, to a 'description of nature which is *independent* of our senses and intuition'. But given its axiomatic status, the principle of general invariance *is neither true nor false, but a regulative idea*,

> if, in accordance with Kant's words, we understand by an idea a concept of reason that transcends all experience and through which the concrete is completed so as to form a totality.[31]

---

[30]   Hilbert, *Grundgedanken der Relativitätstheorie*, Göttingen Summer Semester Lectures 1921; as cited by Majer (1995), p. 284.
[31]   Hilbert (1926), p. 190.

As Ulrich Majer in particular has emphasized, by employing the 'method of ideal elements' in his proof-theory (regarded as a strictly finite means to prove the consistency of transfinite mathematics), Hilbert expressly tied the use of ideal elements in mathematics to Kant's regulative use of ideas.[32] And, while Hilbert allowed that such elements could be introduced either through mathematical construction or as axioms,[33] the axiomatic method, naturally, prefers the latter. In virtue of their ideality, and so severance from experience and intuition, axioms of invariance play a hypothetical role in cognition, no longer constitutive of experience, but informing and guiding the idea of physical objectivity.

This completes Hilbert's revision of the Kantian a priori. By the early 1920s, Hilbert had termed his revised understanding of the a priori 'the finite point of view' (*die finite Einstellung*). But Hilbert's work on 'Foundations of Physics' in 1915–17 shows in addition that Majer is correct in concluding that

> Hilbert's 'finite point of view' is not restricted to mathematics or meta-mathematics, but is stated as a *universal principle of epistemology*.[34]

Hilbert took from Kant the methodology or standpoint that objective cognition can only be understood as conditioned by a priori structures of the mind, but he refashioned the boundaries of the a priori somewhat differently:

> The a priori is thereby nothing more and nothing less than a basic attitude or expression for certain essential preconditions of thought and experience. However the boundaries between that we possess a priori on the one hand, and that, on the other, for which experience is necessary, we must draw other than Kant; Kant far overestimated the role and the scope of the a priori.

We see therefore: in the Kantian theory of the a priori (*Apriori-Theorie*) there is still contained anthropomorphic slag

---

[32] Majer (1993a).

[33] E.g., Hilbert (1992), p. 91: 'The transition to the broader system [containing ideal elements] either can be effected in a constructive manner, in which the new elements are developed through mathematical construction from the older ones, or in an axiomatic manner, in which the new system is characterized through relational properties. In the second case, it requires a proof that the supposition of a system with the desired condition does not in itself lead to contradiction.'

[34] Majer (1993b), p. 191.

(*Schlacken*), from which it must be freed, and after such removal only that a priori attitude (*apriorische Einstellung*) is left, which also lies at the foundation of pure mathematical knowledge: it is essentially that finite attitude characterized by me in different essays.[35]

In sum, Hilbert's two communications on 'Foundations of Physics' are a complex epistemological response to generally covariant field physics, hitherto unrecognized, and directly tied to his employment of the 'axiomatic method'. In accordance with that method, Hilbert understood the significance of the principle of general covariance within the broad framework of the Transcendental Dialectic. A product of the faculty of pure theoretical reason in its 'hypothetical' employment, the axiom of general invariance posits a regulative ideal of systematic unity, and possesses an objective but indeterminate validity. Hilbert's setting of gravitation and electromagnetism within the frame of the 'axiomatic method' is a significant example illustrating how invariance principles may be methodologically interpreted as the projection of a necessary postulate of the systematization or unity of nature grounded in the basic structure of human reason and cognition. It would seem from Wigner's remarks on invariance principles that something along these lines is also what he had in mind.

[35] Hilbert (1930); reprinted in Hilbert (1935), pp. 383, 385.

Objectivity: A Kantian Perspective

ROBERTO TORRETTI

The subject of this paper is objectivity from Kant's point of view: or better, my own perspective on Kant's perspective on objectivity. More precisely, I want to draw attention to some aspects of the latter, which I believe are too narrow and must be widened before we can benefit from a Kantian approach today.

The great and lasting novelty of Kant's approach lies, to my mind, in the notion that objects which are the referents of epistemic discourse, be they things and their attributes, or objective situations and objective developments, are not *given* but *constituted*, articulated in the stream of becoming by our own regulated activity of composition or 'synthesis'. In other words: objectivity is an *achievement*, is not a *gift*. Scientific realists might feel inclined to question the originality of this view, inasmuch as they—who can trace their doctrine all the way back to Parmenides or at least Democritus—also believe that objectivity is an achievement, which can only be attained by painstakingly fighting off the idols that muddle our native subjectivities. But there are big differences between the scientific realist's ready-made world of perfectly definite objects waiting for the scales to fall from our eyes so that we get to see things in their own light as they are in themselves, and Kant's conception of the world as an *Idee* or program for the local, partial, approximate construction of objects by ever imperfect but endlessly perfectible modeling according to *our* lights. Not the least important and surely the most attractive of these differences is that, whereas the scientific realists must relegate the achievement of objectivity to the end of the road, the Kantian scientists can take pride in their daily achievements of contextual, improvable, incomplete, but reasonably working and passably stable objective truths. Thus, for example, from a Kantian perspective, a report that the traffic light in such and such a street corner in Bloomsbury is out of order and does not switch at regular intervals from red to green and back again to red, is a piece of *objective* knowledge although it involves reference to subjective perceptions of colour and does not describe the physical system in question in terms of string theory or whichever will be the final physical theory of everything.

Modern philosophy, from Descartes onwards, and especially in the shape it took in the British Isles, assumes what we may call the

doi:10.1017/S1358246108000052

Roberto Torretti

methodological primacy of subjective *Erlebnisse* (the standard English word for *Erlebnis* is, of course, 'experience'; but one must be careful with this word when speaking about Kant, for it is also employed to translate Kant's term *Erfahrung*, which designates what is for him the very locus of objectivity). On the said assumption, the philosopher accepts the flow of feelings, sensations and fantasies as unquestionably certain, just as it comes and goes, and seeks to build a bridge from it to the so-called 'external world' of objective things and facts. Kant sets out from this same starting point—otherwise he could not have been a partner to the philosophical conversation of his time—but he turned the said quest for objectivity on its head. Instead of looking for a handle in the sensuous manifold, by seizing which one could jump out of the 'stream of consciousness', he contends that no such stream is possible, at any rate not one attended by consciousness, unless it consists in the steady and progressive construction of an objective system of nature.

Kant argues for this in two ways which differ so much in surface structure and apparent intention that their kinship usually eludes the reader. One argument is presented on pp. 99–110 of the first edition of the *Critique of pure reason*,[1] and forms the core of Section 2 of 'On the deduction of the pure concepts of the understanding'. This passage was deleted, like several others, in the second edition,[2] not—says Kant (on p. XLII thereof)—because he no longer agreed with them, but to make room for the addition of other passages. One of these is labelled 'Refutation of idealism', and offers a less profound and ambitious argument to substantially the same effect (B 274-279). The gist of this argument is the following. To be compatible with *self*-awareness, without which no *mere* awareness is possible, the flight of *Erlebnisse* in time must be referred to *steady* and therefore *spatial* objects. Readers who reach this point of the second edition will be acquainted with the table of the categories, the 'deduction' of their objective validity, the 'schematism' by which they operate the constitution of objects and the principles that govern this operation; so Kant can take for granted everything that, according to him, is implied in the reference of *Erlebnisse* to objects. The argument in the first edition precedes almost all these

[1]   Kant (1781). References to this edition will be designated by KrV A, followed by the page number. All translations from this work are by the author (RT).
[2]   Kant (1787). References to this edition will be designated by KrV B, followed by the page number. All translations from this work are by the author (RT).

sections and therefore must go deeper into the question of constitution.

Roughly stated, the argument in KrV A proceeds as follows: absolutely nothing is *simple* in the stream of *Erlebnisse*;[3] therefore, fragments of the stream can be sensed only if they are run through and held together in 'the synthesis of apprehension'. To bring this about in the midst of the stream's incessant flow, apprehension must be assisted by recollection. Thus, for a melody to be heard, every segment of it must somehow be remembered at the time the last note comes forth. Yet, as Kant pointedly remarks, if there is no awareness that what is being noticed now is one and the same thing that was noticed a moment ago, the entire reproduction in the sequence of *Erlebnisse* will be in vain. The requisite identification is achieved by 'the synthesis of recognition in a concept'. 'Every cognition—says Kant—requires a concept, no matter how imperfect or unclear it might be. By nature, a concept is always something (...) that serves as a rule.' Indeed a concept can only work for the recognition, reproduction and apprehension of *Erlebnisse* insofar as it grasps the regular patterns of the *Erlebnis* manifold and thereby represents 'the synthetic unity in the awareness thereof'.[4] On the other hand, recognition, that is, awareness of the identity of that which is being successively grasped, cannot take effect without awareness of the identity of the very act of grasping. This form of awareness, that is, *self-awareness*, is called by Kant *apperception* (after Leibniz). It is the key to Kant's conception of objectivity. Let me quote just one convoluted but pivotal passage of the first *Critique*:

The original and necessary awareness of the identity of oneself is at the same time awareness of an equally necessary unity of the

---

[3]   KrV A 784/B 812, A 772/B 800. See also vol. 28, pp. 281f. and vol. 8, p. 208 of *Kant's gesammelte Schriften*, (Berlin: De Gruyter). Henceforth I shall refer to this edition as Ak, followed by volume and page number, with a colon separating both numbers. Translations from this work are by the author (RT).

[4]   The last five lines of the main text are in part a translation, in part a paraphrase of the following passage: 'Alles Erkenntniß erfordert einen Begriff, dieser mag nun so unvollkommen oder so dunkel sein, wie er wolle; dieser aber ist seiner Form nach jederzeit etwas Allgemeines, und was zur Regel dient. So dient der Begriff vom Körper nach der Einheit des Mannigfaltigen, welches durch ihn gedacht wird, unserer Erkenntniß äußerer Erscheinungen zur Regel. Eine Regel der Anschauungen kann er aber nur dadurch sein, daß er bei gegebenen Erscheinungen die nothwendige Reproduction des Mannigfaltigen derselben, mithin die synthetische Einheit in ihrem Bewußtsein vorstellt' (KrV A 106).

Roberto Torretti

composition of all appearances according to concepts, that is, to rules that not only make them reproducible with necessity, but also, in so doing, *determine an object for their intuition*, that is, the concept of something wherein they are necessarily interconnected. For the mind could never think of its own identity in the manifold of its ideas (*Vorstellungen*) (...) if it did not have before its eyes the identity of its act, which subordinates all synthesis of apprehension (...) to a transcendental unity and makes its regular interconnection a priori possible.[5]

Right after this passage, Kant declares that henceforth we shall be able to better characterize the abstract notion of an *object* in general, that is, what he calls 'the transcendental object'.[6] This turns out to be neither more nor less than the intellectual support that holds the identity of the mind's act before the mind's 'eye'.

The pure concept of this transcendental object (which in effect is always in all our cognitions the same unspecified X) is what can generally procure a relation to an object, that is, objective reality, to all our empirical concepts. This concept cannot contain any definite intuition, and therefore concerns exclusively that unity which must be found in a manifold of cognition insofar as it stands in relation to an object. This relation, however, is nothing else than the necessary unity of consciousness, and with it also of the synthesis of the manifold through the

[5] 'Also ist das ursprüngliche und nothwendige Bewußtsein der Identität seiner selbst zugleich ein Bewußtsein einer eben so nothwendigen Einheit der Synthesis aller Erscheinungen nach Begriffen, d.i. nach Regeln, die sie nicht allein nothwendig reproducibel machen, sondern dadurch auch ihrer Anschauung einen Gegenstand bestimmen, d.i. den Begriff von Etwas, darin sie nothwendig zusammenhängen: denn das Gemüth könnte sich unmöglich die Identität seiner selbst in der Mannigfaltigkeit seiner Vorstellungen und zwar a priori denken, wenn es nicht die Identität seiner Handlung vor Augen hätte, welche alle Synthesis der Apprehension (die empirisch ist) einer transscendentalen Einheit unterwirft und ihren Zusammenhang nach Regeln a priori zuerst möglich macht' (KrV A 108. I include here all the words I have represented by ellipsis in the translation).
[6] Speaking of 'the transcendental object of sense intuition' (*das transscendentale Obiect der sinnlichen Anschauung*), Kant says in Reflection 5554: 'This is no real object or given thing, but a concept in relation to which appearances have unity' (*Dieses ist aber kein reales obiect oder gegeben Ding, sondern ein Begrif, auf den in Beziehung Erscheinungen Einheit haben.*—Ak 18: 230).

84

common function of the mind that is capable of combining it in one idea.[7]

This radically innovative and for many people shocking conception of objectivity is both clarified and strengthened by Kant's words in Reflection 5643:

> We know an object only as something in general, for which the given intuitions are merely predicates. How they can be the predicates of something else cannot be known by comparing them with it, but only through the manner how consciousness of the multiple in general can be regarded as necessarily combined in one consciousness. The multiple is unified in the idea of an object. All intuitions are merely ideas; **the object to which they are referred lies in the understanding**.[8]

In his letter to Marcus Herz, on 21 February 1772, Kant told his friend he had asked himself for the ground of the reference of our

---

[7] 'Der reine Begriff von diesem transscendentalen Gegenstande (der wirklich bei allen unsern Erkenntnissen immer einerlei $= X$ ist) ist das, was allen unsern empirischen Begriffen überhaupt Beziehung auf einen Gegenstand, d.i. objective Realität, verschaffen kann. Dieser Begriff kann nun gar keine bestimmte Anschauung enthalten und wird also nichts anders als diejenige Einheit betreffen, die in einem Mannigfaltigen der Erkenntniß angetroffen werden muß, so fern es in Beziehung auf einen Gegenstand steht. Diese Beziehung aber ist nichts anders, als die nothwendige Einheit des Bewußtseins, mithin auch der Synthesis des Mannigfaltigen durch gemeinschaftliche Function des Gemüths, es in einer Vorstellung zu verbinden' (KrV, A 109).

[8] 'Wir kennen ein obiect nur als ein Etwas überhaupt, dazu die gegebene Anschauungen nur Prädicate sind. Wie diese nun von einem Dritten die praedicate seyn können, kan durch ihre Vergleichung nicht erkannt werden, sondern durch die Art, wie in einem Bewustseyn das Bewustseyn des Manigfaltigen überhaupt als nothwendig verbunden angesehen werden könne. In der Vorstellung eines obiects ist das Manigfaltige vereinigt. Alle Anschauungen sind nur Vorstellungen; das Obiect, darauf sie bezogen werden, liegt im Verstande' (Ak 18: 283). Cf. also this passage from Reflection 5642: 'Wenn wir zur Warheit noch etwas mehr erfodern als den durchgängigen zusammenhang der Anschauungen nach Gesetzen des Verstandes, worin wolten wir sie denn setzen, wenn dieses nicht Zugleich die Vorstellung eines bestimmten obiects wäre. *Soll es ausser dem noch in Übereinstimmung mit etwas anderm, was nicht in unsern Vorstellungen liegt, seyn, wie wollen wir es damit vergleichen.* Alle obiecte werden nur durch die Vorstellungen in mir bestimt; was sie übrigens an sich seyn mögen, ist mir unbekannt' (Ak 18: 281; my emphasis).

85

Roberto Torretti

ideas to an object.[9] The argument I have just sketched provides an answer to this question and paves the way for Kant's purported proof that the rules governing the constitution of objects through the threefold synthesis of *Erlebnisse* ultimately—or rather, primarily—are none other than the concepts listed in the 'table of the categories' he had elicited, not without some sleight of hand, from the various classifications of judgments he found in contemporary German textbooks of logic.[10] I cannot go into details but I must emphasize this: *all* that Kant's laborious Transcendental Deduction of the Categories can claim to prove is that *some such* non-empirical concepts are required to spell out subjective appearances in order to read them as objective experience (*Erfahrung*). However, it does not follow from the transcendental deduction that those concepts are contained in a given, finite list, let alone that they cannot increase or vary. Surely Kant, prompted by his religious beliefs, would have sternly denied that they do. But Kant forthrightly acknowledged that 'this peculiarity of our understanding, that it can produce *a priori* unity of apperception solely by means of categories, and precisely by such and so many' admits no further explanation.[11] The great British Kant scholar, H.J. Paton, who was born under Queen Victoria, barely touched on this text in a footnote and left it out of his index of quoted passages.[12] Yet for us today it would be very hard to countenance a Kantian perspective on anything if Kant himself had not openly conceded the groundlessness of Reason.

---

[9] 'Ich frug mich nemlich selbst: aus welchem Grunde beruhet die Beziehung desienigen, was man in uns Vorstellung nennt, auf den Gegenstand?'(Ak 10: 130).

[10] The match between Kant's table of judgments (KrV, A 70/B 95) and his table of the categories (KrV, A 80/B 106) has often been questioned because it requires the addition of singular and indefinite judgments to the then familiar classifications. But when I speak of Kant's sleight of hand I am thinking mainly of the implausible link he establishes between quantification in the natural sciences and the traditional classification of subject-predicate statements into affirmative and universal (A), negative and universal (E), affirmative and particular (I), and negative and particular (O). I, for one, have never been able to see more than a pun on the words 'quantity' and 'quality' in the alleged correspondences between universal, particular and—if you wish— singular judgments and the principle of the axioms of intuition and between affirmative, negative and—if you wish— indefinite judgments and the principle of the anticipations of perception.

[11] See KrV B 145f. Kant's Reason has no further reason, but, like the proverbial rose of Angelus Silesius, 'sie blühet weil sie blühet'.

[12] Paton (1936), vol. 1, p. 536, fn. 1.

By admitting that there is *no reason why* the constitution of objects by the human understanding must follow precisely the patterns listed and described by him, Kant opens a wide door to intellectual pluralism, which indeed has thrived in his wake. However, his conception of the understanding as a closed system of rules with full authority over every cognitive judgment makes it virtually impossible to think that there is more than one form of understanding, expressed in a single fixed 'categorial framework' or 'conceptual scheme'; for thoughts belonging to one such closed intellectual system could not be understood or even recognized as *thoughts* in the context of a different closed system. Now, the very idea of intellectual closure is unpalatable to us, especially if it goes with the idea that the complete set of primary concepts of the understanding is equinumerous with that of the signs of the Zodiac and that of the apostles of Jesus. Moreover, the explosive growth of knowledge in the last two centuries has persuaded us that at least one of Kant's principles of pure understanding is untenable, namely, the Third Analogy of Experience, which proclaims the necessity of instantaneous action at a distance; that he confuses efficient causality with determinism, although the latter is time-symmetric and the former is not; and that the concept of probability, which —in Ian Hacking's phrase—*emerged* in the seventeenth century in the full light of European intellectual history— nevertheless should have a place in a list of primary concepts, for, although one might perhaps think of characterizing probability as quantified possibility, the Kantian definition of real possibility as agreement with the formal conditions of experience leaves no room for quantification.

Such facts have strengthened the impression not infrequent in the twentieth century that Kant's *Critique of pure reason* contains very little that could be of philosophical use to us. As with all major thinkers of the past, this is probably true of what Kant offered as his *doctrine*, but we cannot, in all fairness, say the same of the insights that he so often expresses in passing or which can be read in his books between lines. I shall now quote a short sentence of the 1787 edition of the *Critique* which, when read together with two other passages he wrote in the 1790s, throws an unfamiliar light on the doctrine of the categories and offers a way of bypassing the inconveniences I have mentioned. Kant writes: 'Among all ideas *combination* is the only one that is not given through objects, but can only be performed by the subject itself, because it is an act of its self-activity'.[13] A similar

---

[13] 'Unter allen Vorstellungen die *Verbindung* [ist] die einzige, die nicht durch Objecte gegeben, sondern nur vom Subjecte selbst verrichtet werden kann, weil sie ein Actus seiner Selbstthätigkeit ist' (KrV, B 130).

Roberto Torretti

statement appears in the manuscript about advancements in metaphysics, written in 1791: 'All the ideas (*Vorstellungen*) that constitute an experience (*Erfahrung*) can be counted as belonging to sensibility, with only one exception, namely, the idea of the composite, as such. For composition cannot fall under the senses but we must make it ourselves; thus, it does not belong to the receptivity of the senses, but to the spontaneity of the understanding, as an a priori concept'.[14] If the notion of combination or composition *as such* is, according to Kant, *the only one* that pertains to the understanding alone and 'is not given by objects', then surely all other notions are obtained through the objects constructed—*by combination*—from the stream of *Erlebnisse*. Now, unless I am quite wrong, *all other notions* include the twelve categories. Indeed, Kant himself did not draw this conclusion from his very drastic assertion. Instead, on 11 December 1797, he explained to Tieftrunk that

> The concept of the composite in general is not a particular category, but is contained in all categories [...]. For the composite cannot be intuited as such, but the concept or consciousness of composition (a function which, as synthetic unity of apperception lies at the root of every category) must precede in order that the manifold given to intuition be combined in one consciousness, that is, in order to grasp the object as something composite.[15]

---

[14] 'Alle Vorstellungen, die eine Erfahrung ausmachen, können zur Sinnlichkeit gezählt werden, eine einzige ausgenommen, d.i. die des Zusammengesetzten, als eines solchen. Da die Zusammensetzung nicht in die Sinne fallen kann, sondern wir sie selbst machen müssen: so gehört sie nicht zur Receptivität der Sinnlichkeit, sondern zur Spontaneität des Verstandes, als Begriff a priori' (Ak 20: 275f).

[15] 'Der Begrif des Zusammengesetzten überhaupt ist keine besondere Categorie, sondern in allen Categorien (als synthetische Einheit der Apperception) enthalten. Das Zusammengesetzte nämlich kann, als ein solches, nicht angeschauet werden; sondern der Begrif oder das Bewußtsein des Zusammensetzens (einer Function die allen Categorien als synthetischer Einheit der Apperception zum Grunde liegt) muß vorhergehen, um das mannigfaltige der Anschauung gegebene sich in einem Bewußtsein verbunden, d.i. das Object sich als etwas Zusammengesetztes zu denken, welches durch den Schematism der Urtheilskraft geschieht indem das Zusammensetzen mit Bewußtsein zum innern Sinn, der Zeitvorstellung gemäs einerseits, zugleich aber auch auf das Mannigfaltige in der Anschauung gegebene Andererseits bezogen wird' (Ak 12: 222f).

This might suggest that Kant regarded the twelve categories as *modes* or *specifications* of the concept of the composite in general. But then, by the same token, *all other concepts*, no matter how humble, must also be regarded as such. After all, in strict Kantian orthodoxy one ought to describe them as specifications of the categories. In the manuscript about the real advancements of metaphysics, Kant says: 'There are therefore in the understanding as many concepts a priori under which the objects given to the senses must stand, as there are kinds of composition (synthesis) with awareness, that is, as there are kinds of synthetic unity of apperception of the manifold given in intuition'.[16] If we were bent on making sense of the doctrine of categories, as is presented, say, in §10 of the *Critique*, we would probably have to say that specification by the twelve categories is inherent in or intrinsic to the very notion of composition, and—like Klaus Reich or Béatrice Longuenesse—we would contrive a clever argument to prove that this is so.[17] But if, on the contrary, we perceive the 4 × 3 table of the categories as a millstone around Kant's neck and wish to free him from its burden, we should seize on the opportunity that he himself gave us when he said that the concept of composition is 'in the end, *the only* fundamental concept a priori which, in our understanding, originally underlies all concepts of objects of the senses'.[18] All specification of this concept—in effect the entire task of articulating the stream of *Erlebnisse* to integrate it in the synthetic unity of

---

[16]   'Es werden also so viel Begriffe a priori im Verstande liegen, worunter die Gegenstände, die den Sinnen gegeben werden, stehen müssen, als es Arten der Zusammensetzung (Synthesis) mit Bewußtseyn, d.i. als es Arten der synthetischen Einheit der Apperception des in der Anschauung gegebenen Mannigfaltigen giebt' (Ak 20: 271). Kant obviously believed that the said 'kinds of composition' were none other than his twelve categories.

[17]   Reich (1932) caused a great impression on me when I read it in the 1960s, but it did not last long. On the other hand, Longuenesse (1998) is perhaps the most illuminating and stimulating book about Kant that I have read, especially in its Part Three. Nevertheless, doubts remain as to whether there is more than homonymy between ordinary and scientific concepts of quantity and the 'quantity' of categorical judgments, or that the concept of physical interaction has anything to do with the truth-functional operator of exclusive disjunction. I do, however, agree completely with her description of the structure of Kant's argument in the Transcendental Analytic and her proposals for re-reading the Transcendental Aesthetic, and I believe that nobody who has studied her book can maintain that Kant's doctrine of the categories was implausible or unworthy of a great philosopher.

[18]   Ak 20: 271; my emphasis.

apperception—is then entrusted to the creative interplay between the sensibility and the understanding studied by Kant in the *Kritik der Urteilskraft* and to which he refers in the 1797 letter to Tieftrunk as 'the schematism of the power of judgment'.

According to Kant, the power of judgment operates in two directions: working from the top down, it brings particular *Erlebnisse* under available concepts through which they are grasped as presentations of objects; working from the bottom up, it finds and—if needs be—it creates general concepts suitable for articulating the particulars it discerns in the stream of *Erlebnisse*. This form of operation from the bottom up is evidently indispensable if combination or composition is the only concept that is originally available, whether or not it comes modulated by twelve categories. Kant calls it 'reflection' and ascribes it to *die reflectierende Urteilskraft*, because he remains enthralled by the traditional empiricist—in effect, Aristotelian—view of concept formation. According to this view, a general concept is obtained by *comparison* of particulars, *reflection* about their similarities, and *abstraction* of their common features. This description fits the job of the naturalist who explores a new territory, classifying minerals, or plants, or insects. But concept formation in mathematical physics does not proceed in this way and Kant certainly knew it. Indeed he was perhaps the first philosopher to fully realize that the Aristotelian scheme is insufficient for modern science. But he apparently believed that, just like—in his opinion—Aristotle himself had in one fell swoop reached the end of the road in logic, so had Newton established the principles and basic concepts of physics once and for all. On this assumption it was not unreasonable to come up with 'metaphysical principles of natural science' which reflect the Newtonian achievement but which also match well enough the principles and basic concepts of the human understanding that Kant had gleaned from eigthteenth-century handbooks of ontology. Two centuries later, in the course of which several so-called scientific revolutions have not only occurred but have been discussed *ad nauseam*, this kind of approach is no longer viable. No matter how strong our desire for secure knowledge and stable truths, we must yield to the evidence that science's hunger for new concepts is insatiable and will not be quenched by any closed system of reason. At least in physics, we have seen cohort after cohort of increasingly complex mathematical structures emerge in the light of day, not always in full armour, claiming the right to represent vast families of phenomena within some acceptable margin of imprecision. Concepts of this kind are not meant merely to classify given objects in a received or unprecedented taxonomy, but rather to provide the intellectual setting or, if you wish, the scaffolding for objects to be articulated and displayed. Such concepts cannot be fished out of the stream of impressions, as pre-Kantian empiricists proposed, and this is probably the reason why science-conscious post-Kantian empiricism had to dress up in a 'logical' garb to enjoy a short revival in the twentieth century. Einstein, who had first-hand knowledge of the formation of physico-mathematical concepts, forcefully characterized them as 'freie Erfindungen des menschlichen Geistes', unconstrained inventions of the human mind.[19] I would not presume to say this better than Einstein did. But I shall now venture a tentative proposal linking the exercise of free invention in Einstein's sense with the imaginative interplay between the sensibility and the understanding that Kant discusses in the Schematismus chapter and again in his *Kritik der Urteilskraft*.

To explain my proposal I must lift a restriction I have respected up to this point. Except for a few allusions to the temporal flow of *Erlebnisse* and a brief hint to spatiality as a condition of steadiness, I have intentionally avoided all reference to Kant's notorious doctrine of time and space as the 'forms' of our 'internal' and 'external' sense. I am persuaded that this doctrine was the key that opened the gates of the garden of critical philosophy; but I can also see that for someone who is already inside it, Kant's presentation of this doctrine in the Transcendental Aesthetic is still too close to the pre-critical teaching of the dissertation of 1770 and does not fit the conception of the human understanding presented in the Transcendental Analytic. My point is not merely that, after Lobachevsky and Riemann, Euclidean geometry can no longer be regarded as a condition of the possibility of our experience of physical objects; but rather that Euclidean geometry, in its full richness and complexity, cannot be attributed to a pure intuition which, in Kant's words, is blind (unless it is set to work by and for the understanding). Kant himself clearly hinted that the Transcendental Aesthetic needs revision. He did so in §26 of the 1787 *Critique*, especially in the long footnote to B 160, where he distinguishes between 'the form of intuition' and 'formal intuition', and also in §38 of *Prolegomena*, where a well-known theorem of geometry is described as a law of nature posited by the understanding.[20] However, the section concerning the Axioms of Intuition (A 162-166/B 202-207)—which deals explicitly with the

---

[19]   Einstein, 'Zur Methodik der theoretischen Physik' (*ca.* 1930), in Einstein (1979), p. 115.

[20]   Kant, Ak 4: 320–322. As Longuenesse (1998), p. 213, tersely remarks: 'The goal of the Transcendental Deduction of the Categories

emergence of geometry through the interplay of intellect and sensibility in 'the successive synthesis of productive imagination' (A 163/B 204)—does not actually elucidate the formation of geometrical concepts and axioms, but simply takes it for granted. Indeed, by associating—no matter how vaguely—the 'axioms of intuition' with the categories of quantity, Kant remains beholden to the medieval conception of mathematics as the science of quantity and blissfully unaware of the geometrical significance of non-quantitative properties and relations. Of course, philosophers, though they are often endowed with above average hindsight, are not required to have any foresight at all; and it would be terribly unfair to reproach Kant for not having anticipated the tropical growth of topological, algebraic and order structures that fill the landscape of modern mathematics.

My proposal is to secure maximal freedom for Kant's *productive imagination* or *reflective judgment* by minimizing the limitations imposed on it from either end of its playground, namely, *first*, by the pure forms of sensibility and, *second*, by the pure concepts of the understanding. On the first point, Béatrice Longuenesse had this to say: 'Kant's transcendental account of the pure intuition of space provides no reason to assert that space is necessarily Euclidean, so that Kant needlessly limits the scope of his transcendental Aesthetic and Analytic, when he claims that the representation of space they ground is that of Euclidean geometry'.[21] Indeed, Kant himself acknowledged that 'space is something too uniform and too indeterminate with respect to all particular properties' to comprise a store of geometrical theorems.[22] In a more assertive mood, and following a suggestion of Henri Poincaré,[23] I dare to add that the intuitive 'form' illustrated in every *Erlebnis* merely adumbrates the mathematical notion of a—should we say four-dimensional?—coordinate patch. On the second point, concerning the other end of

---

is "fully attained" only when it leads to a rereading of the Transcendental Aesthetic'.

[21]   Longuenesse (1998), p. 287.

[22]   *Prolegomena*, §38 (Ak 4:321).

[23]   'Je conclurai que nous avons tous en nous l'intuition du continu d'un nombre quelconque de dimensions, parce que nous avons la faculté de construire un continu physique et mathématique; que cette faculté préexiste en nous à toute expérience parce que sans elle, l'expérience proprement dite serait impossible et se réduirait à des sensations brutes, impropres à toute organisations, que cette intuition n'est que la conscience que nous avons de cette faculté'. Poincaré (1912); quoted from Poincaré (1913a), p. 157.

the playground of concept formation, I stand by what Kant said in the texts I quoted earlier: the notion of combination or composition *as such* is *the only one* that pertains to the understanding alone. Within these boundaries, but free from any additional a priori constraints, the power of judgment has plenty of room to improvise and articulate not just the familiar concept pairs *thing* and *attribute, cause* and *effect*, but all the grand conceptual structures employed by mathematical physics or yet to be created by its practitioners.

Kantians who adopt my proposal will no longer be put to shame by the growth of geometry or the turnabouts of mechanics. Thanks to it, Kant's pure reason can take pride on the open-endedness that actual human reason so glaringly displays. More significantly perhaps, we renounce the claim to completeness and invariability that Kant made on behalf of the categories and principles of the understanding. Thereby, we extend to reason itself Kant's intrepid rejection of unconditioned totalities, instead of allowing her to stand as the ultimate transcendental illusion. Open-endedness and detotalization yield two philosophical benefits. First of all, if we admit that scientific concept formation is ever in progress and there is no closed system of basic notions by which it must abide, we can in good faith dismiss the widespread and yet highly unlikely view of the history of science as a series of quantum jumps between incommensurable intellectual systems. The glass-and-steel towers of theory can always communicate with each other across the quicksands of ordinary discourse on which they repose. The second philosophical benefit I see is this: if even the formation of basic concepts remains incomplete, the very idea of a full inventory of predicates by comparison with which every single object might be exhaustively determined makes no sense at all, and the thoroughgoing determination of things asserted by modern pre-critical metaphysics is unthinkable.

Still, before we can say that my proposal is workable we would have to see it at work. How can this be done? One must show, in particular historical cases, how a new concept or structured panoply of concepts issues from those that were previously available—and ultimately perhaps from pre-conceptual intuitions—through an intellectual effort resembling that of Kant's productive imagination or reflective judgment. This is not easy, for mathematicians and theoretical physicists have not been fond of describing the often tortuous paths by which they reached their ideas. I dare say, however, that Riemann's lecture 'On the hypotheses that lie at the foundation of geometry'[24] bears witness to the reflections that took him from common and

---

[24] Riemann (1867). Riemann delivered this lecture in 1854.

more or less intuitive notions of space and quantity to the concepts of differentiable manifold and Riemannian metric. Along similar lines, one could perhaps—reading Hermann Weyl, Élie Cartan and their successors—reconstruct the way from Riemann's ideas to the seemingly forbidding notion of a fibre bundle. Likewise, I believe that the evolution of Einstein's thinking about gravity—from the redis-covery[25] of the equivalence principle in 1907 to the final formulation of geometrodynamics in curved spacetime more than eight years later—can profitably be viewed from such a reformed Kantian perspective.

The three examples I have mentioned concern conceptual inno-vations not directly linked to the nit and grit of laboratory life. They are also quite foreign to the myriad-year old everyday fight for life in which and for which our most common concepts were born. This reminds us of a limitation that Kant's philosophy shares with its predecessors. Kantian objectivity is achieved through the doings of the human understanding,[26] but the understanding is for Kant a handless actor. We ought to manage to consistently think of it as acting from a body in order to properly understand the presence of objects as *pragmata*, as the Greek founders of philosophy spon-taneously called them in their mother tongue.[27]

[25] I say 'rediscovery' because the equivalence principle is already implicit in Corollary VI to Newton's Laws of Motion, as Herbert Stein (1977) pointed out.

[26] 'Intellektuell ist, dessen Begriff ein Tun ist' (Kant, Reflection 4182, Ak 17: 447).

[27] In the discussion that followed the reading of this paper at the UCL conference, Professor Michael Friedman remarked that, as far as he could tell, the effective elucidation and solution of problems in the philosophy of science had gained little or nothing from the consideration of cognition as a form of embodied intelligent action. Replying to his comments, I pro-posed the book by James Woodward (2003)—and the work of his predeces-sors Judea Pearl and Clark Glymour *et al.*—as a harbinger of what one might expect in this field. By linking the origin and meaning of the concept of cause to the live experience of human intervention in the course of things, these authors have not only thrown much light on a famously obscure concept but have also paved the way for understanding the difference between the discrete causal chains we discern everywhere, both in ordinary and in labora-tory life, and the deterministic evolution of closed physical systems governed by the differential equations of mathematical physics.

Einstein, Kant, and the A Priori*

MICHAEL FRIEDMAN

1. Introduction

Kant's original version of transcendental philosophy took both Euclidean geometry and the Newtonian laws of motion to be synthetic a priori constitutive principles—which, from Kant's point of view, function as necessary presuppositions for applying our fundamental concepts of space, time, matter, and motion to our sensible experience of the natural world.[1] Although Kant had very good reasons to view the principles in question as having such a constitutively a priori role, we now know, in the wake of Einstein's work, that they are not in fact a priori in the stronger sense of being fixed necessary conditions for all human experience in general, eternally valid once and for all. And it is for precisely this reason that Kant's original version of transcendental philosophy must now be either rejected entirely or (at least) radically reconceived. Most philosophy of science since Einstein has taken the former route: the dominant view in logical empiricism, for example, was that the Kantian synthetic a priori had to be rejected once and for all in the light of the general theory of relativity.

Yet Hans Reichenbach took the latter route in his first published book: in *Relativitätstheorie und Erkenntnis Apriori* (1920) he proposed instead that Kantian constitutively a priori principles of geometry and mechanics should be *relativized* to a given time in a given theoretical context. Such principles still function, throughout the development from Newton to Einstein, as necessary presuppositions for applying our (changing) conceptions of space, time, and motion to our sensible experience, but they are no longer eternally valid once and for all. For example, while Euclidean geometry and the Newtonian laws of motion are indeed necessary conditions for giving empirical meaning to the Newtonian theory of universal gravitation, the situation in Einstein's general theory relativity is quite different. The crucial mediating role between abstract mathematical

---

[1]   For details on Kant's understanding of Euclidean geometry and the fundamental principles of Newtonian mechanics see Friedman (1992a).

doi:10.1017/S1358246108000064   ©The Royal Institute of Philosophy and the contributors 2008
Royal Institute of Philosophy Supplement **63** 2008   95

Michael Friedman

theory and concrete sensible experience is now played by the light principle and the principle of equivalence, which together insure that Einstein's revolutionary new description of gravitation by a four-dimensional geometry of variable curvature in fact says something about concrete empirical phenomena: namely, the behavior of light and gravitationally interacting bodies.

In my recent book, *Dynamics of Reason* (2001a), I have taken up, and further developed, Reichenbach's idea. But my implementation of this idea of relativized constitutively a priori principles (of geometry and mechanics) essentially depends on an historical argument describing the developmental process by which the transition from Newton to Einstein actually took place, as mediated, in my view, by the parallel developments in scientific philosophy involving Hermann von Helmholtz, Ernst Mach, and Henri Poincaré. However, since this argument depends on the concrete details of the actual historical process in question, it would therefore appear to be entirely contingent. How can it possibly be comprehended within a properly *transcendental* philosophy? Indeed, once we have given up on Kant's original ambition to delineate in advance the a priori structure of all possible scientific theories, it might easily seem that a properly transcendental argument is impossible. We have no way of anticipating a priori the specific constitutive principles of future theories. It appears that all we can do is wait for the historical process to show us what emerges a posteriori as a matter of fact. So how, more generally, can we develop a philosophical understanding of the evolution of modern science that is at once genuinely historical and properly transcendental?[2]

Let us begin by asking how Kant's original transcendental method is supposed to explain the sense in which certain fundamental principles of geometry and mechanics are, in fact, both a priori and necessary. This method, of course, appeals to Kant's conception of the two rational faculties of sensibility and understanding. The answer to the question 'how is pure mathematics possible?' appeals to the necessary structure of our pure sensibility, as articulated in the Transcendental Aesthetic of the *Critique of Pure Reason*. The answer to the question 'how is pure natural science possible?' appeals to the necessary structure of our pure understanding, as articulated in the Transcendental Analytic. Yet there is an obvious objection to this procedure: how can such proposed transcendental explanations inherit the (assumed) a priori necessity of the sciences

---

[2]   I am especially indebted to Charles Parsons for raising this problem of historical contingency and stimulating me to take it very seriously.

whose possibility they purport to explain unless we can also somehow establish that they are the *unique* such explanations?[3] From our present point of view, for example, it does not appear that Kant's explanation of the possibility of pure mathematics is uniquely singled out in any way; on the contrary, our greatly expanded conception of purely logical or analytic truth suggests that an appeal to the faculty of pure sensibility may, after all, be explanatorily superfluous. Indeed, from the point of view of the anti-psychological approach to such questions that dominated much of twentieth-century analytic philosophy, it appears that all consideration of our subjective cognitive faculties is similarly explanatorily superfluous.

In Kant's own intellectual context, however, explanations of scientific knowledge in terms of our cognitive faculties were the norm—for empiricists, rationalists, and (of course) Aristotelians. Everyone agreed, in addition, that the relevant faculties to consider were the senses and the intellect; what was then controversial was the precise nature and relative importance of the two. Empiricist views, which denied the existence of the pure intellect or its importance for scientific knowledge, were, for Kant, simply out of the question, since they make a priori rational knowledge incomprehensible.[4] Moreover, the

[3]   Kant often makes such claims to explanatory uniqueness, for example, in the Transcendental Exposition of the Concept of Space added to the second [B] edition (B41): 'Therefore, only our explanation makes the *possibility of geometry* as an a priori synthetic cognition comprehensible. Any mode of explanation that does not achieve this, even if it appeared to be similar to ours, can be most securely distinguished from ours by this criterion' (translation by MF). I am indebted to Dagfinn Føllesdal for emphasizing to me the importance of the problem of uniqueness in this connection.

[4]   Thus, in considering the questions 'how is pure mathematics possible?' and 'how is pure natural science possible?' in § VI of the Introduction to the second edition of the *Critique*, Kant simply takes it for granted that the actual existence of these sciences puts the existence of synthetic a priori knowledge entirely beyond all doubt. In particular, in considering Hume's skepticism concerning the necessity of the causal relation—which then leads to skepticism about the possibility of any a priori metaphysics—Kant blames this result on Hume's insufficiently general understanding of the problem (B20): '[H]ume would never have arrived at this assertion, which destroys all pure philosophy, if he had kept our problem before his eyes in its [full] generality; for he would then have seen that, according to his argument, there could also be no pure mathematics (for it certainly contains synthetic a priori propositions), and his good sense would then surely have saved him from this assertion' (translation by MF). Similarly, while considering (in § 14 of the second edition) the circumstance that neither Locke nor Hume posed the problem of the

Michael Friedman

conception of the pure intellect that was most salient for Kant was that of Leibniz, where the structure of this faculty is delineated, in effect, by the logical forms of traditional Aristotelian syllogistic. But this conception of the pure intellect, Kant rightly saw, is entirely inadequate for representing, say, the assumed infinite extendibility and divisibility of geometrical space, which had recently proven itself to be both indispensable and extremely fruitful in Newtonian mathematical physics.[5] Nevertheless, Newton's own conception of space as the divine sensorium was also unacceptable on theological and metaphysical grounds, and so the only live alternative left to Kant was the one he actually came up with: space is a pure form of our sensibility (as opposed to the divine sensibility), wherein *both* (infinitely iterable) geometrical construction *and* the perception of spatial objects in nature (like the heavenly bodies) then become first possible.

It is of course entirely contingent that Kant operated against the background of precisely these intellectual resources, just as it is entirely contingent that Kant was born in 1724 and died in 1804. Given these resources, however, and given the problems with which Kant was faced, the solution he came up with is not contingent. On the contrary, the intellectual situation in which he found himself had a definite 'inner logic'—mathematical, logical, metaphysical, and theological—which allowed him to triangulate, as it were, on a practically unique (and in this sense necessary) solution.

Beginning with this understanding of Kant's transcendental method and its associated rational necessity, we can then see a way forward for extending this method to post-Kantian developments in both the mathematical exact sciences and transcendental philosophy. We can trace out how the 'inner logic' of the relevant intellectual situation evolves and changes after Kant in response to both new developments in the mathematical exact sciences themselves and the manifold and intricate ways in which post-Kantian scientific philosophers attempted to reconfigure Kant's original version of transcendental philosophy in light of these developments. That each of

---

transcendental deduction, and instead attempted a psychological or empirical derivation of the pure concepts of the understanding, Kant concludes (B127–8): 'But the *empirical* derivation which both fell upon cannot be reconciled with the actuality of the a priori scientific cognition that we have—namely of *pure mathematics* and *universal natural science*—and is thus refuted by this fact [*Faktum*]'.

[5] Again, see Friedman (1992a), chapters 1 and 2 for details.

98

these successive new intellectual situations has its own 'inner logic' implies that the enterprise does not collapse into total contingency. In addition, the fact that they successively evolve out of, and in light of Kant's original system suggests that it may still count as transcendental philosophy. In my reconceived version of transcendental philosophy, therefore, integrated intellectual history of both the exact sciences and scientific philosophy takes over the role of Kant's original transcendental method.

2. Helmholtz and Poincaré

Hermann von Helmholtz's neo-Kantian scientific epistemology, for example, had deep roots in Kant's original conception. In particular, Helmholtz developed a distinctive conception of space as a 'subjective' and '*necessary* form of our external intuition' in the sense of Kant; and, while this conception was certainly developed within Helmholtz's *empirical* program in sensory psychology and psycho-physics, it nevertheless retained important 'transcendental' elements.[6] More specifically, space is 'transcendental', for Helmholtz, in so far as the principle of free mobility (which allows arbitrary continuous motions of rigid bodies) is a necessary condition for the possibility of spatial measurement and, indeed, for the very existence of space and spatial objects. Moreover, the condition of free mobility represents a natural generalization of Kant's original (Euclidean) conception of geometrical construction, in the sense that Euclidean constructions with straight-edge and compass, carried out within Kant's form of spatial intuition, are generated by the group of specifically Euclidean rigid motions (translations and rotations). The essential point, however, is that free mobility also holds for the classical non-Euclidean geometries of constant curvature (hyperbolic and elliptic), and so it is no longer a 'transcendental' and 'necessary' condition of our spatial intuition, for Helmholtz, that the space constructed from our perception of bodily motion obeys the specific laws of Euclidean geometry. Nevertheless, Helmholtz's generalization of the Kantian conception of spatial intuition is, in an important sense, the *minimal* (and in this sense unique) such generalization consistent with the nineteenth-century discovery of non-Euclidean geometries.[7]

---

[6] For Helmholtz's characteristic combination of empirical (or 'naturalistic') and transcendental (or 'normative') elements, see Hatfield (1990). For my reading of Helmholtz's conception of space and geometry, see Friedman (1997); (2000).

Michael Friedman

The great French mathematician Henri Poincaré in turn transformed Helmholtz's conception. In particular, Poincaré's use of the principle of free mobility (which plays a central role in his philosophy of geometry) is explicitly framed by a hierarchical conception of the mathematical sciences, beginning with arithmetic and proceeding through analysis, geometry, mechanics, and empirical physics—where, in particular, each lower level of the hierarchy (after arithmetic) *presupposes* that all earlier levels are already in place.[8]

This hierarchical conception of the mathematical sciences underlies Poincaré's fundamental disagreement with Helmholtz. For Helmholtz, as we have seen, the principle of free mobility expresses the necessary structure of our form of external intuition, and, following Kant, Helmholtz views all empirical investigation as necessarily taking place within this already given form. Helmholtz's conception is Kantian in so far as space has a 'necessary form' expressed in the condition of free mobility, but it is also empiricist in so far as which of the three possible geometries of constant curvature obtains is determined by experience. For Poincaré, by contrast, although the principle of free mobility is still fundamental, our actual perceptual experience of bodily 'displacements' arising in accordance with this principle is far too imprecise to yield the empirical determination of a specific mathematical geometry: our only option, at this point, is to *stipulate* Euclidean geometry by convention, as the simplest and most convenient idealization of our actual perceptual experience. In particular, experiments with putatively rigid bodies, for Poincaré, involve essentially physical processes at the level of mechanics and experimental physics, and these sciences, in turn,

[7]   Bernhard Riemann's general theory of manifolds includes spaces of *variable* curvature not satisfying the condition of free mobility, and it is for precisely this reason that Hermann Weyl later attempted to generalize Helmholtz's approach to comprehend the (four-dimensional) (semi-)Riemannian geometries of variable curvature used in Einstein's general theory of relativity. Moreover, as I explain in Friedman (2000), pp. 209–211, Weyl, too, conceived his work as a generalization of Kant's original theory of space as an (a priori) *'form of experience'*. The important point here, however, is that Helmholtz is 'closer' to Kant's original theory (in so far as his generalization preserves the possibility of geometrical constructions analogous to Euclid's), whereas Weyl's work arises only as a further generalization, in turn, of Helmholtz's.

[8]   This hierarchical conception is developed especially clearly in Poincaré (1902). For details see Friedman (1999), chapter 4; (2000).

presuppose that the science of geometry is already firmly in place. In the context of Poincaré's hierarchy, therefore, the principle of free mobility expresses our necessary freedom to choose—by a 'convention or definition in disguise'—which of the three classical geometries of constant curvature is the most suitable idealization of physical space.

One of the most important applications of Poincaré's hierarchical conception involves his characteristic perspective on the problem of absolute space and the relativity of motion explained in his discussion of the next lower level in the hierarchy: (classical) mechanics. Poincaré's key idea is that what he calls the (physical) 'law of relativity' rests squarely on the 'relativity and passivity of space' and therefore reflects the circumstance, essential to free mobility, that the space constructed from our experience of bodily displacements is both homogeneous and isotropic: all points in space, and all directions through any given point, are, necessarily, geometrically equivalent.[9] Thus, Poincaré's conception of the relativity of motion depends on his philosophy of geometry, and this is especially significant, from our present point of view, because Poincaré's ideas on the relativity of motion were also inextricably entangled with the deep problems then afflicting the electrodynamics of moving bodies that were

[9]   The 'law of relativity' is first introduced in Chapter V, 'Experience and Geometry', of Poincaré (1902), p. 96, English translation (1913b), p. 83: 'The laws of the phenomena which will happen [in a material system of bodies] will depend on the state of these bodies and their mutual distances; but, because of the relativity and passivity of space, they will not depend on the absolute position and orientation of this system. In other words, the state of the bodies and their mutual distances will depend only on the state of the same bodies and their mutual distances at the initial instant, but they will not depend at all on the absolute initial position of the system and its absolute initial orientation. This is what I shall call, for the sake of brevity, *the law of relativity*'. Moreover, 'in order fully to satisfy the mind', Poincaré continues, the phenomena in question should also be entirely independent of 'the velocities of translation and rotation of the system, that is to say, the velocities with which its absolute position and orientation vary' (1902), p. 98, English translation (1913b), p. 85. Thus, because of 'the relativity and passivity of space', the absolute position or orientation of a system of bodies in space can have no physical effect whatsoever, and neither can any *change* (velocity) of such absolute position or orientation. In emphasizing that Poincaré's treatment of the relativity of motion rests squarely on his philosophy of space and geometry, I am in very substantial agreement with the excellent discussion in DiSalle (2006), § 3.7.

Michael Friedman

eventually solved (according to our current understanding) by Einstein's special theory of relativity.

I shall return to Einstein below, but I first want to emphasize that the connection Poincaré makes between his philosophy of geometry and the relativity of motion represents a continuation of a problematic originally prominent in Kant. Helmholtz, as we have seen, transformed Kant's philosophy of space and geometry, and Ernst Mach, among others, participated in a parallel transformation of Kant's approach to the relativity of motion, which finally eventuated in the modern concept of an inertial frame of reference.[10] Neither Helmholtz nor Mach, however, established any kind of conceptual connection between the foundations of geometry and the relativity of motion, which at the time appeared to be entirely independent of one another. On Kant's original approach to transcendental philosophy, by contrast, the two were actually very closely connected. While Kant's answer to the question 'how is pure mathematics possible?' essentially involved his distinctive perspective on Euclidean constructive operations, his answer to the question 'how is pure natural science possible' involved an analogous constructive procedure by which Newton, from Kant's point of view, arrived at successive approximations to 'absolute space' via a definite sequence of rule-governed operations starting with our parochial perspective here on earth and then proceeding to the center of mass of the solar system, the center of mass of the Milky Way galaxy, the center of mass of a system of such galaxies, and so on *ad infinitum*.[11] Indeed, the way in which Kant thereby established a connection between the problem of space and geometry and the problem of the relativity of motion was intimately connected, in turn, with both the overarching conception of the relationship between sensibility and understanding that frames his transcendental method and his characteristic perspective, more generally, on the relationship between constitutive and regulative transcendental principles.[12]

[10] For the nineteenth-century development of the concept of an inertial frame, see DiSalle (1988), (1991); for Mach's place in this development, see DiSalle (2002).

[11] Kant develops this interpretation of 'absolute space' in his *Metaphysische Anfangsgründe der Naturwissenschaft* (1786), published between the first (1781) and second (1787) editions of the *Critique of Pure Reason*. For details see Friedman (1992a), chapters 3 and 4, and also the Introduction to my (2004) translation of Kant's work.

[12] In particular, 'absolute space' for Kant is a regulative idea of reason, defined by the forever unreachable 'center of gravity of all matter' which we can only successively approximate but never actually attain.

Now it was Mach, as I have suggested, who first forged a connection between Kant's original solution to the problem of 'absolute space' and the late nineteenth-century solution based on the concept of an inertial frame of reference.[13] And it is clear, moreover, that Poincaré was familiar with this late nineteenth-century solution as well. It is also clear, however, that Poincaré's attempt to base his discussion of the relativity of motion on his philosophy of geometry runs into serious difficulties at precisely this point; for Poincaré is here forced to distinguish his 'law of relativity' from what he calls the 'principle of relative motion'. The latter applies only to inertial frames of reference, moving uniformly and rectilinearly with respect to one another, while the former applies to non-inertial frames of reference in a state of uniform rotation as well: it follows from the 'relativity and passivity' of space, for Poincaré, that uniform rotations of our coordinate axes should be just as irrelevant to the motions of a physical system as uniform translations. Therefore, the full 'law of relativity', as Poincaré says, 'ought to impose itself upon us with the same force' as does the more restricted 'principle of relative motion'. Poincaré must also admit, however, that the more extended 'law of relativity' does not appear to be in accordance with our experiments (e.g., Newton's famous rotating bucket experiment).[14]

[13] Kant's construction of 'absolute space', from a modern point of view, yields better and better approximations to a cosmic inertial frame of reference defined by the 'center of gravity of all matter'. Such a cosmic frame, in which the fixed stars are necessarily at rest, also counts as a surrogate for Newtonian 'absolute space' in Mach's treatment. For details, see again DiSalle (2002).

[14] Poincaré formulates 'the principle of relative motion' in Chapter VII, 'Relative Motion and Absolute Motion', of *La Science et l'Hypothèse* (1902), p. 135, English translation (1913b), p. 107: 'The motion of any system whatsoever must obey the same laws, whether it be referred to fixed axes, or to movable axes transported by a rectilinear and uniform motion. This is the principle of relative motion, which imposes itself upon us for two reasons: first, the most common experience confirms it, and second, the contrary hypothesis is singularly repugnant to the mind'. This, of course, is the principle of what we now call Galilean relativity, which was originally formulated by Newton as Corollary V to the Laws of Motion, and then played a central role in the recent literature on inertial frames of reference (see the references cited in note 10 above). However, as Poincaré is well aware, such Galilean relativity holds only for (uniform) rectilinear motions and does not extend, therefore, to the case of (uniform) rotational motion Poincaré also wishes to subsume under his 'law of relativity'. Nevertheless, Poincaré says, 'it seems that [the principle of relative

Michael Friedman

3. Einstein

It is for this reason that Einstein's appeal to what he calls the 'principle of relativity' in his 1905 paper on special relativity is independent of Poincaré's 'law of relativity', and it is also independent, accordingly, of Poincaré's conventionalist philosophy of geometry. Einstein's principle is limited, from the beginning, to inertial frames of reference (moving relative to one another with constant velocity and no rotation), and his concern is to apply this (limited) principle of relativity to both electro-magnetic and mechanical phenomena. Thus, whereas Poincaré's 'law of relativity' involves very strong a priori motivations deriving from his philosophy of geometry (based on the 'relativity and passivity of space'), Einstein's 'principle of relativity' rests on the emerging experimental evidence suggesting that electro-magnetic and optical phenomena do not in fact distinguish one inertial frame from another. Einstein 'conjectures' that this experimentally suggested law holds rigorously (and for all orders), and he proposes to 'elevate' it to the status of a presupposition or postulate upon which a consistent electrodynamics of moving bodies may then be erected:

> Examples of this sort [the relatively moving conductor and magnet—MF], together with the unsuccessful attempts to discover any motion of the earth relative to the "light medium," suggest that the phenomena of electrodynamics as well as mechanics possess no properties corresponding to the idea of absolute rest. They suggest rather that, as has already been shown to the first order of small quantities, the same laws of electrodynamics and optics will be valid for all frames of reference for which the equations of mechanics are valid. We will elevate [*erheben*] this conjecture (whose content will be called the "principle of relativity" in what follows) to the status of a postulate [*Voraussetzung*], and also introduce another postulate, which is only apparently irreconcilable with it, namely, that light is always propagated in

---

motion] ought to impose itself upon us with the same force, if the motion is varied, or at least if it reduces to a uniform rotation' (1902), pp. 136–7, English translation (1913b), p. 108. Thus, Poincaré's a priori commitment to the law of relativity, derived from the homogeneity and isotropy of space, stands in *prima facie* contradiction with the well-known experimental limitations of the principle of relative motion (Poincaré presents a sophisticated analysis of this apparent contradiction in the following discussion, which I shall have to pass over here).

empty space with a definite velocity c which is independent of the state of motion of the emitting body. These two postulates suffice for attaining a simple and consistent theory of the electrodynamics of moving bodies based on Maxwell's theory for stationary bodies. (1905), pp. 891-2, Engl. translation (1923), pp. 37-8.

Hence, Einstein's understanding of the principle of relativity is also independent of Poincaré's carefully constructed hierarchy of the mathematical sciences, and it is for precisely this reason, I suggest, that Poincaré himself could never accept Einstein's theory.[15]

Nevertheless, it appears overwhelmingly likely that, although Einstein did not embrace Poincaré's conventionalist philosophy of geometry, Einstein's use of the principle of relativity was explicitly inspired by Poincaré's more general methodology described in *La Science et l'Hypothèse*—according to which the fundamental principles of mechanics, in particular, are 'conventions or definitions in disguise' arising from 'experimental laws' that 'have been elevated into principles to which our mind attributes an absolute value'.[16]

---

[15]   In his 1912 lecture on 'Space and Geometry', appearing in Poincaré (1913a), Poincaré explicitly considers what we now call the four-dimensional geometry of Minkowski space-time, and he clearly states his preference for an alternative formulation of the Lorentzian type—where, in particular, both the Newtonian laws of mechanics and 'the relativity and passivity of space' retain a foundational role. Thus, from a modern point of view, while Poincaré's most fundamental 'law of relativity' is a purely geometrical principle, expressing the necessary symmetries of three-dimensional (homogeneous) space, Einstein's 'principle of relativity' expresses the symmetry or invariance properties of the laws of Maxwell-Lorentz electrodynamics—which we now take to be the symmetries of Minkowski space-time. The central problem with Poincaré's hierarchy, from this point of view, is that it makes the three-dimensional geometry of space prior to the four-dimensional geometry of space-time: compare again DiSalle (2006), § 3.7 for a similar diagnosis.

[16]   This idea is stated as a key part of Poincaré's 'General Conclusions' to his discussion of (classical) mechanics (1902), p. 165, English translation (1913b), p. 125: '[The fundamental principles of mechanics] are conventions or definitions in disguise. Yet they are drawn from experimental laws; these laws, so to speak, have been elevated [*érigées*] into principles to which our mind attributes an absolute value'. Later, in *Geometrie und Erfahrung* (1921), Einstein explicitly uses the language of 'elevation' [*erheben*] in connection with precisely Poincaré's conventionalism (1921), p. 8, English translation (1923), p. 35: 'Geometry (*G*) [according to Poincaré's standpoint] asserts nothing about the behavior of actual things, but only geometry together with the totality (*P*) of physical laws. We can

In Einstein's case, the experimental law in question comprises the recent results in electrodynamics and optics, and Einstein now proposes to 'elevate' both the principle of relativity and the light principle (which together imply that the velocity of light is invariant in all inertial frames) to the status of 'presuppositions' or 'postulates'. These two postulates together then allow us to 'stipulate' a new 'definition of simultaneity' (based on the assumed invariance of the velocity of light) implying a radical revision of the classical kinematics of space, time, and motion. In particular, whereas the fundamental kinematical structure of an inertial frame of reference, in classical mechanics, is defined by the Newtonian laws of motion, (a revised version of) this same structure, in Einstein's theory, is rather defined by his two postulates.[17]

A central contention of Kant's original version of transcendental philosophy, as we know, is that the Newtonian laws of motion are not mere empirical laws but a priori constitutive principles on the basis of which alone the Newtonian concepts of space, time, and motion can then have empirical application and meaning. What we have just seen is that Einstein's two fundamental 'presuppositions' or 'postulates' play a precisely parallel role in the context of special relativity. But we have also seen significantly more. For Poincaré's conception of how a mere empirical law can be 'elevated' to the status of a 'convention or definition in disguise' is a continuation, in turn, of Kant's original conception of the constitutive a priori. Whereas Helmholtz's principle of free mobility generalized and

---

say, symbolically, that only the sum $(G) + (P)$ is subject to the control of experience. So (G) can be chosen arbitrarily, and also parts of (P); all of these laws are conventions. In order to avoid contradictions it is only necessary to choose the remainder of (P) in such a way that (G) and the total (P) together do justice to experience. On this conception axiomatic geometry and the part of the laws of nature that have been elevated [*erhobene*] to conventions appear as epistemologically of equal status' (I shall return to *Geometrie und Erfahrung* below). To the best of my knowledge, this striking language in Einstein's 1905 paper (together with its reappearance in 1921) has not been previously noted in the literature.

[17] The crucial point, in this connection, is that Newton's third law—the equality of action and reaction—implicitly defines the relation of absolute simultaneity in a classical inertial frame, in so far as it allows us to coordinate action-reaction pairs related by the Newtonian law of (instantaneously propagated) gravitation. Einstein's two postulates take over precisely this role in the case of his new, relativized relation of simultaneity defined by (continuously propagated) electro-magnetic processes.

extended Kant's original theory of geometrical construction within our 'subjective' and *'necessary* form of external intuition', Poincaré's idea that specifically Euclidean geometry is then imposed on this form by a 'convention or definition in disguise' represents an extension or continuation of Helmholtz's conception. In particular, Euclidean geometry is applied to our experience by precisely such a process of 'elevation', in which the merely empirical fact that this geometry governs, very roughly and approximately, our actual perceptual experience of bodily displacements gives rise to a precise mathematical framework within which alone our properly *physical* theories can subsequently be formulated.[18]

This same process of 'elevation', in Einstein's hands, then makes it clear how an extension or continuation of Kant's original conception can also accommodate new and surprising empirical facts—in this case, the very surprising empirical discovery (to one or another degree of approximation) that light has the same constant velocity in every inertial frame. It now turns out, in particular, that we can not only impose already familiar and accepted mathematical frameworks (Euclidean geometry) on our rough and approximate perceptual experience, but, in appropriate circumstances, we can also impose entirely unfamiliar ones (the kinematical framework of special relativity). Einstein's creation of special relativity, from this point of view, thus represents the very first instantiation of a relativized and dynamical conception of the a priori—which, in virtue of precisely its historical origins, has a legitimate claim to be considered as genuinely constitutive in the transcendental sense. What vindicates this claim, therefore, is a reconceived version of transcendental philosophy where precisely the kind of constructive philosophical history

[18] Euclidean geometry is singled out, for Poincaré, in that it is both mathematically simplest and very naturally corresponds—roughly and approximately—to our pre-scientific experience of bodily displacements. Just as Helmholtz's conception, as I have suggested, is the minimal extension of Kant's original conception consistent with the discovery of non-Euclidean geometries, Poincaré's conception is the minimal extension of Helmholtz's consistent with the more sophisticated group-theoretic version of the principle of free mobility due to Sophus Lie, the new perspective on the relativity of motion due to the modern concept of an inertial frame, and, most importantly, the apparently paradoxical new situation in electrodynamics arising in connection with precisely this relativity of motion—where, in particular, Poincaré's hierarchical conception of the mathematical sciences allows him to retain the foundational role of both Euclidean spatial geometry and the laws of Newtonian mechanics in the face of what we now call Lorentzian (as opposed to Galilean) relativity .

Michael Friedman

I have been trying to exemplify takes the place of Kant's original transcendental method. In particular, that the 'inner logic' of the successive intellectual situations in question proceeds against the background of, and explicitly in light of Kant's original theory is what makes this enterprise properly 'transcendental'.

Yet Einstein's creation of the general theory of relativity in 1915 involved an even more striking engagement with Poincaré's conventionalist methodology, which, I contend, makes the transcendentally constitutive role of this theory's fundamental postulates (the light principle and the principle of equivalence) even more evident.

The first point to make, in this connection, is that the principle of equivalence (together with the light principle) plays the same role in the context of the general theory that Einstein's two fundamental 'presuppositions' or 'postulates' played in the context of the special theory: namely, they define a new inertial-kinematical structure for describing space, time, and motion. Because Newtonian gravitation theory involves an instantaneous action at a distance (and therefore absolute simultaneity), it was necessary after special relativity to develop a new theory of gravitation where the interactions in question propagate with the velocity of light. And Einstein solved this problem, via the principle of equivalence, by defining a new inertial-kinematical structure wherein the freely falling trajectories in a gravitational field replace the inertial trajectories described by free particles affected by no forces at all. The principle of equivalence, in this sense, replaces the classical law of inertia holding in both Newtonian mechanics and special relativity. But the principle of equivalence itself rests on a well-known empirical fact: that gravitational and inertial mass are equal, so that all bodies, regardless of their mass, fall with exactly the same acceleration in a gravitational field. In using the principle of equivalence to define a new inertial-kinematical structure, therefore, Einstein has 'elevated' this merely empirical fact (recently verified to a quite high degree of approximation by Lorand von Eötvös) to the status of a 'convention or definition in disguise'—just as he had earlier undertaken a parallel 'elevation' in the case of the new concept of simultaneity introduced by the special theory.[19]

---

[19] Friedman (2001a), pp. 86–91, develops more fully the parallel between these two cases of 'elevating' a mere empirical fact to the status of a (relativized) a priori principle by first examining the relationship between the invariance of the velocity of light (as recently verified in the Michelson-Morley experiment) and Einstein's new definition of simultaneity, and then the relationship between the equality of gravitational and

Nevertheless, Einstein did not reach this understanding of the principle of equivalence all at once. He first operated, instead, within an essentially three-dimensional understanding of special relativity, and he proceeded (in the years 1907–1912) to develop relativistically acceptable models of the gravitational field by considering the inertial forces (like centrifugal and Coriolis forces) arising in non-inertial frames of reference within this framework.[20] It was in this context, in particular, that Einstein finally (in 1912) came upon the example of the uniformly rotating frame (the rotating disk), and it was at this point (and only at this point) that he then arrived at the conclusion that the gravitational field may be represented by a non-Euclidean geometry. This use of non-Euclidean geometry, however, was essentially three-dimensional, limited to purely *spatial* geometry, and Einstein did not arrive at the idea of a four-dimensional non-Euclidean geometry—where *space-time* geodesics represent freely falling trajectories affected only by gravitation—until he had generalized his conception to what we now call the four-dimensional (semi-)Riemannian geometries of variable curvature.[21]

It was in precisely the context of this line of thought finally that Einstein found that he now had explicitly to oppose Poincaré's conventionalist philosophy of geometry. Yet Einstein's argument—as described in *Geometrie und Erfahrung* (1921)—was far from a simple rejection of Poincaré's methodology in favor of straightforward 'empiricism'.[22] For Einstein also famously says, in the same work, that '*sub specie aeterni*' Poincaré is actually correct—so that, in particular, Einstein's reliance on a Helmholtzian conception of 'practically rigid bodies' is here merely provisional. I have suggested, therefore, that we can best understand Einstein's procedure as one of delicately situating himself *between* Helmholtz and Poincaré. Whereas Einstein had earlier followed Poincaré's general conventionalist methodology in 'elevating' the principle of relativity (together with the light principle) to the status of a 'presupposition' or 'postulate', he here follows Helmholtz's empiricism in rejecting Poincaré's

---

inertial mass (as recently verified in the Eötvös experiments) and the principle of equivalence.

[20]   See Norton (1985) for the details of Einstein's early applications of the principle of equivalence.

[21]   I discuss at length the crucial importance of the rotating disk example in the development of Einstein's thought—following Stachel (1980)—in Friedman (2001a), (2002).

[22]   For a detailed analysis of *Geometrie und Erfahrung*, against the background of both Helmholtz and Poincaré, see Friedman (2001a), (2002).

more specific philosophy of geometry in favor of 'practically rigid bodies'.

Einstein does not explicitly mention Helmholtz in *Geometrie und Erfahrung*. However, in a closely related article on 'Non-Euclidean Geometry and Physics', Einstein makes it perfectly clear that the opposition he has in mind is precisely that between Helmholtz and Poincaré:[23]

> Either one accepts that the "body" of geometry is realized in principle by the solid bodies of nature, if only certain prescriptions are maintained regarding temperature, mechanical stress, and so on; this is the standpoint of the practicing physicist. Then a natural object corresponds to the "interval" of geometry, and all propositions of geometry thereby attain the character of assertions about real bodies. This standpoint was represented especially clearly by Helmholtz, and one can add that without it establishing the [general—MF] theory of relativity would have been practically impossible. Or, one denies in principle the existence of objects that correspond to the fundamental concepts of geometry. Then geometry alone contains no assertions about objects of reality, but only geometry together with physics. This standpoint, which may be more perfect for the systematic presentation of a completed physics, was represented especially clearly by Poincaré. On this standpoint the total content of geometry is conventional; which geometry is to be preferred depends on how "simple" a physics can, by its use, be established in agreement with experience. (1925), pp. 18–9.

It does not follow, however, that Einstein is also rejecting his earlier embrace of Poincaré's general conventionalist (or perhaps we should say 'elevationist') methodology. Indeed, Einstein had already sidestepped Poincaré's specific philosophy of geometry in the case of special relativity, and for essentially the same reason he explicitly opposes it here: Poincaré's rigid hierarchy of the sciences, in both cases, stands in the way of the radical new innovations Einstein himself proposes to introduce.[24]

---

[23] Ryckman (2005), § 3.3, emphasizes the importance of this passage in relation to the earlier argument of *Geometrie und Erfahrung*.

[24] As I suggested, Einstein could not embrace Poincaré's philosophy of geometry even in 1905, since it privileges a priori the three-dimensional geometry of space over the *de facto* symmetries of the laws of motion (which, on our current understanding, express the four-dimensional geometrical symmetries of space-time). Einstein's divergence from Poincaré on this point is even stronger in general relativity; for, not only do we now use

But why was it necessary, after all, for Einstein to engage in this delicate dance between Helmholtz and Poincaré? The crucial point is that Einstein thereby arrived at a radically new conception of the relationship between the foundations of (physical) geometry and the relativity of space and motion. These two problems, as we have seen, were closely connected in Kant, but they then split apart and were pursued independently in Helmholtz and Mach. In Poincaré, as we have also seen, the two were perceptively reconnected once again, in so far as Poincaré's hierarchical conception of the mathematical sciences incorporated both a modification of Helmholtz's philosophy of geometry and a serious engagement with the late nineteenth-century concept of inertial frame. Indeed, it is for precisely this reason, as we now see, that Poincaré's scientific epistemology was so important to Einstein. Einstein could not simply rest content with Helmholtz's 'empiricist' conception of geometry, because the most important problem with which he was now faced was to connect the foundations of geometry with the relativity of motion. But Einstein could not rest content with Poincaré's conception either, because his new models of gravitation had suggested that geometry has genuine physical content.

4. Conclusion

Einstein's radically new way of reconfiguring the relationship between the foundations of geometry and the relativity of motion therefore represents a natural (but also entirely unexpected) extension or continuation of the same conception of dynamical and relativized constitutive a priori principles he had first instantiated in the creation of special relativity. Just as he had earlier shown how an extension or continuation of Kant's original conception could accommodate new and surprising empirical facts (the discovery of the invariance of the velocity of light), Einstein here shows how a further extension of this same tradition can do something very similar in facilitating, for the first time, the application of a non-Euclidean geometry to nature. In this case, however, it is not the relevant empirical fact

---

non-Euclidean geometries to describe both space and space-time, but we have also definitively given up (in both cases) the homogeneity and isotropy (constant curvature) of the underlying geometry. Einstein thereby ultimately arrived at a radically new conception of physical geometry envisioned by neither Helmholtz nor Poincaré. For details, see again Friedman (2002).

Michael Friedman

(the well-known equality of gravitational and inertial mass) that is surprising, but the entirely unforeseen connection between this fact and the new geometry. And what makes this connection itself possible, for Einstein, is precisely the principle of equivalence—which thereby constitutively frames the resulting physical space-time geometry of general relativity in just the same way in which Einstein's two fundamental 'presuppositions' or 'postulates' had earlier constitutively framed his mathematical description of the electrodynamics of moving bodies in special relativity. Whereas the particular geometry in a given general relativistic space-time is now determined empirically (by the distribution of mass and energy in accordance with Einstein's field equation), the principle of equivalence itself is not empirical in this sense. This principle is instead *presupposed*—as a transcendentally constitutive condition—for any such geometrical description of space-time to have genuine empirical meaning in the first place.

The historicized version of transcendental philosophy I am attempting to exemplify therefore sheds striking new light, I believe, on the truly remarkable depth and fruitfulness of Kant's original version. Kant's particular way of establishing a connection between the foundations of geometry and the relativity of motion—which, as we have seen, lies at the heart of his transcendental method—has not only lead, through the intervening philosophical and scientific work of Helmholtz, Mach, and Poincaré, to a new conception of the relativized a priori, first instantiated in Einstein's theories. It has also led, through this same tradition, to a radically new reconfiguration of the connection between geometry and physics in the general theory of relativity itself. There can be no question, of course, of Kant having 'anticipated' this theory in any way. The point, rather, is that Kant's own conception of the relationship between geometry and physics (which was limited, of necessity, to Euclidean geometry and Newtonian physics) set in motion a remarkable series of successive reconceptualizations of this relationship (in light of profound discoveries in both pure mathematics and the empirical basis of mathematical physics) that finally eventuated in Einstein's theory.

Contingent Transcendental Arguments for Metaphysical Principles[1]

HASOK CHANG

Introduction

One of Kant's lasting contributions to epistemology was to demonstrate the presence of a priori elements in empirical knowledge. However, grave doubts have been cast on the Kantian enterprise since later mathematics and physics have rejected some key elements of what Kant had regarded as a priori knowledge. In this paper, I propose a way forward in updating Kantian transcendental arguments in order to open up the a priori to adaptations to particular epistemic circumstances. My proposal is to identify transcendental arguments that have contingent conditions, in the following form: '*If* we want to engage in a certain epistemic activity, *then* we must presume the truth of some particular metaphysical principles'.

I am not a Kant scholar, and this paper is not intended as an exegesis of any works of Immanuel Kant. Rather, what I want to do is to take some central insights from Kant's work and adapt them freely to give them more immediate relevance to contemporary philosophy of science.

Aside from explaining my own proposal, I would like to draw a comparison-and-contrast with Michael Friedman's notion of the relativized a priori. I also want to trace an affinity between my proposal and C. I. Lewis's system of 'conceptual pragmatism', in which he advances a 'pragmatic conception of the a priori'. I will in fact begin with a critical exposition of Friedman's and Lewis's ideas in the first part of the paper. Then I will move on to my own ideas.

[1] Acknowledgements: I would like to thank many people whose critical and constructive commentary or practical assistance helped me develop these ideas, particularly Roberto Torretti, Grant Fisher, Henk de Regt, Sabina Leonelli, Michela Massimi, Alirio Rosales, Michael Friedman, Tom Ryckman, Eric Schliesser, Matthew Lund, Mieke Boon, Henk Procee, Hans Radder, and Chiara Ambrosio.

doi:10.1017/S1358246108000076

Hasok Chang

Part A. What to do about the instability of metaphysics: Friedman and Lewis

It is regrettable that Kant fell into the trap of thinking that systems of knowledge like Euclidean geometry and Newtonian mechanics were necessarily and universally true. Looking at Kant from a little distance makes one thing clear: his location in the Newton-enraptured eighteenth century must have exerted a strong hold on his imagination. This Kantian predicament is uncomfortably close to Philipp Frank's assessment of the poverty of philosophical opposition to new scientific ideas: what parade as deep metaphysical truths are often simply 'petrified' remains of outdated scientific theories. In Frank's view, science needs to educate metaphysics, not *vice versa*.[2]

Kant was, of course, not alone in this sort of error; there are many other cases from the history of science showing the pernicious effect of metaphysical beliefs that are leftovers from earlier scientific theories. In his opposition to orthodox quantum mechanics, Albert Einstein pleased himself by declaring that 'God does not play with dice'; but how did he have this (not only direct but apparently exclusive) access to God, while Niels Bohr would seem to have been denied the direct telephone line? Erwin Schrödinger's objection to quantum jumps, the Cartesians' objection to Newtonian action at a distance, and other similar cases all illustrate the same point. Scientific reactionaries protest that a new theory does not make sense, that it is unintelligible; these cries of unintelligibility cease to resonate with new generations of scientists, who grow up with the new theory and find it just as intelligible (or unintelligible) as any other theory.[3] If metaphysics is to serve as a guide for scientific work, we must try to do something about the lack of stability displayed by metaphysical beliefs.

A1. Michael Friedman's historicized universalism

It is in this connection that Friedman's pioneering work on a Kantian interpretation of scientific change has been so important. Friedman stresses the hidden continuity in scientific change, even revolutionary change. Accepting the basic historical reality of Kuhnian paradigm shifts, Friedman still detects continuity and progress at the level of

---

[2]   Frank (1949), ch. 12, pp. 207–215.
[3]   See De Regt and Dieks (2005), pp. 159–162, for an instructive discussion of the context-dependence of intelligibility.

constitutive principles. In *The Dynamics of Reason*, toward the end of the third lecture, Friedman issues quite a strong and definite prescription on how scientific change should be made:

> How is it possible to venture a transformation of our present constitutive principles resulting in a genuine conceptual change or shift in paradigm? How, more specifically, can the proposal of a radically new conceptual framework be, nonetheless, both rational and responsible? In accordance with our threefold perspective on inter-paradigm convergence we can now say the following: first, that the new conceptual framework or paradigm should contain the previous constitutive framework as an approximate limiting case, holding in precisely defined special conditions; second, that the new constitutive principles should also evolve continuously out of the old constitutive principles, by a series of natural transformations; and third, that this process of continuing conceptual transformation should be motivated and sustained by an appropriate new philosophical meta-framework, which, in particular, interacts productively with both older philosophical meta-frameworks and new developments taking place in the sciences themselves.[4]

When paradigm change is made in this way, we can have '*a convergent sequence* of successive frameworks or paradigms, approximating in the limit (but never actually reaching) an ideal state of maximally comprehensive communicative rationality in which all participants in the ideal community of inquiry agree on *a common set of truly universal, trans-historical constitutive principles*'.[5]

Some questions must be raised about this universalizing picture of inquiry and scientific progress presented by Friedman. Why are universality and trans-historicity taken for granted as ideals we must all aspire to? Universality is clearly something that Kant himself aspired to, and Friedman's text perhaps reveals an unquestioning acceptance of Kantian universalism even as he renounces the immutability of Kantian categories. But in this 'post-modern' age, we cannot escape the pluralist question: what would be so wrong with having different parts of the human epistemic community pursuing the study of nature on the basis of different sets of constitutive principles? Would that not be more in keeping with the promotion of human freedom? And would having multiple lines of inquiry not be more conducive to more discoveries being made and preserved? There is

---

4   Friedman (2001a), p. 66.
5   Friedman (2001a), p. 67; emphases added.

Hasok Chang

at least a serious debate to be had about these questions.[6] Paul Feyerabend, Karl Popper and others detested Kuhn's view of normal science for its insistence on the monopoly enjoyed by the ruling paradigm within a given scientific discipline, but Kuhn at least allowed different sorts of paradigms for different scientific fields. It seems that Friedman's ideal does not allow that plurality; instead, there seems to be an expectation that mathematical physics must provide the constitutive principles that all other sciences must build on.[7]

Similarly, when it comes to trans-historicity, why is it that a new conceptual framework or a new set of constitutive principles should be tied to the existing one so closely as Friedman dictates? The empiricist impulse would be to say that there is nothing wrong with abrupt change as long as the new set of constitutive principles come with appropriate theories that account for observed phenomena, phenomena as framed through the new constitutive principles. And is it impossible that we may actually achieve better results by introducing new constitutive principles in a discontinuous way, when the results are judged by various criteria such as empirical adequacy, useful applications, simplicity, explanatory power, etc.? These sentiments underlie the argument by Frank mentioned above, and they receive the boldest expression in Feyerabend's argument for 'counter-induction' as a method of escaping from the grip of an old cosmology.[8]

A2. C. I. Lewis on the pragmatic a priori

In trying to formulate my own answers to all those questions, I find the work of Clarence Irving Lewis very helpful.[9] Lewis was a curious

[6] Kellert *et al.* (2006) represents a significant start on the debate on scientific pluralism.

[7] See, for example, the discussion of the Chemical Revolution in Friedman (2001a), pp. 124–5.

[8] Feyerabend (1975), chs. 2–3, and pp. 65–8, 77–8.

[9] Since C. I. Lewis is no longer a household name even among professional philosophers, I give here a few basic facts of his life, taken from his autobiographical notes in Schilpp (1968). Lewis was born in 1883 in Stoneham, Massachusetts, son of a shoemaker. He studied at Harvard, where his teachers included Josiah Royce and William James. After a brief spell teaching English, he returned to Harvard for graduate study, completing his Ph.D. in 1910. In 1911 he went to the University of California at Berkeley to teach philosophy, and composed *The Survey of Symbolic Logic*

kind of Kantian, who reportedly said: 'I am a Kantian who disagrees with every sentence of the *Critique of Pure Reason*.'[10] His best-known work, the 1929 book titled *Mind and the World Order*, will be the focus of my attention here.[11] In an apparently anti-Kantian move, Lewis denies that there are any synthetic a priori principles. He declares: *'The a priori is not a material truth, delimiting or delineating the content of experience as such, but is definitive or analytic in its nature'*.[12] For him, all a priori principles follow from the nature of the concepts we choose to craft and use:

> The paradigm of the a priori in general is the definition. It has always been clear that the simplest and most obvious case of truth which can be known in advance of experience is the explicative proposition and those consequences of definition which can be derived by purely logical analysis. These are necessarily true, true under all possible circumstances, because definition is legislative.[13]

He adds: 'the powerful sweep and consequence of purely logical analysis has not been understood. The clearest example of this power of analysis is to be found, of course, in mathematics. The historical importance of mathematics as a paradigm of a priori truth needs no emphasis'.[14] And yet, Lewisian a priori principles in science are not mere tautologies; they do serve as significant laws of nature, in a way that I think is perfectly consonant with Friedman's views on what constitutive principles do. Interestingly, Lewis chose Einstein's definition of simultaneity in special relativity to help make his point about the role of definitions:

> As this example well illustrates, we cannot even ask the questions which discovered law would answer until we have first by a priori stipulation formulated definitive criteria. Such concepts are not

---

to help his teaching. He returned to Harvard in 1920, where he taught until his retirement in 1953. He gave an account of his 'conceptual pragmatism' in his *Mind and the World Order* in 1929, and published *An Analysis of Knowledge and Valuation* in 1946. He died in 1964.

[10]   Beck (1968), p. 273.
[11]   I do hope to engage in a more general study of Lewis's ideas, following up on some recent scholarship such as Rosenthal (2007) and Murphey (2005).
[12]   Lewis (1929), p. 231; emphasis original.
[13]   Lewis (1929), pp. 239–240.
[14]   Lewis (1929), pp. 240–241.

verbal definitions nor classifications merely; they are themselves laws which prescribe a certain behaviour to whatever is thus named. Such definitive laws are a priori; only so can we enter upon the investigation by which further laws are sought.[15]

A3. Friedman vs. Lewis on the a priori

A very instructive comparison and contrast can be drawn between Friedman's and Lewis's views of the a priori. There are three points that I would like to highlight, summarized in Table 1.

Lewis recognizes, as does Friedman, that 'there will be no assurance that what is a priori will remain fixed and absolute throughout the history of the race or for the developing individual'. What he emphasizes in that situation is the freedom of the human inquirer: 'If the a priori is something made by the mind, mind may also alter it'; and 'the determination of the a priori is in some sense like free choice and deliberate action'.[16] In fact he seems to take it as definitive of the a priori that it 'has alternatives',[17] and maintains that an aspect of our mind about which we truly have no choice would not even be recognized at all.[18] For Lewis, 'The necessity of the a priori is its character as legislative act. It represents a constraint imposed by the mind, not a constraint imposed upon mind by something else'.[19] There may be no direct contradiction between Lewis's remarks and Friedman's

Table 1 Friedman and Lewis on the a priori

	Lewis	Friedman
Lack of permanence	Free choice	Tempered by connections with previous principles
Historicity	Shift between permanent elements	Natural transformations
Criteria of judgments	Pragmatic	Generality and adequacy

[15] Lewis (1929), p. 256.
[16] Lewis (1929), pp. 233–234.
[17] Lewis (1929), p. 232.
[18] Lewis (1929), p. 236.
[19] Lewis (1929), p. 197.

statements about the a priori, but the difference of emphasis is very clear. Even when Lewis quotes Einstein, which he does at length, it is only to hear Einstein concluding that the definition of simultaneity in special relativity is 'a *stipulation* which I can make of my own free-will'.[20] Lewis's emphasis on the freedom of choice tends to go against, or at least allow a deviation from, the universalizing aspect of Friedman's prescription, which I have noted as less than compelling.

On the other hand, Lewis's liberal notion of the a priori can actually provide more stability to knowledge than achievable under Friedman's scheme. Because the Lewisian a priori is analytic, its truth is fixed and not subject to re-evaluation. As Lewis puts it: 'That only can be a priori which is true *no matter what*'.[21] So, while Friedman accommodates historical change by demanding an orderly transformation of a priori principles, Lewis does it by allowing changes in preferences among all available conceptual structures, each of which remains fixed. When Lewis says that the a priori can be altered by the mind, he does not mean that each given a priori principle can change its content; rather, we switch our allegiance from one to another, as we do when we elect a new political leader. Confusion may be created by the same *word* being used to denote what are actually different concepts, as Kuhn showed so nicely with historical examples like the term 'planet' before and after the Copernican Revolution and the term 'mass' in classical mechanics and special relativity. We should not mistake such verbal confusion as something profound about the nature of the a priori. Along with the permanence of each version of a priori knowledge, also comes the permanence of empirical knowledge, once it has been achieved:

> New ranges of experience such as those due to the invention of the telescope and microscope have actually led to alteration of our categories in historic time. The same thing may happen through more penetrating or adequate analysis of old types of experience—witness Virchow's redefinition of disease. What was previously regarded as real—e.g., disease entities—may come to be looked upon as unreal, and what was previously taken to be unreal—e.g., curved space—may be admitted to reality. But when this happens *the truth remains unaltered and new truth and old truth do not contradict*. Categories and concepts do not literally change; they are simply given up and replaced by new ones.[22]

---

20 Quoted in Lewis (1929), p. 256.
21 Lewis (1929), p. 197; emphasis original.
22 Lewis (1929), p. 268; emphasis original.

Finally, Lewis is adamant that the choice of a priori principles, right down to the principles of logic,[23] are made by pragmatic criteria:

while the a priori is *dictated* neither by what is presented in experience nor by any transcendent and eternal factor of human nature, it still *answers to* criteria of the general type which may be termed pragmatic. The human animal with his needs and interests confronts an experience in which these must be satisfied, if at all. Both the general character of the experience and the nature of the animal will be reflected in the mode of behavior which marks this attempt to realize his ends. This will be true of the categories of his thinking as in other things. And here, as elsewhere, the result will be reached by a process in which attitudes tentatively assumed, disappointment in the ends to be realized, and consequent alteration of behavior will play their part.[24]

Lewis adds:

If we were jelly-fish in a liquid world, we should probably not add at all, because the useful purposes served by such conceptions would be so slight. Still if some super-jelly-fish should invent arithmetic by a *jeu d'esprit* (as Hamilton invented quaternions) he would find nothing in any possible experience to controvert it, and he might with some profit apply it to his own distinct ideas.[25]

Contrast this with Friedman's criteria in judging the goodness of the transformations of constitutive principles: 'we can thus view the evolution of succeeding paradigms or frameworks as a convergent series, as it were, in which we successively refine our constitutive principles in the direction of ever greater generality and adequacy'.[26] And although we are not in possession of 'truly universal principles of human reason', we can imagine 'that our present constitutive principles represent one stage of a convergent process, as it were, in that they can be viewed as approximations to more general and adequate constitutive principles that will only be articulated at a later stage'.[27] I would again question the undisputed desirability of generality, and I am not sure what exactly Friedman means by the

---

[23]   Lewis (1929), p. 247: 'the ultimate criteria of the laws of logic are pragmatic. Indeed, how could they be anything else?'
[24]   Lewis (1929), p. 239; emphases added.
[25]   Lewis (1929), p. 252.
[26]   Friedman (2001a), p. 63.
[27]   Friedman (2001a), p. 64.

'adequacy' of a constitutive principle. Adequacy may cover, in part, what Lewis means by pragmatic criteria. What is more certain is the affinity between Lewis's views and Poincaré's conventionalism. Lewis says that although a priori principles cannot be rendered false come what may, 'If experience were other than it is, the definition and its corresponding classification might be inconvenient, useless, or fantastic....'[28] In a wording strongly reminiscent of Poincaré, Lewis notes that the pragmatic choices are 'questions of convenience or of value'.[29]

Part B. Metaphysical principles and epistemic activities

B1. The connection between metaphysical principles and epistemic activities

Having made a brief review of Friedman's and Lewis's ideas on how to accommodate historical change in the realm of a priori knowledge, I am now ready to present my own ideas. And here I must begin with a brief complaint about Lewis: I think his pragmatism does not go far enough to deliver the full potential of his approach. He does consider what knowledge can do for 'the human animal with his needs and interests'; however, in his conception of knowledge itself he is for the most part traditional, seeing it as an abstract system consisting of concepts, laws, and empirical statements. What I would like to do is make a full development of Lewis's idea of the 'pragmatic a priori'. I propose to carry Lewis's major insights into an analysis of knowledge as a process of inquiry, which consists of 'epistemic activities of an embodied and conceptualizing subject', to use a phrase from Alirio Rosales.[30] My line of thinking is also highly consonant with Marjorie Grene's revision of Kant with an emphasis on the knower as an agent.[31] Taking Lewis at his word when he says that the a priori is pragmatic, I see a priori principles as necessary conditions for carrying out certain epistemic activities. This is a line of thought I initially developed in more detail in another paper,[32] which I will condense and update here.

28 Lewis (1929), p. 240.
29 Lewis (1929), p. 248.
30 Private communication, June 2007.
31 Grene (1974), ch. 5.
32 Chang (in press).

I also want to stress that there are Kantian undertones in the basic insight I am trying to develop. This is particularly true on Henry Allison's interpretation of Kant's epistemology, according to which Kant was trying to elucidate the 'intellectual conditions of human cognition'.[33] Kant linked the categories with the 'universal logical functions of thinking'. What he called 'functions of thinking' can be linked with my idea of 'epistemic activities'. However, in my view Kant was wrong in thinking that he had given a complete treatment of the functions of thinking. Or perhaps the trouble is that he only dealt with what he considered truly universal in all human judgment, leaving out many activities of the mind which are only contingently required depending on one's current aims and circumstances. On the other side, the Kantian impulse was to elevate to the status of universality any types of judgment he found sufficiently widespread. We can escape both of these difficulties by acknowledging that there is a large element of choice in the types of epistemic activities we enter into. I would like to say the synthetic a priori only exists in a contingent way—not as universal conditions of human cognition, but as local conditions of particular brands of cognition.

B1.1. How counting requires discreteness

The basic idea of my proposal can be illustrated most effectively through a very simple example, to begin with. If we want to engage in the activity of counting, then we have to presume that the things we are trying to count are discrete. In other words, the metaphysical principle of discreteness is required in the activity of counting, and enables that activity. What we have here may be considered a peculiar type of transcendental argument—laying out the necessary conditions of something that we may or may not choose to do, rather than investigating the preconditions of what is accepted as given. In other words, I am proposing to modify Kant's transcendental arguments for the synthetic a priori into a contingent form: '*if* we want to do X, *then* we must presume Y.' Let me stress several aspects of this situation:

> (1) It is obvious that the necessity here is *conditional*: it is only if we count things that discreteness has to be presumed. (Whether or not we ought to engage in counting is a separate question—recall Lewis's jelly-fish).

---

[33] Allison (2004), pp. 11ff, and chapter 6.

(2) The principle of discreteness says nothing about whether the *world in itself is* discrete or not, only that we need to *take* it as such if we are going to count things.

(3) What underlies the sense of necessity here is impossibility: we can try, but we just cannot count anything in an utterly undifferentiated continuum. The nature of that impossibility is interesting. It is a *pragmatic impossibility*, which is a notion I will take as a primitive rather than try to analyze it further in terms of other notions, which I think are less basic.[34]

(4) The difference between *empirical truth* and *pragmatic necessity* should be clear. A given bit of the universe may or may not contain discrete pieces; if it does, then that domain is in fact discrete, which would be an empirical truth; that would be a fact, with no necessity about it. The necessity of discreteness only comes with our *commitment* to count.

(5) The denial of a metaphysical principle, while we are engaged in the activity that requires it, generates a sense of *unintelligibility*. If we are trying to count things that we cannot grasp as discrete, that makes no sense; it is an unintelligible activity that we are engaged in.

B1.2. How single value is necessary for testing-by-overdetermination
As a slightly more subtle example of a metaphysical principle, take what I call the *principle of single value*. This principle states that a real physical property can have no more than one definite value in a given situation; or, that two correct value-ascriptions about the same situation cannot disagree with each other, when we are concerned with a real physical property.[35] Consider what we get when we violate the principle of single value. Someone says: 'The length of this stick is both *2m* and *3m*.' 'No,' we would respond, 'the value has to be one or the other, not both at once.'

[34] I want to argue that other types of impossibility are actually grounded in pragmatic impossibility, being metaphorical extensions of the latter. This is why it would be futile to try to analyze pragmatic impossibility further. In working out the notions of necessity and possibility sketched here, I would like to build connections to Roberto Torretti's ideas on the subject, as expressed in Torretti (1990), chapter 5.
[35] See Chang (2001), pp. 11, 18. In experimental practice, 'disagreeing' means differing so much as to go beyond the admitted margin of error. I have shown how this principle has done useful work, although it might seem entirely vacuous (Chang 2001, pp. 17–22).

(Even quantum mechanics in its Copenhagen Interpretation stops short of saying that a particle can have multiple positions at once; a particle can only have non-zero probabilities of detection in various places).

What are the grounds of the validity of this single-value principle? The first thing to note is that it is not an empirical generalization. To see that point, imagine trying to test the principle by experiment. If we went around taking measurements of various quantities to check that we get a single value each time, that would seem as silly as testing 'All bachelors are unmarried' by collecting a bunch of bachelors and checking each one carefully to see if he is married. Worse, if someone reported a counter-instance (say, that his weight is both 60 kg and 70 kg), our reaction would be total incomprehension. We would have to say that such an observation is 'not even wrong', and we would feel compelled to engage in a metaphysical discourse to persuade this person that he is not making any sense. The principle of single value is not a logical truth, either. One can easily imagine variables that have multiple values, especially in the realm of non-physical quantities and designations: for example, names of persons or places, or multi-valued functions in mathematics.

Still, where we do recognize it as valid, the principle of single value clearly seems to have a necessity about it. What could be the source of this necessity? I would like to propose that the necessity of the principle of single value comes from the requirements of testing.[36] Let me elaborate on that idea. Take an ordinary situation in which a theory is tested, in the simplified view given by the hypothetico-deductive model. We derive a prediction from the theory, and check it against observation. If the predicted and observed values differ, we decide that there is something false about the theory. This is usually regarded as a matter of simple deductive logic, but we are actually making a tacit reliance on the principle of single value. We predict that the temperature here at 10am today will be 15°C; our observation says it is 20°C. If the temperature could be both 15°C *and* 20°C, there would be no refutation here. To put it formally: there is no logical contradiction between 'T = 15°C' and 'T = 20°C', until we also put in the principle of single value, which gives 'If T = 20°C, then T ≠ 15°C'. Now we do have a contradiction, because we have 'T = 15°C' and

[36]   Chang (2001), pp. 18–22. I thank Roberto Torretti (private communication, March–April 2005) for getting me to think about this point in a fresh way.

'T $\neq$ 15°C'.[37] Without the principle of single value, we cannot engage in this kind of testing. More generally, the principle of single value is required for what I call testing-by-overdetermination, in which we determine the value of a quantity in two different ways. If the values match, that gives credence to the basis on which we made the two determinations; if the values do not match, then we infer that there is some problem in our starting assumptions. The two determinations could be the familiar prediction–observation pair, or two observations, or even two theoretical determinations. So, what we engage in is *attempted overdetermination*, which is really just an elaborate way of saying 'checking'.

To summarize: we need to subscribe to the principle of single value *if* we want to engage in testing-by-overdetermination. In other words, the *necessity* of the principle of single value springs from our commitment to testing-by-overdetermination. Or, single-valuedness is necessary for enabling the activity of testing-by-overdetermination. What we have is a pragmatic necessity—a necessity arising from the requirements of epistemic action, not some kind of hyper-truth that pertains to a proposition.

B2. Preliminary list of principle–activity pairs

So far we have examined two epistemic activities, and found a metaphysical principle that is required for each activity (single value for testing, discreteness for counting). This picture can now be broadened: to each well-defined basic epistemic activity, there is an associated metaphysical principle that makes it performable and intelligible.

The proposed one-to-one pairing of epistemic activity and metaphysical principle might seem too neat, artificial and contrived. But it will seem more natural if we recognize two things. First, the one-to-one correspondence only applies to the most basic epistemic activities; complex ones will require multiple principles. Second, in the principle–activity pairing, the metaphysical principle and the epistemic activity are mutually constitutive. A general link between ontology and epistemology will be easily granted, in the sense that the appropriate method of studying something is surely linked with the nature of that something. Here I am pointing to the purest and

---

[37]   Lewis (1929), p. 246, puts it: 'The law of contradiction tells us that nothing can be both white and not white, but it does not and can not tell us whether black is not white. ....'

Hasok Chang

strongest version of that link: a distinct type of epistemic activity has its particular type of object, the essential characteristic of which is defined by the fundamental metaphysical principle associated with the activity. At the same time, the nature of the activity is shaped by the basic character of its objects. So the conditional statement that if we want to engage in activity X then we must presume the truth of principle Y, becomes analytic.

Table 2 gives a list of basic epistemic activities and their associated metaphysical principles that I have started compiling. Even a brief consideration of these pairings will reveal some quite interesting consequences of this way of thinking. About the first two activity–principle pairs I have already said enough. (There is just one brief note I must add on the second pair: there are other modes of 'testing', including a 'trial run', which can be made without a specific prior prediction of the outcome. This is why I must specify what I have in mind here as 'testing-by-overdetermination'). The remaining activity–principle pairs deserve some brief explanations.

(Rational) Prediction – The principle of uniform consequence
('principle of induction' or 'determinism')
In order to make any rational predictions (as opposed to random guessing, or prophecy by oracle or divine illumination), we must take it for granted that the same initial circumstance will always have the same outcome. Induction is just this 'principle of uniform consequence' in action. As Wesley Salmon points out in his critique of Popper,[38] an attempt to do away with induction disables the activity of rational prediction. This is why we cannot seem to get away from induction, no matter what its logical deficiencies are. Induction is not merely a custom, nor an optional piece of scientific methodology, but a necessary condition for rational prediction. This is a more robust justification of induction as a practice than the 'pragmatic' argument given by Hans Reichenbach: in Reichenbach's view, induction is justified as a practice that would give us success if we could have success at all; my view is that induction is necessary regardless of any prospect of success, as long as we engage in the activity of rational prediction.[39]

In a similar vein, it is instructive to view indeterminism or determinism as more than a mere metaphysical belief. Determinism is a

[38] See Salmon (1988), from which I also take the phrase 'rational prediction'.
[39] Reichenbach (1935), English transation (1971), pp. 469ff.

Table 2 A partial list of activity–principle pairs

Epistemic activity	Metaphysical principle
Counting	Discreteness
Testing-by-overdetermination	Single value
(Rational) Prediction	Uniform consequence
(Contrastive) Explanation	Sufficient reason
Narration	Subsistence
(Linear) Ordering	Transitivity
Voluntary action	Agency
Intervention	Causality
Empathy	Other minds
Observation	Externality/Objectivity
Identification	Identity of indiscernibles
Assertion	Non-contradiction

commitment to engage in the activity of rational prediction in every individual case. That commitment was one important aspect of Einstein's insistence that quantum mechanics was incomplete, and it is shared by those who are still pursuing hidden-variable theories. But the justification for determinism is not as strong as the justification for induction in general, because it is possible to live with rational predictions only in a statistical sense.

(Contrastive) Explanation – The principle of sufficient reason
The activity of explaining why something (as opposed to something else) happened requires the assumption that when there is an observed difference, there is a reason behind it. I will call this the principle of sufficient reason, since it can be considered a weak version of that old metaphysical principle.[40] This principle of sufficient reason provides a very broad schema of explanation ('X rather than Y, because C', or, 'X rather than Y, because A rather than B'). This schema is fully compatible with the subsumption model of explanation, and it is more general in that it does not require the *explanans* to contain any laws or even to be more general than the *explanandum*. And the explanatory factor may be causal, or anything else. As with testing, I should note that there are other modes of explanation than the contrastive.

[40] Depending on the exact formulations, it could be that the principle of sufficient reason is just the contrapositive of the principle of uniform consequence.

Hasok Chang

Narration – The principle of subsistence

Next, consider the activity of narration. What is required for telling a story? It might be thought that something to do with time would be the most fundamental principle of narrative. But, contrary to expectation, it is not time-ordering that provides the most basic metaphysical principle behind narration. A narrative requires entities or persons whose identities last through time, which 'house' the changes that are narrated. Otherwise, we cannot even formulate narrative strands like 'someone ran down the street'. Paradoxically, without postulating *something* that lasts, it is impossible to describe any change. In the context of physical science, this principle of persistence (or better, subsistence) manifests itself as more specific assumptions, such as that fundamental particles persist without alteration ('atomism'), or that there is a substance or quantity that is conserved (mass, energy, etc.).

This, incidentally, is why the Big Bang makes an unintelligible narrative about the origin of the universe; I am not saying that the science behind Big Bang cosmology is unintelligible, but only that it is impossible to make an intelligible narrative about the Big Bang itself. The Book of Genesis at least offers an intelligible narrative about the origin of the universe (though one that I personally do not believe), since there is God, whose identity lasts through the act of creation. But if we demanded a story about how God came to be, we would run into the same unintelligibility as with the Big Bang. The story of ultimate origin is untellable, much as Kant taught us in his antinomies of reason, though for a slightly different reason from what he gave.

(Linear) Ordering – The principle of transitivity[41]

If we want to put a set of entities into an ordered sequence, we must assume that the method of ordering (or, the relation that forms the basis of ordering) is transitive. This applies not only to numerical ordering, but all other kinds of linear sequencing such as time-ordering, status-based hierarchies, chemical affinity tables, and completely non-quantitative cases such as alphabetical ordering.

---

[41] My thinking about this particular activity–principle pair was inspired by the work of Georgette Taylor on affinity tables in eighteenth century chemistry.

Voluntary action – Agency
Engaging in voluntary action makes no sense unless we presume that our will directs certain parts of ourselves to move in certain ways.[42] That presumption may be called the principle of agency.

Intervention – Causality
Similarly, intervening in the world with our own actions requires a presumption that our actions do make things happen; I am calling that the principle of causality for want of a better word, but this needs to be distinguished from the notion of 'causality' that putatively obtains in the interaction of things between each other, which I think is only a metaphorical projection of the causality in our own direct actions. Agency and causality together provide the most fundamental schemata for our bodily actions.

Empathy – Other minds
In the activity of understanding other people's intentions and emotions (which I have called 'empathy' for lack of a better word), one needs to presume that there are other minds who possess intentions and emotions like one's own.

Observation – Externality/Objectivity
Similarly, the activity of observation makes no sense unless we presume that there are entities 'out there' whose manifestations we cannot control at will. The last two activity–principle pairs give us the most fundamental constituents of the world: external objects and other minds.

Identification – Identity of indiscernibles
The identification of an object (or a property) *as* something of any given description must be based on something like Leibniz's principle of the identity of indiscernibles.[43] The principle itself can be divorced from various uncertain uses that Leibniz himself (and others) made of it.

---

[42]   Whether the will itself is free or not is a separate question. Along vaguely Kantian/Jamesian lines I would imagine that the freedom of the will is a metaphysical principle concomitant to the activity of making moral judgments (cf. Carlson 1997, pp. 374–375).

[43]   I thank Roberto Torretti for this suggestion.

Hasok Chang

Assertion – Non-contradiction

Even the principle of non-contradiction may be a metaphysical principle, associated with the epistemic activity of asserting a proposition.[44] It may seem odd to call a logical principle *metaphysical*, but we can think of non-contradiction as the essential nature of propositions involved in any reasoning. A new light may be thrown on the nature of logical necessity as well: the principle of non-contradiction is necessary because of a pragmatic impossibility, namely that we find it impossible to assert something without avoiding the assertion of its direct denial.

This is only a partial list, and I expect there will be more activity–principle pairs to be found. But already, thinking through this list gives me a whole new way of thinking and many interesting insights about some very familiar and fundamental issues in philosophy.

B3. Complex epistemic activities

In real life, we hardly ever engage in such simple and elementary epistemic activities as appearing in the above list. What we actually have, even in the practice of mathematics or theoretical physics, are mostly very complex and specific activities—such as, say, predicting the frequencies of molecular radiation by solving the Schrödinger equation using certain techniques of approximation. I think it is going to be a very interesting and informative challenge to extend my analysis to complex epistemic activities in various areas. A complex activity will involve multiple basic activities, each with its attendant metaphysical principle. Therefore, all of those metaphysical principles have to be satisfied for the complex activity to be performable and intelligible.

There are some very interesting and common conjunctions of basic epistemic activities which play essential roles in science and everyday life. For example, the activity of giving mechanical explanations can be seen as a synthesis of contrastive explanation, narration, and (imagined) intervention. The construction of physical objects is another crucial activity, but it cannot be conceived fully in terms of the basic activities and principles I have discussed so far in this paper. It involves first of all the assumption that every object is 'located' in space and time ('physicalism' as meant by Otto Neurath). We also presume that all sensations attributed to one and the same object are harmonious with each other (e.g., a big sharp edge felt in gently running a finger along a completely smooth-looking surface

---

[44] I had conceived the relevant epistemic activity here as deductive inference, but have revised my view on Roberto Torretti's suggestion.

is not intelligible). Quite possibly there is a presumption of causality, too, embodied in the notion of a physical object. We can see that the analysis of a complex epistemic activity is a challenging task that will require imagination as well as care.

It would be wrong to think of a complex activity as made up of basic activities in an atomistic way. All distinct activities to which we give definite characterization are abstractions from what we actually do. Although it is often instructive to think of a complex abstraction as constructed from simpler abstractions, it would be a mistake to build up a whole universe of activities from basic activities.[45] Rather, the important thing to note is the relationships holding between the domains of applicability of various activity-descriptions. If an act that qualifies as an instance of activity A always qualifies as an instance of activity B as well, but not *vice versa*, we can say that activity B is more basic than activity A. Applying that idea to the basic epistemic activities that I have discussed so far, I find that some of them are more basic than others. For example, testing-by-overdetermination always involves assertion. Therefore, assertion is a more basic activity than testing-by-overdetermination, and the latter requires the principle of non-contradiction in addition to the principle of single value. Similarly, hardly any other activity can take place without identification.

It is beyond the scope of this paper to enter into a detailed analysis of any particular complex activities. But it seems clear to me that thinking along these lines provides a good framework for analyzing scientific practice, thus providing a new direction for a philosophy of science that engages better with the actual happenings in science, both historical and contemporary. I am currently engaged in developing such a philosophy of scientific practice.

B4. Pragmatic roots of necessity and ontology

I would like to close with some further reflections on the concept of necessity. I believe that necessity is a concept rooted in human action, which we project metaphorically onto the rest of nature—sometimes sensibly, and sometimes not. The ignoring of this human, pragmatic context is the main reason why we have such trouble understanding the notion of necessity, as we try to render

---

[45]   The limitations are similar for any other kind of compositional reductionism. See, for example, the anti-reductionist arguments in Dupré (1993), chapter 4.

'necessary truth' as some sort of hyper-truth, with the help of possible-worlds semantics and such. Instead, I would like to propose that something is 'necessarily true' if it *needs* to be *taken* as true for the purpose of some epistemic action (here I deviate from Lewis, who still seems to take necessary truth as truth in all possible worlds.)

Necessity also does not imply universality. Metaphysical principles are not truly universal, as their necessity remains conditional on our commitment to engage in their associated epistemic activities. Even with some of the most basic epistemic activities, there are situations in which we would decline to engage in them. First, we may judge that the activity in question is not useful enough to bother with. Second, nature may be such that it is impossible for us to perform the activity (Lewis sees this as a matter of applicability of our concepts). Recall Lewis's jelly-fish, on both counts. Or imagine the prospect of attempting to make rational predictions in an utterly chaotic situation, or in a world ruled by a malicious controller bent on frustrating us. There is an element of choice and judgment in epistemic activity, just as in any other kind of human activity. Necessity is omni-present in human action, but not in a uniform way.

This is, again, the key difference I see between my way of thinking and the legacy of Kant. In my scheme there are no eternal and universal categories, since we are not compelled to engage in all the same basic epistemic activities all the time. It is a mistake to treat the activity-dependent conditions of performability and intelligibility as unconditional metaphysical truths. Even compared to William Whewell's scheme, in which the categories evolve with the general development of science,[46] or Friedman's system of the relativized a priori in which revolutions are allowed,[47] my scheme is distinct in allowing more freedom to epistemic communities and even individuals in their choice of epistemic activities, and in taking the pragmatic performability of activities as the ultimate basis of necessity. This expands and completes Lewis's idea of the freedom in the a priori.

Conclusion

In summary, I have proposed a novel way of extending Kant's legacy in order to accommodate the problem of scientific change. Albeit

[46] For a convenient selection of Whewell's writings relevant to this issue, with a brief introduction, see Kockelmans (1968), pp. 47–79.
[47] Friedman (2001a), esp. part 2, ch. 1.

with undiminished admiration for Michael Friedman's effort to understand how a continuous evolution of the a priori dimension of physical knowledge is possible underneath the appearance of haphazard and radical shifts of paradigms, I follow C. I. Lewis in emphasizing our freedom in choosing our a priori, in our continual effort to meet pragmatic needs. I supplement Lewis's position with a reframing of the a priori as the pragmatically necessary preconditions of the epistemic activities we choose to carry out. The fully pragmatist notion of the a priori that I propose has some far-reaching implications in epistemology and metaphysics.

It is satisfying to see how our basic metaphysical conceptions arise from the way we engage with the world. The most fundamental part of ontology is not abstracted from what we passively observe; rather, it emerges and becomes established as an essential ingredient in our successful epistemic activities.[48] A whiff of scientific realism can be derived from that insight: if some of our epistemic activities are successful, that must be some sort of indirect vindication of the metaphysical principles presumed in those activities.[49] But this vague sense of vindication is all we can have, and it only points to an inarticulable harmony between the state of the world and our metaphysical principles. There is a Kantian insight here: nature in itself (not what Kant called 'nature', which consists of phenomena) is not the object of our epistemic activities; our activity-based ontology is not a direct representation of nature (or, the Kantian 'thing in itself'). As Henri Bergson put it: 'The bodies we perceive are, so to speak, cut out of the stuff of nature by our *perception*, and the scissors follow, in some way, the marking of lines along which *action* might be taken'.[50] When nature 'speaks' to us, it is only through the outcomes of our epistemic activities. That is not to deny that nature enters and rules our life, by determining which epistemic activities are pragmatically possible and profitable. But metaphysical principles do not give us the kind of direct representation of nature that the correspondence theory of truth would have us seek.

[48]   See Carlson (1997) for an insightful argument that there were significant Kantian elements in William James's thinking, despite the latter's renunciation of Kantianism.

[49]   This is reminiscent of Duhem's argument that when we witness the extensive organization of phenomena through a successful theory, 'it is impossible for us to believe that this order and this organization are not the reflected image of a real order and organization'. See Duhem (1906), English translation (1962), pp. 26–8; he also cites Poincaré in that discussion.

[50]   Bergson (1907), English translation (1911), p. 12; emphases original.

Arithmetic from Kant to Frege: Numbers, Pure Units, and the Limits of Conceptual Representation

DANIEL SUTHERLAND

There is evidence in Kant of the idea that concepts of particular numbers, such as the number 5, are derived from the representation of units, and in particular pure units, that is, units that are qualitatively indistinguishable. Frege, in contrast, rejects any attempt to derive concepts of number from the representation of units. In the *Foundations of Arithmetic*, he softens up his reader for his groundbreaking and unintuitive analysis of number by attacking alternative views, and he devotes the majority of this attack to the units view, with particular attention to pure units.[1] Since Frege, the units view has been all but abandoned. Nevertheless, the idea that concepts of number are derived from the representation of units has a long history, beginning with the ancient Greeks, and was prevalent among Frege's contemporaries. I am not interested in resurrecting the units view or in righting wrongs in Frege's criticisms of his contemporaries. Rather, I am interested in the program of deriving concepts of number from pure units and its history from Kant to Frege. An examination of that history helps us understand the units view in a way that Frege's criticisms do not, and in the process uncovers important features of both Kant's and Frege's views. I will argue that, although they had deep differences, Kant and Frege share assumptions about what such a view would require and about the limits of conceptual representation. I will also argue that they would have rejected the accounts given by some of Frege's contemporaries for the same reasons. Despite these agreements, however, there is evidence that Kant thinks that space and time play a role in

---

[1] Frege (1884), English translation (1950). Frege commits a total of 27 sections at the beginning of the *Foundations* to attacking his contemporaries on the concept of number. He begins with his crucial arguments that number is neither a property of external things nor something subjective, a theme that reappears throughout his polemic. He then devotes the next 16 sections to attacking the idea that numbers could be derived from units (10 sections attack pure units in particular, and two are specifically directed against an appeal to space and time).

doi:10.1017/S1358246108000088

Daniel Sutherland

overcoming the limitations of conceptual representation, while Frege argues that they do not.

Because this paper examines views from Kant to Frege, in other respects it must remain fairly focused. For example, it concentrates on accounts of number concepts themselves, and only indirectly considers accounts of arithmetical operations. Furthermore, Kant thought that temporal succession and the representation of order are central to arithmetical cognition, but I will highlight the role of space and the representation of collections. This paper is an exploration of one theme found in Kant's statements about arithmetical cognition; a complete account of Kant's views will substantially qualify the view I attribute to him here.

This paper will begin with some background concerning Kant's philosophy of mathematics and Greek mathematics before turning to Frege's contemporaries and how Kant would have evaluated them. It will then take up Frege's criticisms of his contemporaries and the relation between Frege's and Kant's views. Finally, it will consider what each has to say about the possibility of a role for space or time.

1. Kant and concepts of number from pure units

Kant's philosophy of mathematics rests on his theory of magnitudes. Before the nineteenth-century arithmetization of mathematics placed natural numbers at its foundation, it was common to describe mathematics as the science of magnitudes, a view that can be traced to the Greek mathematical tradition, in particular to the Eudoxian theory of proportions found in Euclid's Books V and VII.[2] The Eudoxian theory provides a general treatment of magnitudes that does not presuppose numbers and yet covers both continuous magnitudes such as lines, planes, and volumes, and discrete magnitudes, such as numbers.[3] Magnitudes are homogeneous within their kinds; that is, magnitudes

---

[2]   Friedman (1992a), pp. 110–3, points out the connection between Kant's theory of magnitudes and the Eudoxian theory. I develop a broader interpretation of Kant's theory of magnitudes and its relation to the Eudoxian theory in Sutherland (2004).

[3]   Although the theory treats both continuous and discrete magnitudes, the treatment of the continuous and the discrete are split between Books V and VII respectively. Algebra traces its origin through an arithmetical tradition leading back to Diophantus, but the development of algebra and its application to geometry in the early modern period led to its being viewed as a universal mathematics of all magnitudes, corresponding to the

that are homogeneous can be composed to constitute more of exactly the same kind—lines with lines, areas with areas, and so on.

Kant follows the Greek conception when he defines a magnitude as a homogeneous manifold, but he moves beyond it to provide a deeper analysis of homogeneity and a theory of our cognition of homogeneous manifolds. In Kant's view a homogeneous manifold exhibits numerical difference without qualitative difference. In other words, a homogenous manifold consists of a manifold of parts that are qualitatively identical.[4] This fact about homogeneous manifolds has important consequences for our cognition of them. Kant states in the Amphiboly of the *Critique of Pure Reason* that Leibniz's Principle of the Identity of Indiscernibles (PII) could not be disputed if objects were cognized solely by means of the understanding, and hence by means of concepts alone, without the aid of intuition (A263–4/B319–20).[5] This important counterfactual asserts a fundamental limitation of conceptual representation—our inability to represent numerical diversity with qualitative identity by means of concepts alone. Kant emphasizes this limitation by asserting that an attempt to use concepts alone to represent a multiplicity of identical things inevitably collapses into the representation of just one thing.[6]

Eudoxian theory that bridges both continuous and discrete magnitudes. For a fuller discussion of this point, see Sutherland (2006).

[4] For a defense of the claim that Kant's analysis of homogeneity is an extension of the Greek notion of homogeneity, see Sutherland (2004).

[5] Quotations from the *Critique of Pure Reason* closely follow, with occasional modifications, the Paul Guyer and Allen Wood (1997) translation. All other references to Kant's work will be to volume and page number, separated by a colon, of the Akademie edition of *Kants gesammelte Schriften*.

[6] Kant states:

According to mere concepts of the understanding, it is a contradiction to think of two things outside of each other that are nevertheless fully identical in respect of all their inner determinations (of quality and quantity); it is always one and the same thing thought twice (numerically one) (Ak 20:280).

A few pages later Kant adds that conceptual representation alone would 'bring the whole of infinite space into a cubic inch and less ...' (20:282). This work is translated as 'What Real Progress Has Metaphysics Made in Germany since the Time of Leibniz and Wolff?', in H. Allison and P. Heath (eds.), (2002) *Theoretical Philosophy after 1781*, The Cambridge Edition of the Works of Immanuel Kant (Cambridge: Cambridge University Press), 337–424.

Daniel Sutherland

Consequently, concepts on their own cannot represent a homogeneous manifold.

In contrast, Kant denies that PII is true of appearances, because they are objects of intuition, and intuition allows us to represent numerical difference with qualitative identity.[7] Since intuition can represent numerical difference without qualitative difference, it allows us to represent a homogeneous manifold, which I have argued elsewhere is in Kant's view a fundamental role for intuition in mathematical cognition.[8]

It is more difficult to see what role intuition should play in Kant's philosophy of arithmetic than in his geometry. The representation of succession is undoubtedly fundamental, but the role of intuition in representing discrete magnitudes is also central. When Kant discusses arithmetical cognition in the *Critique of Pure Reason*, he refers to discrete magnitudes such as fingers or dots on a page, which are both discrete and spatially disconnected (B15-6). They are related to our representation of units in some way similar to the way that a drawn triangle is related to our a priori construction of a triangle.[9]

Kant's treatment of discrete magnitudes suggests another important connection between Kant and Greek mathematics. Reconstructing the

[7]   Kant makes this clear in the Amphiboly, which emphasizes this feature of space and at the same time its composability:

> (...) multiplicity and numerical difference are already given us by space itself as the condition of outer appearances. For a part of space, although completely similar and equal to another part, is nevertheless outside of it, and is for that very reason a different part from that which abuts it to constitute a larger space (A264/B320).

He reaffirms this later in the Amphiboly, stating:

> The concept of a cubic foot of space, wherever and however often I think it, is in itself always completely the same. Yet two [distinct] cubic feet of space are nevertheless distinguished in space merely through their locations (*numero diversa*) (A282/B338).

[8]   See Sutherland (2004). Geometry provides the paradigm for the role of intuition in the representation of a homogeneous manifold. To quickly summarize the broader view: the categories of quantity—unity, plurality, and allness—are used to cognize the part-whole relations of continuous regions in space, which provides a mereological basis for our cognition of the composition relations among the parts of space. (It is worth noting that the role of intuition in allowing us to represent a homogeneous manifold has been overlooked, but it is not the only role for intuition in mathematical cognition).

[9]   I will come back to this relation below.

Greek conception of number is a formidable challenge; I will limit myself to highlighting a few relevant features.[10]

The Greek term for number, '*arithmos*', had different senses. The thinnest sense seems to have been nothing more than a particular *collection* of things, such as the number of sheep in a particular field or the number of shoes in my closet, in roughly the way we think of a particular set. This notion of *arithmos* presupposes a choice of unit, such as a shoe or pairs of shoes. Another closely related sense of *arithmos* was the number that resulted from enumerating the members of a collection, which is sometimes called the 'counting-number' of the counted collection. It, too, presupposes the choice of a unit, which is often called a 'counting-concept.'[11] There is also a further conception of number apart from a kind of thing, one that is based on collections of 'pure' units. The motive for pure units may arise from the desire for a general representation of number apart from any kind of thing counted.[12] The close connection of *arithmos* to particular collections of things and the notion of number as a collection of units were influential into the nineteenth century.

We can distinguish two sorts of purity that are included in the generality to which pure units aspire. Consider the seven samurai. In the first sort of purity, we would like the units to represent any seven samurai, not the seven masterless samurai who defended a small village in the sixteenth century. This requires that the units of the collection are 'equal and not in the least different from each other,' as Plato puts it.[13] The units could still have the characteristics common

---

[10]   My comments rely primarily on Jakob Klein (1968), especially Chapter 6; §1 of Stein (1990); and William Tait (2005), especially §9.

[11]   Interpretation is difficult, but *arithmos* in this sense might conceivably belong *only* to the particular collection counted, so that the eight of these sheep would be distinct from the eight of those sheep. Rogers Albritton first suggested to me that considering numbers as abstract particulars is at the very least an interpretative possibility that requires consideration. Klein seems at least to make room for this reading; see Klein (1968), 46–7. However, *arithmos* as counting number might be thought of as a species under which collections of a particular size fall, so that the eight of these sheep is the same eight as the eight of those sheep. On this view, particular number words, such as 'eight' can be viewed as a common name of collections of a particular size. See Stein (1990), 163–4, and Tait (2005), 238–9.

[12]   The generality of such a representation might be thought a necessary presupposition of the enumeration that results in counting-numbers, and hence it might be thought to be more fundamental. See Klein (1968), 49.

[13]   Plato's *Republic*, trans. by G. Grube, (Indianapolis: Hackett, 1974, revised by C.D.C. Reeve in 1992), 526 A; quoted in Klein (1968), 24.

to all the things counted (that is, belonging to the Japanese warrior class) but the units would not be distinguished from each other by any further characteristics (such as being old, or short, or hot-headed). In the second sort of purity, we would like to represent seven of anything, be they seven samurai, seven swans-a-swimming, or the seven habits of highly effective people. This requires that the units also have no characteristics common to any particular *kind* of thing, such as being a samurai. Of course, if a pure unit has no characteristics at all other than being a unit, then both kinds of generality would be achieved, but the first kind of generality raises particular challenges for a conception of number based on units. How can we represent the units of a collection as distinct from each other without representing them with distinguishing characteristics? If we do not represent any distinguishing characteristics, then we are only left with the representation of a samurai, for example, with nothing to distinguish seven of them. But if we represent each samurai with distinguishing properties, then we lose the generality of the representation, and it will only represent a collection of samurai with those particular distinguishing characteristics. There is, then, a *prima facie* tension between a completely general representation of number by means of units and the particular characteristics required to distinguish those units. I will call this the 'pure plurality problem'.

The idea that number is based on pure units bears a striking resemblance to what I have said about Kant's appeal to a homogeneous manifold of discrete units. In Kant's view, concepts on their own could never represent a collection of units as distinct and yet without distinguishing characteristics, since concepts on their own represent by means of qualities, which are distinguishing characteristics. Intuition, on the other hand, allows us to represent pure numerical difference without specific difference, which is just what is required for the representation of pure units.

Before saying more, I would like to lay to rest a possible confusion. First, the units I have described would be pure in the sense of being completely free of qualitative differences. This is not to be confused with Kant's notion of purity in relation to the a priori, which requires that there be no admixture of anything empirical. Any sense of purity associated with the a priori is in addition to purity in the sense of being qualitatively identical, and unless I explicitly indicate otherwise, I will mean the latter. For all I have said, someone might think that we could in some way rely on empirical experience, perhaps in combination with abstraction, to represent pure units. Second, Kant indeed holds that arithmetic is a priori and hence not dependent on particular empirical experience for its justification, even if we use empirical intuitions such as fingers as an aid. He holds that, despite the aid of empirical intuition in their representation, number concepts themselves are pure in the sense of a priori. In that case, however, what is it that the intuition of the fingers aids us in representing when 'seeing the number 12 arise' (B16)? It is plausible that in Kant's account, at least part of the answer is the pure intuition of different locations in space underlying the empirical intuition of the fingers. The resulting representation of units would be pure in both senses—qualitatively identical and free of empirical content.

What textual evidence do we have that Kant thinks that arithmetical cognition in particular rests on the representation of pure—that is, qualitatively identical—units? In addition to referring to fingers and dots on a page in his discussion of the role of intuition in arithmetical cognition (B16), Kant also refers to strokes and beads of an abacus:

> (…) the concept of magnitude seeks its standing and sense in number, but seeks this in turn in the fingers, in the beads of an abacus, or in strokes and points that are placed before the eyes. The concept is always generated a priori, together with the synthetic principles or formulas from such concepts (…) (A240/B299).

Kant states explicitly that these empirical representations aid us in forming an a priori representation of the synthesis of units. It would be natural to suppose that an a priori and fully general representation of numbers based on units would have no admixture of the empirical in it, and hence would retain none of the distinguishing empirical characteristics of fingers or dots or beads or strokes, representing instead qualitatively identical units.

Comparison to Kant's comments on the relation between a drawn triangle and the a priori representation of a triangle is helpful on this point. Kant states that

> The individual drawn figure is empirical, and nevertheless serves to express the concept without damage to its universality, for in the case of this empirical intuition we have taken account only of the action of constructing the concept, to which many determinations, e.g., those of the magnitude of the sides and the angles, are entirely indifferent, and thus we have abstracted from these differences, which do not alter the concept of the triangle (A714/B742).

A similar attention to construction in the case of arithmetic and hence a similar abstraction from the 'entirely indifferent' properties of units would lead to a representation of units as qualitatively identical. In other words, our fingers would be an aid to the a priori

Daniel Sutherland

representation of units distinguished only by their difference in spatial location.[14]

Kant's descriptions of arithmetical cognition as cognition of magnitudes provide more direct evidence of this view. Any reference to magnitudes is a reference to a homogeneous manifold in intuition, and as I mentioned above, in Kant's view a homogeneous manifold consists of qualitatively identical elements. Moreover, Kant repeatedly describes arithmetical cognition as a synthesis of *homogeneous* units in particular. In the Schematism of the *Critique of Pure Reason*, for example, Kant states that 'the pure schema of magnitude (*quantitas*) is a representation that summarizes the successive addition of one to one (homogeneous)' (A142–3/B182; see also A164/B205, A242/B300).

In Kant's time, however, there was also another, less stringent notion of homogeneity that was often mentioned as a condition of counting. Counting was said to require that one employs a counting-concept under which all the things to be counted fall; to count a collection of jaguar and tapir, for example, one would have to ascend at least to the concept of mammal, say, and count the items under this concept. As mentioned above, the counting-concept requirement is found in ancient Greek arithmetic, but the role of counting-concepts should not be restricted to acts of counting; any representation of a collection was thought to require a common concept under which the elements fall. In Kant's time, the things that fall under such a concept were said to be homogeneous with respect to that concept. Clearly, this sort of homogeneity does not require that the units be qualitatively identical.[15]

I believe, however, that it is precisely here that Kant, following his deeper analysis of the Greek notion of homogeneity, introduces a *further* notion of homogeneity whose representation is required for a priori knowledge in geometry and arithmetic. This homogeneity is the property of numerical difference without specific difference, a property of magnitudes that intuition allows us to represent. The fact that intuition allows us to represent this further kind of homogeneity constitutes a fundamental role for intuition in all mathematical cognition.[16] This account of homogeneity derives further support from, on the one hand, the conception of early modern

---

[14] I say more below about only attending to the action of construction in my discussion of schemata below.
[15] Interpreting Kant's notion of homogeneity along these lines is prominent in various interpretations, in particular Longuenesse (1998).
[16] For a more detailed defense of this view, see Sutherland (2004).

algebra as a science of magnitude common to geometry and arithmetic, and on the other, the connection between early modern algebra and the Eudoxian theory of proportions.[17] Kant's deeper notion of homogeneity does not displace the common-concept sense of homogeneity; the representation of a collection of seven samurai still requires the common concept of samurai. Nevertheless, a full account of our representation of seven samurai as a collection of seven also requires the deeper notion of homogeneity.[18]

There is another interpretive possibility that seems to obviate the representation of pure units. Kant distinguishes between images and schemata. As an example of an image of the number five, Kant refers to five points set alongside one another. The schema, in contrast, allows us to think of a number in general and is a universal procedure of imagination for providing an image for a number concept. In the case of arithmetic, Kant states

> (. . .) the pure *schema* of magnitude (*quantitas*), as a concept of the understanding, is *number*, a representation which summarizes the successive addition of one to one (homogeneous). Thus number is nothing other than the unity of the synthesis of the manifold of a homogeneous intuition in general, because I generate time itself in the apprehension of the intuition (A142–3/B182).

These passages can leave the impression that arithmetical cognition is based only on a rule of successive synthesis in time, and hence suggest that the representation of pure units in space, which might seem to fall on the side of images, are strictly speaking unnecessary. Indeed, these passages may be taken as evidence of a rather abstract view of

[17]   For more on this additional support, see Sutherland (2006).
[18]   There are two cases to consider. First, if we call to mind a general representation of any seven samurai, then we do not want to represent the individual samurai as possessing particular distinguishing properties, and the deeper homogeneity of intuition allows us to accomplish this. Second, if we have seven particular samurai before us and we wish to represent them as seven, the homogeneity of intuition may allow us to abstract from their distinguishing properties, in the way that we can appeal to our fingers in the representation of $5 + 7 = 12$. In both cases, however, the account may be more complicated; it may be that once we have attained pure a priori concepts of numbers and pure a priori cognition of arithmetical truths such as $5 + 7 = 12$, we can directly apply those concepts (and truths) to particular collections. Either way, however, there is a further issue that I will address below: Kant may think that the role of the homogeneity of intuition is to allow the concepts of number to arise or to establish their objective validity in a way that does not undermine their generality.

Daniel Sutherland

arithmetic as mere rules or techniques of calculation for finding the magnitudes of objects.[19] Most importantly, however, is the point Kant makes explicit in the geometrical case: the schema of a triangle is a rule of the synthesis of imagination for the construction of pure figures in space, and its being a rule rather than an image accounts for the generality of the conclusions we base on geometrical constructions (A140–1/B179–80). There are important differences between the generality of geometrical claims and arithmetical claims such as $5 + 7 = 12$, as Kant himself emphasized. Yet, if Kant appeals to schemata to explain the generality of geometrical claims, it seems possible that he also appeals to schemata to explain any generality underlying particular arithmetical claims or particular numerical concepts. In short, if the generality of mathematical claims rests on schemata (understood as rules for construction) rather than images, then it seems there is no need to represent pure units to achieve a fully general representation of number.[20] If successful, Kant's appeal to rules to explain generality would circumvent the pure plurality problem that arises from an attempt to explain the generality of our representation of five, for example, through the representation of pure units.

This shows that Kant's view is more sophisticated and complex than the simple pure units view outlined above. While Kant does appeal to schema to explain the generality of mathematical claims, the representation of pure units still plays an essential role in our cognition of fundamental a priori arithmetical truths, such as $5 + 7 = 12$. At the very least, Kant seems to think that the representation of pure units is required for us to acquire the concepts of number (to 'see the number 12 arise') or to establish the objective validity of our basic arithmetical concepts, and to do so in a manner that preserves the generality achieved by appealing to schemata. In short, what Kant claims in the Schematism is compatible with the further claim that when we take things like fingers as an aid in our pure a priori cognition of $5 + 7 = 12$, our taking them as representations of pure units is part of the schema of number itself. In fact, this last possibility is suggested by the Schematism passage just quoted, which refers to the successive addition of '(one to one) homogeneous', that is, homogeneous units.

---

[19] Friedman (1992a), pp. 112–22, develops this line of thought with some care. For important modifications to this view, see Friedman (2000).

[20] Friedman (1992a), pp. 122–29, identifies the schemata for geometrical constructions with Euclidean constructions, and points out that in Kant's view, the problem of deriving general conclusions from particular geometrical figures is solved by an appeal to schemata rather than images (p. 90).

144

I have given textual and interpretive grounds for thinking that in Kant's view, arithmetical cognition requires the representation of pure units. As with so many of Kant's views, one could wish for clearer expressions of it in the *Critique*. Kant comes close to making the qualitative identity of units explicit in the Discipline of Pure Reason, where he states:

> The general synthesis of *one and the same* [von einem und demselben] in time and space, and the magnitude of an intuition in general (number) that arises there from, is a business of reason through the construction of concepts, and is called mathematical (A724/B752, my emphasis).

On my interpretation, the explicit mention of multiple instantiations of 'one and the same in time and space' is a reference to units distinguished only by their location in time and space and to Kant's discussion of numerically distinct indiscernibles in the Amphiboly.

The clearest statement of the pure units view is not found in Kant himself, but in his foremost defender and expositor Johann Schultz. His *Prüfung der Kantischen Critik der reinen Vernunft*, published in 1789, is an examination and defense of Kant's philosophy with a particular emphasis on his philosophy of mathematics. Schultz's work and the correspondence between them are valuable resources for insights into Kant's views.[21]

As is well known, Schultz disagrees with Kant in thinking arithmetic is grounded in axioms, in particular, the axioms of commutivity and associativity.[22] Schultz states that the fact that mathematics

---

[21]   Schultz had been Kant's student and later wrote a review of Kant's *Inaugural Dissertation* that influenced the development of Kant's thought. Encouraged by Kant, he published a summary and explanation of Kant's views (Schultz, 1784). Kant thought well enough of it that at one point he planned to use it as a textbook for his metaphysics course. Schultz (1789) is less of a summary and includes more philosophical analysis. (Here below, all references to Schultz are to this latter work with page numbers in brackets). In addition, Schultz wrote at least seven reviews supporting Kant's philosophy.

Schultz lived in Königsberg and became its court chaplain; he also received a professorship in mathematics at the university, most likely with Kant's support. The two would have had opportunity to converse, but they nevertheless communicated at least in part through letters; we have at least a dozen from Kant to Schultz. See Kuehn (2001), and James C. Morrison introduction to the English translation of Schultz (1784).

[22]   Schultz (1789), 221–3, also identifies two postulates of arithmetic, both of which concern magnitudes and emphasize homogeneity. In

rests on intuition can be shown both from the nature of its axioms and postulates and from the concept of counting itself. We can set aside Schultz's views on the axioms and postulates, for it is what he says about the concept of counting that is of particular interest to us. Schultz states:

> When I am to add 5 to 7, for example, I must first individually represent to myself the units of the number 5, and hence represent $1 + 1 + 1 + 1 + 1$. Now every one of these units, the *quantity as well as the quality*, thus in itself, is completely identical [*ganz einerlei*], and thus the understanding cannot differentiate them by the smallest *inner* characteristic, consequently it cannot differentiate them through concepts. It is therefore only possible through *outer* or *sensible* characteristics, that is, through those that do not consist in a concept but an *intuition* (...) Things that in respect of their inner characteristics are perfectly identical [vollkommen einerlei], and hence completely indistinguishable for the mere understanding, we cannot distinguish in any other way than by representing them either *at different places of space* or *in different points in time* (225–6).

This passage reflects Kant's own claims about the limits of conceptual representation and provide strong indirect evidence that Kant thought that our representation of numbers depends in some way on the representation of pure units.[23]

More would be required to defend and elaborate this interpretation of Kant. In particular, one would need to fill out the account of the Schematism and explain the relation between the representations of temporal succession and of pure units, but I will not attempt to do so here. Instead, I would like to concentrate on the idea that our concepts of number depend on the representation of units—its historical influence and its fate—from Kant to Frege. When discussing Kant in what follows, I will focus on his views on the limitations on conceptually

---

keeping with my interpretation Schultz is attempting to articulate the way in which Kant's philosophy of arithmetic rests on Kant's more general theory of magnitudes.

[23]   Schultz also echoes Kant when he describes the consequences of attempting to represent pure units without appealing to intuition:

> The help of *intuition* is required, without which the concept of their *plurality* would be wholly impossible; rather, the understanding would have to think them all together as absolutely [schlechterdings] *eadem numero*, that is, as *only one* (226).

representing pure units and the role of intuition in overcoming those limitations.

2. Numbers from units in Frege's contemporaries

Those of Frege's contemporaries who appealed to units were inclined to empiricism and, in so far as they considered the basis of mathematical cognition, leaned toward empirical psychology. Several espoused versions of formalism. In general, they do not appear to be particularly interested in Kant. In considering how Kant would react to them, I will set aside his most obvious criticism of empiricism: that no account that relies on empirical experience for justification of mathematical claims can explain the a priori status of mathematics. Likewise, in considering Frege's criticisms I will set aside arguments against the psychologism and subjectivism of mental abstraction as well as his arguments against formalism. I will instead focus on the way in which Frege's contemporaries thought that concepts of number were derived from the representation of units, and how Kant and Frege would or did respond to that view in particular.

Before I begin, a few points about terminology will be helpful. First, the German term '*Anzahl*' was used in rough correspondence to the Greek notion of *arithmoi*, that is for a collection or a counting-number of a particular collection. The German term '*Zahl*' was also used in this way, but '*Zahl*' was first and foremost used for the notion of an individual number, such as the number 5, apart from any collection; some who wrote on mathematical foundations reserved it for the latter. Usage was by no means settled, however, and these terms were used in different ways, sometimes even interchangeably.[24] To help avoid confusion, I will use 'number' only to translate '*Zahl*' and will leave '*Anzahl*' untranslated.

Second, in its most general use the German term '*gleich*' was and remains highly ambiguous. It is often translated 'equal,' though it is also often translated 'identical', which is itself ambiguous. In many contexts, it is probably best translated by the correspondingly ambiguous term 'same'. When describing a relation between two or

---

[24] I am setting aside debates about various connotations that have been attributed to *Anzahl* and *Zahl* by philologists; the distinction I describe is paramount. For more details on these disputes, see Stosch (1772); Adelung (1793); Eberhard (1819), among others.

more things, '*gleich*' has at least five distinct senses, three of which correlate with three senses of identity:

1. Similar, that is, the same with respect to some property, relation, or circumstance; e.g. the same in color;
2. Equal, that is, the same with respect to particular quantitative properties; e.g. the same in length or volume;
3. Practically Identical, that is, the same with respect to all readily noticeable intrinsic properties; e.g. the sameness of some identical twins;
4. Qualitatively Identical, that is, completely the same with regard to all intrinsic properties; e.g. the sameness of two identical rain drops (supposing that they in fact share all intrinsic properties);
5. Strictly or Numerically Identical, that is, one and the same; e.g. the sameness of Cicero and Tully.

Only the fifth sense of equal and identical are absolute; the first four senses are all notions of equal or identical in some respect, that is, in respect to some property or kind of property.[25] One must keep these possible senses of equality and identity in mind when reading Frege's contemporaries.

There is, however, a further use of '*gleich*' that is crucial to take into account:

6. Equipollent, that is, the elements of one collection stand in a one−to−one correspondence with the elements of another collection.

This is also a notion of 'equality in some respect,' but this sort of equality asserts a one−to−one correspondence between the elements of one collection and the elements of another without further conditions on the elements themselves. This sense of equality *between collections* must be sharply distinguished from any requirement of sameness *among elements of a collection*. '*Gleich*' is used for both. Moreover, it would be easy to run them together, since the relation of equipollence and the representation of pure units might both be thought to play a role in the representation of the natural numbers. As we will see in the next section, failing to carefully distinguish them can lead to misunderstandings.

With these preliminaries aside, let us turn to Frege's contemporaries. Rudolph Lipschitz opens his 1877 *Lehrbuch der Analysis* with

[25]   I would like to thank William Tait for prompting me to make this last point explicit.

a discussion of number comprising just two short paragraphs.[26] He states that the concept of *Anzahl* arises from regarding separated things and neglecting their characteristics, adding that one who wishes to obtain an overview of certain given things will begin with a certain thing and add a new thing to the earlier ones. This procedure is called counting and results in a fully determinate concept of number [*Zahl*] for a particular collection of given things.

Lipschitz is so brief that it is hard to be sure of his position. In fairness, it should be noted that some of those whom Frege attacks, and in particular Lipschitz, do not show great interest in the foundations of arithmetic, and seem eager to get on to analysis, analytic functions, or other topics. Regardless, Lipschitz does not acknowledge the need for generality. From the Kantian perspective, Lipschitz simply fails to see what would be required of a general concept of number based on units and hence fails to address the pure plurality problem.[27]

I turn next to Ernst Schröder. His 1873 *Lehrbuch der Arithmetik und Algebra* sets out to give an account of the natural numbers, or *natürlichen Zahlen*, but immediately begins with the conditions of counting, and instead discusses *Anzahl*, where that is understood as a number of things.[28]

Schröder calls anything that is to be counted a unit [*Einheit*] (5), and says that the conditions of counting require that units be distinguished from each other in our representation of them through some characteristic (3). Counting also requires that the objects appear to us to be similar [*ähnlich*] to each other, though this similarity condition is extremely minimal, for it can be satisfied by any accidental relation, such as being counted by us. Schröder slides from similarity [*ähnlich*] to equality [*gleich*] when he states that the question of the *Anzahl* of things arises only when the things are viewed as equal to each other; clearly, he has in mind the minimal understanding of '*gleich*' as similarity, corresponding to sense 1 listed above.

Schröder distinguishes between the equality among units of a collection and equality between collections. The latter is defined as an equipollence between two collections, that is, two collections are said to occur 'in equal *Anzahl* [*in gleicher Anzahl*]' when there

---

26   Lipschitz (1877).
27   It is possible that Lipschitz would simply reject the pure plurality problem; his views might approach those of Mill in this respect. Unfortunately, a discussion of Mill is beyond the scope of this paper.
28   Schröder (1873). All references to Schröder will be to this work (page numbers in brackets).

Daniel Sutherland

is a 1–1 correspondence between their members (8). This, however, imposes no further conditions on the elements themselves.

Since Schröder's account of the notion of equality among units is extremely minimal and does not rule out distinguishing characteristics, his units are not pure. From a Kantian perspective, Schröder's treatment of *Anzahl* fails to acknowledge the need for a general representation of units.

This is only half of Schröder's account, however, for he has a different characterization of number itself, that is, *Zahl*. (It is noteworthy that Frege does not refer to this second characterization in his criticisms). Schröder states that number arises by means of drawing a stroke [*Strich*] corresponding to each element in a collection. He calls the strokes 'ones' or 'oners,' which are represented in his text by the numeral '1'.[29] He states that a natural number is a sum of oners, where by 'sum' he appears to simply mean a collection.[30] Thus, a number is a special case of a collection in which the units are oners, which are used to illustrate a particular collection of units in respect of their plurality.

Oners, like any other collection of units, can also stand in relations of equipollency. The convenience of numbers in determining equipollency relations among collections recommends them and leads to their use as a measure of frequency or plurality.

After saying that number is an illustration of units in respect of their frequency, Schröder states that with collections of oners, the very least of things is illustrated—'so little, that if the one is left out, nothing at all would remain'. He concludes that 'the abstraction in the illustration–process of counting is the greatest,' and entails the greatest simplification of representations (6). While numbers are identified with the collections of oners themselves, the maximal abstraction involved in illustrating units by means of them leaves no distinguishing properties. Hence in this context, Schröder means qualitative identity, which corresponds to sense 4 of '*gleich*'

---

[29] I will use 'oners' because Schröder prefers 'einer' to 'eins' and because it will help avoid confusion between the numeral one and the (or a) number one.

[30] In a collection, the oners are separated from each other by plus signs (p. 5), a representation of number he calls their '*Urform*' (p. 22). Note that Schröder says that the sum of oners is a natural number, not that it has a natural number. Schröder holds that the numbers consisting of distinct collections of oners are themselves distinct even when they are equipollent. In this respect, his *Zahl* resembles the first interpretation of Greek *arithmos* mentioned in footnote 11 above.

listed above, and we are left with a general representation of pure units.[31]

It is important to note that this maximal abstraction is not the result of the traditional understanding of abstraction that might, for example, proceed from the concept of a Clydesdale to the concepts of horse, animal, extended body, and being. One of the most interesting features of Frege's predecessors is that they depart from the traditional conception of abstraction to make room for a numerical kind of abstraction that suits the needs of mathematics. Unfortunately, Schröder does not further describe or defend the nature of this numerical abstraction. For the sake of argument let us grant that through some sort of numerical abstraction, we can get to a collection of oners.

Schröder's account lays claim to a completely general representation of units while simply assuming that those units remain distinguished. Since the maximal abstraction is intended to leave behind all distinguishing properties, however, there is nothing left to render the units distinct. Hence, Schröder does not provide a solution to the pure plurality problem. As Kant might put it, Schröder attempts to have his cake and eat it too.[32]

[31]   One might think that in Schröder's view, we could take the oners themselves as pure units, that is, that we could represent them while abstracting from all their distinguishing properties other than their spatial relations, in the way that I have suggested Kant may think of using dots on a page. It is not entirely clear what the illustration relation consists in, but I think that on the most sympathetic reading of Schröder's position consistent with his claims of maximal abstraction, the oners represent pure units. As noted in §1 above, there are two sorts of purity at stake in the representation of pure units: a lack of distinguishing characteristics among a collection of units, and a lack of any distinguishing characteristics at all. Oners may have (or at least approximate) the first sort of purity, while clearly failing to achieve the second. See footnote 32 for more on oners and the first sort of purity. I would like to thank Charles Parsons, whose comments led me to distinguish the oners and the units they illustrate.

[32]   It is possible that the distinctness of the oners is intended to represent the distinctness of units illustrated by means of them (see footnote 31). In practice, we distinguish between strokes or between tokens of the numeral '1' by their location in space and time, not by any qualitative differences, such as imperfections or the darkness of their ink. It is possible that Schröder may make at least implicit appeal to space to distinguish the numeral tokens, thereby implicitly adopting the Kantian position. Nevertheless, he nowhere states that a necessary condition of reaching a general representation of number is distinguishing between oners by spatial or temporal location alone. He does say that the fact that number

Daniel Sutherland

Stanley Jevons presents a quite different approach in *The Principles of Science* of 1874.[33] Jevons states that 'with difference arises plurality' and that '[N]umber is but another name for *diversity*' (175). Jevons distinguishes between concrete number and abstract number; the former corresponds to *arithmoi* and *Anzahl*—for example, three horses—while the latter refers to numbers *simpliciter*, like the number three.

Unlike Schröder, Jevons explicitly distinguishes numerical abstraction from logical abstraction. The latter gives us a conceptual representation of an abstract quality, as when we abstract from several objects that are red to the conception of the quality redness (33). In this sort of abstraction, we 'drop out of notice the very existence of difference and plurality' among the red objects (178). In contrast, numerical abstraction consists in abstracting from 'the character of the difference from which plurality arises, retaining merely the fact' (177; see also 178). In keeping with this conception of numerical abstraction, he describes abstract number as merely '*the empty form of difference* (177)'. Jevons holds that leaving out both the kinds of objects numbered and any specification of their differences while retaining the fact of their differences accounts for the generality of number. He is explicit that the notions of both concrete and abstract number specify that the units counted are to be distinguished, while leaving unspecified what characteristics will distinguish them (177–8). In short, Jevons explicitly embraces a concept of number that appeals to *indeterminate* distinguishing characteristics, and he singles out a special form of abstraction that results in such a concept. We seem to have found a solution to the difficulty reconciling the generality of number with the need for distinguishing characteristics, a solution that does not require the representation of pure units, and hence avoids the pure plurality problem.

Jevons' solution is not without its own difficulties, however. It is essential to the generality of concepts that they represent indeterminately, that is, that they need not specify all the properties an object might have. But this is a different sort of indeterminacy from that which Jevons proposes. For example, the concept of being a shape requires that an object have specific characteristics, being completely bounded in space, say, while it simply leaves out the characteristics

---

consists of spatially separated components that can be generated at any time brings advantages (p. 9), but that is as far as he goes.

[33] Jevons (1874). All references to Jevons here below will be to this text (page numbers in brackets).

corresponding to a particular shape. In contrast, a concept that results from Jevons' numerical abstraction retains the fact of difference, which requires that each unit must have the characteristic of *having (or lacking) one or more characteristics that, in coordination with the one or more characteristics that each of the other units have (or lack), is sufficient to distinguish it from each of the other units.* The traditional understanding of conceptual representation, according to which characteristics simply represent particular qualities, simply does not make room for this sort of indeterminacy.

One might well respond: so much for the traditional understanding of a concept, which is also inadequate for other sorts of conceptual representation, and I would agree. What we are interested in, however, is how matters were viewed by Kant and others up to and including Frege. In general, Kant's discussions of concepts reflect a traditional understanding of the constitution of concepts. It seems likely that Kant at least implicitly rules out Jevons' approach, and hence Jevons' solution to the pure plurality problem.

The last text I will consider is Johannes Thomae's 1880 edition of *Elementare Theorie der Analytische Functionen*, which begins with the assumption that we can count.[34] He states that counting rests on our ability to abstract from the peculiarity [*Eigentumlickheit*] of the individuals of a collection of objects and then give successive names to different collections of such objects. He thinks that we can abstract from all peculiarity of objects without collapsing the collection. As a result, each unit is represented as equal to every other, and the concept of number arises from the counting of such units (1). In his view, the equality of units consists in their substitutability, which in turn consists in their lack of distinguishing properties after abstraction. Significantly, however, Thomae also states that abstraction does not remove the differences in spatial or temporal location of the units (1). Thus, Thomae holds the view I have attributed to Kant and is found in Schultz, according to which spatial and temporal location allow us to represent otherwise indistinguishable units and thereby contribute to solving the pure plurality problem.[35]

---

[34] Thomae (1880/1898). All references to Thomae will be to this work (with page numbers in brackets).

[35] Thomae significantly revised his account of number concepts in the 1898 edition, greatly expanding it and attempting to take into account the work of Dedekind and Frege, and in particular Frege's criticisms. He seems not to have really grasped the importance of Frege's advances; he still holds to a units view based on the purported empirical abstraction found in childhood concept acquisition, and he even states that his new

Daniel Sutherland

3. Frege and Kant on the limits of conceptual representation

I would now like to turn to Frege's arguments in the *Foundations of Arithmetic* against the possibility of representing units in a way that allows concepts of number to be based on them.[36] There are two terminological obstacles to understanding him. First, Frege rejects any conception of a number *n* as simply a collection of *n* things or as a property of a particular collection of *n* things.[37] It is therefore not surprising that Frege uses '*Zahl*' only for individual numbers. As we saw above, '*Anzahl*' was commonly used for collections of things rather than individual numbers, but Frege departs from common usage and often uses '*Anzahl*' as a synonym for '*Zahl*', which widens the distance between him and those he attacks.[38]

Second, Frege's use of '*gleich*' and its cognates raises particular difficulties. As noted in the previous section, '*gleich*' is multiply ambiguous. Because Frege treats numbers as singular objects and rejects a notion of a number *n* as a collection of *n* things or a property of a particular collection of *n* things, by his lights, it strictly speaking makes no sense to say that the number of planets is *equal* to the number of coins in my pocket; if it is true, then the number of planets is *one and the same* number as the number of coins in my pocket. Both senses, however, can be expressed by '*gleich*'.

---

account does not differ substantially from Frege's. Nevertheless, he makes interesting further points relevant to the units view, which I will unfortunately not be able to explore here.

[36] Frege has various arguments undermining an appeal to units, including arguments that 0 and 1 cannot be accounted for and that arithmetical operations cannot be made to correspond to the union and dissolution of units, but most of his attention is directed against the possibility of representing the units and it is on this argument that I will focus.

[37] Frege does think of a cardinal number *n* as the object that is the collection of concepts under which exactly *n* things fall, but that is another matter.

[38] See, for example, the headings preceding §55 and the heading to §62. I noted above that Frege does not acknowledge the distinct accounts Schröder gives of *Anzahl* and *Zahl*; this may reflect Frege's conviction that there is no distinct account to be given. I am indebted to William Tait (2005), 38–9 and 242–3, for a helpful treatment of Frege's view of number, identity, and equality in contrast to the views of those Frege discusses. Tait believes that Frege's rejection of the conception of number as a collection leads him to misread Euclid, Hume, and Schröder; see footnote 40 below for a discussion of Hume and footnote 42 below for a discussion of Schröder.

Similarly, '*Gleichung*' is usually translated as 'equation,' which connotes an equality, but Frege maintains that an equation expresses a strict identity. In order to make Frege's views clear, Austin translates '*gleich*' as identical and '*Gleichung*' as identity.[39]

Unfortunately, this leads to misunderstandings. Austin translates '*gleich*' as 'identical' even where Frege is quoting or referring to the views of others, when they certainly do not mean one and the same, but mean something less than strict or numerical identity.[40] Any translation of these terms is beset with perils, of course. Nevertheless, translating '*gleich*' as 'identical' can lead to a misleading portrayal of the philosophers Frege discusses, if one has in mind strict or numerical identity.

There is a further issue about the meaning of '*gleich*' that is of even greater importance. As noted in the previous section, '*gleich*' is used for both equality between collections of things (i.e., equipollence) and for the purported requirement of equality or sameness among the distinct elements of a collection. It is crucial to distinguish between them. In the latter case as in the former, if we translate '*gleich*' as 'identical,' we cannot understand 'identical' to mean one and the same, or we will again misconstrue what Frege's contemporaries had in mind. In fact, in the latter case, we will make complete nonsense of their claims, because it is an obvious contradiction for elements of a collection to be both distinct and one and the same.

Now, 'identical' is itself ambiguous (as is reflected in the list of senses of '*gleich*' in the previous section). It can mean one and the same, that is, strict or numerical identity, which is probably the primary way a philosopher hears it today. But in a looser sense

---

[39] See Austin's (1950) English translation of Frege (1884), p. II, note.

[40] For example, when Hume articulates what has become known as 'Hume's Principle,' he states that those numbers (i.e. collections of things) that can be put into a one-to-one correspondence are called equal. When Frege discusses Hume's Principle in §63, he uses the term '*gleich*,' and goes on to discuss '*Gleichheit*'. As Tait (2005), p. 239, has argued, Frege seems to misread Hume here. Hume is using 'number' to refer to collections, and the relevant notion of *gleich* is of equality between collections, but Frege seems to take Hume to use 'number' to refer to singular objects and to interpret '*gleich*' as identity. In that case, translating '*gleich*' as 'identity' would capture Frege's misunderstanding of Hume, but it would not be true to what Hume said or meant. In this case, Austin translates '*gleich*' as 'equal,' since that was Hume's original term, and then translates Frege's use of '*Gleichheit*' as 'equality or identity'—the former term is a nod to what Hume in fact said, while the latter is how Austin thinks Frege interpreted him.

it can also mean that two or more things are qualitatively identical, that is, they share all of the same inner properties while remaining distinct—for example, the possibility of two identical rain drops, corresponding to sense 4 of '*gleich*' listed above. In this context, identical units are pure units. Thus, Austin's translation of '*gleich*' as 'identical' allows Frege's contemporaries to mean qualitatively identical when discussing the identity among distinct units of a collection.[41]

What is also important, however, is to allow that Frege himself uses 'identical' in the looser sense when he describes the views of his contemporaries, and not in the sense of strict identity, which he intends for equations or the number belonging to the concepts of equinumerous collections. For if we read him as meaning strictly identical, then he will both misrepresent them and make their views manifestly absurd. It is true that Frege relishes making his opponents' views appear absurd, but to do so by misreading their use of '*gleich*' as strictly identical would be willfully tendentious and weaken his attack. Indeed, if he understood '*gleich*' as strictly and numerically identical, the question that composes the heading to §34—'Are units identical [*gleich*] with one another?'—would have an immediate answer: it is logically impossible for a plurality of units to be one and the same unit. It is far better to understand Frege as allowing the looser, qualitative sense of identity in his attack and as arguing that his opponents' views lead to absurdity.[42]

---

[41] It may be that Austin only has the strict sense of identity in mind, for he seems to have some compunction about rendering Frege's description of Thomae's use of '*gleich*' as 'identical.' In §34, Frege states: 'Thomae calls the individual member of his set a unit, and says that "units are identical to each other" ...'. Austin usually stays very close to the original, but in this case he drops the quotation and renders it: 'Thomae ... says *in so many words* that units are identical with each other ...' (my italics). If Austin also had the looser sense of identity in mind, he could have translated Frege more directly. This, of course, assumes that Thomae had this looser sense of identity in mind, as I argued above, but perhaps Austin was unsure of Thomae's meaning.

It is worth noting that in §34, Frege quotes three passages from Thomae and Lipschitz in a way that suggests the first and second passage are from Thomae and the third from Lipschitz. Austin breaks up the sentence and clearly attributes the second passage to Thomae, although it in fact belongs to Lipschitz.

[42] Tait (2005), p. 242, maintains that Frege understands '*gleich*' to mean strict identity, and that Frege imposes this reading on those he discusses. In Frege's §36 discussion of Hume's principle, where '*gleich*' is applied to equipollent collections, I think he is most likely correct; see footnote 40 above. Tait does not, however, explicitly distinguish between this use of '*gleich*'

Frege's argument strategy is to articulate what would be required for the unit view to succeed and to argue that those requirements cannot be met. He holds that if one is going to appeal to units, then the units must be pure, and that at least tacit recognition of this requirement motivates both the use of the maximally neutral word 'unit' and the appeal to identity (§34). Thus Frege and Kant are in complete agreement on the purity requirement. Moreover, both would agree that if someone, for example Lipschitz, does not acknowledge the need for pure units, then he is overlooking the requirements of a completely general representation of number by means of units.

Frege next argues that the units would also need to be distinct from each other, for where there is no diversity, there is no number (§35). Finally, he asserts that you cannot have the required sameness of units and a diverse collection of units at the same time. He cites Jevons, who refers to tokens of the numeral '1' with hash marks to insure that each refers to a distinct unit, and then states in his characteristically crisp polemic:

The symbols

$$1', 1'', 1'''$$

tell the tale of our embarrassment. We must have identity [*Gleichheit*], hence the 1; but we must have difference—hence the strokes; only unfortunately, the latter undo the work of the former (§36; see also §38).

Frege asserts that if we were to derive the concept of number from units, they would have to be identical and diverse at the same time, which is impossible. The reference to impossibility might suggest that Frege has strict identity in mind. But in that case, when Frege states that we 'must have identity', he is certainly not speaking for Jevons or any other adherent of the pure units view, who would only claim that we require qualitative identity. In fact, as mentioned above, this would make Jevons' view patent nonsense. If, on the other hand, Frege instead means qualitative identity, then he appears to hold that qualitative identity would lead to strict identity, which in turn excludes diversity.

---

and its application to elements among a collection, and he does not explicitly consider the possibility that Frege uses 'identity' in the looser sense when describing the purported identity of units among a collection that his opponents, such as Schröder, espouse.

Daniel Sutherland

This is similar to the position that Kant adopts when he considers objects as conceived by the understanding alone: you cannot represent the required units in their purity and represent them as diverse if you represent them merely by means of concepts. Thus, if we focus on Kant's views on representing by means of concepts alone, Frege and Kant agree that the requirements for representing pure units leave one in a bind (I will consider what each would think about appealing to space or time below). Both would claim that Schröder implicitly appeals to a notion of pure units without paying the price of abstracting from all distinguishing characteristics; hence, they would agree that Schröder is trying to have his cake and eat it too, and has not solved the pure plurality problem.

Let us look more closely at why Frege thinks that the units view is untenable. He describes the core of the difficulty with indistinguishable units in §36, where he says that units deprived of their distinguishing characteristics would collapse into one and be numerically identical (§39). Frege appears to be assuming some version of Leibniz's principle of the identity of indiscernibles. Section 34 provides evidence that he does; Frege asks why, in the view he is attacking, we ascribe identity to objects that are to be numbered. Frege seems to allow that identity comes in degrees and can be incomplete, which suggests that he is referring to qualitative identity. He then rules out the complete identity of two objects. Hence, Frege appears to assert that complete qualitative identity entails strict identity—the principle of the identity of indiscernibles.

Further evidence is found in §65, in which Frege states that all the laws of identity are contained in universal substitutability. The context makes it clear that Frege is here talking about strict, numerical identity. But if substitutability is the mark of strict identity, then it seems that qualitative identity would entail numerical identity, and hence some version of the principle of the identity of indiscernibles.[43]

This strengthens the parallel to Kant's views. As noted above, Kant states that if we only represented objects by means of concepts, then the principle of the identity of indiscernibles could not be disputed. And Kant, like Frege, describes the consequences as a kind of collapsing of the distinct units into one (§39).

There is one more important point of agreement between them. At several places in the *Foundations*, Frege describes traditional abstraction resulting in a general concept. In §34, for example, he states that if we disregard the distinguishing properties of a white cat and

---

[43] This would be so if qualitative identity implied substitutability. It is on the basis of §65 that Tait (2005), p. 235, ascribes the principle of identity of indiscernibles to Frege.

a black cat, our abstraction arrives at the concept 'cat' (see also §§44, 45, and 48). There are disagreements about Frege's views on abstraction, but we need not resolve whether Frege endorses traditional conceptual abstraction or merely concedes it for the sake of argument. The important point is that, even if he introduces traditional abstraction only for the sake of argument, he does so to contrast it with and to rule out a special form of abstraction that would result in number (e.g., §44). Moreover, Frege explicitly rejects the conception of numerical abstraction put forth by Jevons, that is, the possibility of abstracting to a concept which, in Jevons' terms, 'retains the fact of difference,' and 'implies the existence of the requisite differences' without specifying them.

Why does Frege reject Jevons' suggestion? He quotes Jevons' claim that numerical abstraction 'consists in abstracting the character of the difference from which plurality arises, retaining merely the fact'. Frege then states that if we attempt to abstract from the distinguishing characteristics '(...) we should never get so far as to distinguish the things at all, and consequently could not retain the fact of the existence of the differences either (...)' (§44).[44] Frege is reasserting his view that abstracting from distinguishing properties would lead to a collapse of the units into one. In other words, he rules out the possibility of characteristics that simply 'retain the fact of difference'.

Frege might be read as objecting to the process of numerical abstraction itself. Even if it is only for the sake of argument, however, Frege allows traditional conceptual abstraction in order to distinguish it from numerical abstraction, so what rules out numerical abstraction in particular? It seems to me unlikely that Frege has a worked out theory of mental activity that would distinguish between the former and the latter. More importantly and decisively, his earlier objection in §39 against units that are pure and yet distinct does not mention abstraction at all; nor do his discussions of Jevons in §36 and §38, where he focuses on the impossibility of units being pure yet distinguishable. He seems to think that the problem is not with the means of attaining a representation of pure units, but with the purported pure units themselves; in arguing against Jevons, he simply does not allow for Jevons' kind of characteristics. Thus, Frege seems to agree with Kant in rejecting characteristics that specify further characteristics indeterminately. It would seem that both Frege and Kant reject Jevons' solution to the problem for the same

[44]   Frege's argument is somewhat more complicated than this summary suggests; he presents a dilemma, and I am drawing out what he says concerning the first horn.

Daniel Sutherland

reason: a shared assumption concerning the limits of conceptual representation.[45]

4. Frege and Kant on the role of space and time

I would now like to turn to Frege's main argument that we cannot overcome the limits of conceptual representation by appealing to space or time to represent pure units. His argument presses a dilemma (§41). The first horn concerns the possibility of representing points of space as qualitatively identical. Frege states that only in themselves, apart from their relations, are points of space qualitatively identical. But, he adds, 'if I am to think of them together, I am bound then to consider them in their collocation in space, or else they fuse irretrievably together into one'. Thus, points of space in themselves may be qualitatively identical, but they cannot be represented as distinct.

It seems that the homogeneity of points of space might support the claim that, in themselves, they are qualitatively identical. What, however, is the basis for Frege's claim that these qualitatively identical points will fuse into one? It appears that Frege either implicitly appeals to the principle of identity of indiscernibles, or thinks that this is a self-evident property of points of space, one that could be described as a case of the identity of indiscernibles.[46] Regardless,

---

[45]   It is perhaps surprising to attribute to Frege a limitation on conceptual representation; his views on what is conceptually representable would appear to be, if anything, quite liberal. Nevertheless, it seems to me that Frege's argument points in this direction.

[46]   Asserting a version of PII applied to points of space would be a departure from the traditional understanding of the principle. Leibniz only applies PII to substances or real beings and their phenomenal manifestations: monads, 'pieces of matter,' atoms, and sensible things such as leaves and drops of water. In his view, PII does not apply to abstractions or ideal beings, and because he holds that spaces and times are merely ideal, he does not think that PII applies to them (as Tait (2005), fn. 29, points out). In fact, Leibniz states that points of space and time are distinct despite being indistinguishable, and he even compares them to pure units in §27 of Leibniz's Fifth Paper of the *Leibniz–Clarke Correspondence*; see H. G. Alexander (1956). Kant would also reject the application of PII to points of space, but for a different reason. In his view, PII does not apply to *any* objects of sensibility, whether or not they are substances, and that includes qualitatively identical parts of space and points of space. Kant focuses on parts of space. In his view points are limits of spaces and hence

160

Frege simply seems to assume that there is no possibility of a primitive distinctness among points of space in themselves. One might think, for example, that points of space, though qualitatively identical, have *haecceities* (or something analogous) that distinguish them one from another. This would be a contentious claim, of course. Nevertheless, the success of his main line of argument against the units view depends on his ability to close off the possibility of appealing to space and time, and without further argument for his assumption, his main line of attack is threatened.[47]

Despite these worries, however, the heart of Frege's argument appears on the second horn of the dilemma, where he claims that points of space can only be distinguished by their relations.[48] He adds:

---

presuppose parts of space, and the same diversity without specific difference holds for them as for qualitatively identical parts of space.

[47] Frege's statement concerning points of space reads:

It is only in themselves, and neglecting their spatial relations, that points of space are identical to one another [*einander gleich*]; if I am to think of them together, I am bound then to consider them in their collocation in space, or else they fuse irretrievably into one (§41).

The phrases '*neglecting* their spatial relations' and 'if I am to *think* of them together [zusammenfassen]' and 'I am bound to *consider* them' leave open the possibility that Frege intends to be discussing *only our representation* of points of space rather than points of space themselves. This would be consistent with his argument strategy; that is, with his attempt to show that Schröder, Jevons, and Thomae cannot *represent* units as both pure and distinct, and hence cannot account for our *representation* of number by appealing to our representation of units. If Frege is making a point about our representation of points of space, then he may be implicitly invoking an intensionalized version of PII—that is, if someone represents x and y as indistinguishable, then that person represents x and y as identical. Nevertheless, as noted in the previous section, Frege asserts an un-intensionalized version of PII in §34, and §65 seems to support it as well. On balance, I think that it is likely that Frege implicitly applies un-intensionalised PII to points of space in §41. I would like to thank Walter Edelberg for suggesting intensionalized versions of PII to me and pressing me for clarification. Un-intensionalized and intensionalized versions of PII are closely related to each other in both Leibniz and Kant; there is much more to say on this point than I can include in this paper.

[48] One can question whether Frege's position makes sense. William Tait has argued that relations between points of space will not distinguish those points unless the relations themselves can be distinguished, which

Daniel Sutherland

All these [spatial and temporal relations] are relationships which have absolutely nothing to do with number as such. Pervading them all is an admixture of some special element, which number in its general form leaves far behind (§41).

In short, Frege argues that the spatial relations that distinguish pure units will undermine the generality of the representation of number, because this spatiality will have to be represented in the concept of number.[49]

How would Kant respond? First, I think that Kant agrees with Frege that qualitatively identical parts and points of space are distinguished by their relations to one another.[50] Thus, despite qualms about Frege's handling of the first horn of the dilemma, I believe Kant would find himself on the second horn. Second, Kant would deny that the relations distinguishing qualitatively identical parts of space must be represented in the concept. Kant makes room for the diversity of pure units despite their indistinguishability by, in effect, drawing a distinction between conceptual and intuitive distinguishability. The former is all that is required for the purity of pure units: conceptual indistinguishability gives us the required generality, while intuitive distinguishability accounts for the diversity of these units.

Frege might reject Kant's attempt to avoid importing a 'special element' into the concept of number by appealing to intuition. He holds that *any* means sufficient to distinguish units, whether it be spatial relations or something else, would have to be specified in the concept of their collection, and hence in the concept of number. The nature of the distinguishing property is immaterial; either it is represented in the concept or it is not. On the one hand, Kant appeals to spatial relations among parts of space to distinguish units, and on the other, he simply omits this difference from the

---

presupposes the distinctness of points of space. Yet Frege has just denied that points of space in themselves are distinct, see Tait (2005), p. 235. If an adequate response to this criticism can be given, it will depend upon difficult issues concerning the nature of relations, distinctness, and identity, issues that I cannot adequately address in this paper.

[49] In fact, he holds that even a single point of space has something *sui generis* that distinguishes it from, say, a moment in time, and 'of which there is no trace in the concept of number' (§41).

[50] Much more can and needs to be said on this point, but I will have to postpone an explication and defense for another occasion.

concept. In short, Frege might say that Kant himself is trying to have his cake and eat it too.

This criticism simply underscores the differences between Frege and Kant's understanding of conceptual representation and its limits. On the criticism proffered on Frege's behalf, anything representable is in principle conceptually representable, while for Kant this is not the case, and intuitive representation can supplement conceptual representation. There is a further point brought out by the criticism, however. For in Kant's view, the generality of the representation of number is not undermined by supplementing conceptual representation with intuition. Whether Kant is entitled to this claim depends on a deeper analysis of the role of schemata in accounting for the generality of mathematical claims, as well as the role of pure units in allowing particular number concepts to arise and in establishing their objective validity in a way that does not undermine that generality. An answer to the questions raised on Frege's behalf will constrain an acceptable Kantian account of arithmetical cognition.

5. Summary

The idea that arithmetical concepts require the representation of units, and pure units in particular, arose as long ago as Plato, but its history effectively ends with Frege. Barring an overthrow of more than a century of mathematical logic, that is as it should be. Nevertheless, interest in the history of the foundations of mathematics requires that we understand this approach, the pure plurality problem, and attempts to overcome this problem. There is evidence that Kant assigns a role to the representation of pure units in the origin of particular number concepts and in establishing the objective validity of arithmetical claims. His account, however, is not subject to the pure plurality problem because he appeals to pure intuition. Understanding the views of Frege's contemporaries requires untangling ambiguous notions of equality and identity, but doing so reveals attempts to make the units view work by developing the notion of numerical abstraction and loosening the traditional understanding of conceptual representation. Clarifying their views and Frege's own notions of equality and identity allow us to better understand his arguments against them.

A comparison of Kant and Frege on pure units also uncovers unexpected features of their views. They are in closer agreement on the units view than one might have expected, and would criticize it on grounds of the limits of conceptual representation. Yet they deeply diverge on whether an appeal to space and time could make the representation of pure units possible. The core issue dividing them is whether space and time make it possible to distinguish units in a way that does not undermine the generality of the concept of number. Frege claims that they will not, but he assumes that space and time lack primitive distinctness, and his claim requires further argument. Kant thinks that they will, but whether he is entitled to this claim depends on his fuller account of the generality of mathematical cognition.[51]

[51] Parsons (1984) explored Kant's conceptions of magnitude and their relation to mathematical cognition and to the categories of quantity. Friedman (1992a), 110–113, drew a connection between Kant's account of algebra and the Eudoxian theory of proportions and he subsequently encouraged me to explore the connection between the Eudoxian theory and Kant's theory of magnitudes. My work can thus be viewed as an extension of Parsons' and Friedman's lines of investigation and I have benefited greatly from their work. Discussions with William Tait revealed that he had addressed some of the same issues I was exploring. I have benefited immensely from Tait's (2005) paper and from regular discussions with him in the spring of 2007 and 2008. I would also like to thank those who responded to versions of this paper delivered at the Central Meeting of the American Philosophical Association, April 2007; the *Kant and Philosophy of Science Today* conference at the Royal Institute of Philosophy, University College London, July 2007; and the UCSB Department of Philosophy, February 2008. I am particularly grateful to Michael Friedman, Robert Howell, and Charles Parsons for detailed comments, as well as Brandon Look for comments and for sharing a draft of his paper on Leibniz's principle of identity of indiscernibles. Special thanks are due the members of the UIC Philosophy of Mathematics Reading Group, especially Bill Hart and Walter Edelberg, for their many insightful remarks, which substantially improved both my understanding of the philosophical issues and this paper. I am also grateful to Marcus Giaquinto for discussion and for comments on the penultimate draft. Finally, I would like to acknowledge the generous support of the National Science Foundation; this paper is based upon work supported by them under Grant No. 0452527.

Intuition and Infinity: A Kantian Theme with Echoes in the Foundations of Mathematics

CARL POSY

Introduction

Kant says patently conflicting things about infinity and our grasp of it. Infinite space is a good case in point. In his solution to the First Antinomy, he denies that we can grasp the spatial universe as infinite, and therefore that this universe can be infinite;[1] while in the Aesthetic he says just the opposite: 'Space is represented as a given infinite magnitude'(A25/B39). And he rests these upon consistently opposite grounds. In the Antinomy we are told that we can have no intuitive grasp of an infinite space,[2] and in the Aesthetic he says that our grasp of infinite space is precisely intuitive.[3]

My main aim in what follows is to resolve this apparent internal conflict. I will discuss Kant's theory of intuition, its Leibnizian background, and how Kant turned that Leibnizian inheritance into separate theories of empirical (sensory) intuition and mathematical intuition. I will argue that these theories interact differently with Kant's notion of infinity—why for Kant there *is* mathematical infinity, but there is not empirical infinity, and why, indeed, empirically there are several different ways to be *non-infinite*—and I will point out how that bifurcation will dissolve his apparent inconsistency. In the end, I will show how Kant subtly distinguishes between the space of the Antinomy and the space of the Aesthetic.

---

[1] 'I cannot say, therefore, that the world is *infinite* in space ... Any such concept of magnitude, as being that of a given infinitude, is empirically impossible, and therefore, in reference to the world as an object of the senses, also absolutely impossible' (A520/B549).

Note: Except as indicated, I will use the Kemp Smith (1929) translation of the *Critique of Pure Reason* (New York: St. Martin's).

[2] 'Now we have the cosmic whole only in concept, never, as whole in intuition' (A519–520/B546–7).

[3] 'Consequently, the original representation of space is an *a priori* intuition, not a concept' (A25/B39–40).

doi:10.1017/S135824610800009X

Carl Posy

But I have a secondary aim as well: I want to display the echoes of this Kantian treatment of infinity and intuition in a famous modern foundational debate in the philosophy of mathematics, the Hilbert–Brouwer *Grundlagenstreit* of the 1920s. By the time of this debate, infinity had firmly roosted in all of mathematics: infinite sets, infinite sequences, and, of course, the continuum, which combines both factors, were seen to lie at the heart of all mathematics. This posed a challenge for thinkers like Brouwer and Hilbert who struggled to show how this modern infinitary mathematics could be anchored in human intuition.

Let me point out that Hilbert and Brouwer tackled this challenge oppositely. Brouwer, pushed human intuition into the heart of mathematics, and changed that heart accordingly. He banned indirect existence proofs; he filled mathematics with exotically generated objects and with subtle intentional distinctions; and he even outright contradicted known mathematical theorems (for him there are no fully defined discontinuous functions). Hilbert, by contrast, was committed to every aspect of the new infinitary mathematics; and he kept it all. From the very beginning of his career he embraced indirect existence proofs, he clung throughout to all the standard theorems, and his ε-symbol brought infinitary thought into mathematical language itself. Human intuition, for him, serves as an outside anchor (in formal systems and their consistency proofs) securing the unfettered heart of mathematics, which proceeds on its own.

Though I spoke of a 'foundational debate', I should say that this conflict was anything but a polite debate. There was a political battle,[4] and there were rhetorical excesses by both sides and their supporters. Hilbert accused Brouwer of a crotchety and emasculating fundamentalism about existence, which would become a 'dictatorship of prohibitions' that 'robs mathematics of [its] most valuable treasures'.[5] Brouwer accused Hilbert of a 'thoughtless use' of non-constructive methods, and of abandoning true intuition in favor of the false security of linguistic expressions and consistency proofs.[6] And, indeed, Hilbert's non-constructive ε-symbol is perhaps the flagship of this approach, and a direct taunt for a Brouwerian constructivist. But behind the pyrotechnics were deep mathematical and philosophical differences. And the main thing I want to argue is that, once we properly understand Kant's views about this issue

[4] See van Dalen (1990) for an account of the political side of this confrontation.
[5] Hilbert (1922).
[6] Brouwer (1928).

of intuition and infinity, we will find that ***both sides are conceptually Kantian***!

This sort of cross-generational comparison is perforce a tapestry of textual exegesis together with reconstructive interpretation. I will do a bit of each in what follows, far from the whole story, but enough, I hope, so that I will be in a position to identify the Kantian components of both Brouwer's and Hilbert's programs in the foundations of mathematics. In addition, in the spirit of this volume, I will mention a few more current issues *en route* as well. I will end with a brief methodological remark.

I. Kant's Theory of Empirical Intuition and Infinity

So let us start with a historical and systematic look at Kant's notion of empirical intuition and its interaction with putative empirical infinity. After that I will turn to his notions of mathematical intuition and mathematical infinity. Historically, Kant is taking a Leibnizian picture and adapting it to his own needs; systematically, that adaptation has cognitive, ontological and semantic sides.

1. Leibniz's theory of intuition and its problem

For Leibniz the paradigm of an intuitive grasp is God's grasp of a *complete concept*. This is the Leibnizian theme that Kant will adapt. According to Leibniz, when God contemplates (say) Julius Caesar, He has spread before Himself a full description of all Caesar's properties. The complete concept is an elaborate arrangement of elementary predicates which describes everything there is about Caesar. It is indeed 'predicatively complete'; it contains every relevant predicate or its denial arranged according to the stages of Caesar's life. There is no aspect of Caesar that is not told in his complete concept.[7]

Ontologically, every *proper object* has such a complete concept. Leibniz envisages a complex combinatorial hierarchy of concepts in which we proceed from the more general at the top, downward to the more specific and in which complete concepts lie at the very

---

[7] 'It is the nature of an individual substance or complete being to have a concept so complete that it is sufficient to make us understand and deduce from it all the predicates of the subject to which the concept is attributed', Leibniz (1686a), §8. Indeed, in this context, Leibniz arrogates the medieval notion of *haecceity* to the complete concept.

Carl Posy

bottom (they are *infima species*). This is actually a source of Leibniz's well-known theory about identity: Caesar's complete concept suffices to distinguish Caesar from any other actual or possible entity, because the complete concept of such an entity will necessarily differ in at least one detail somewhere along the line. Any concept that is less complete—any one that leaves out even a single small determination—must be a general concept; for it will apply to at least two distinct objects. It will describe an 'aggregate', which for Leibniz is a deficient sort of entity, not an object. That is why, for him, compound things cannot be objects: their conceptual descriptions will be general. The only true objects are indivisible monads.

Sometimes Leibniz expresses this in terms of unity: aggregates have at best a 'phenomenal unity', which unites several things whose descriptions partially overlap. By contrast Caesar's complete concept provides him with a *true unity*, a principle from which one can deduce everything that there is about Caesar.

Speaking **cognitively**, this divine grasp is **immediate** and **singular**. *Immediate:* because God directly grasps each of the stages and each of the elementary predicates in a single cognitive swoop. He has no need for linguistic abbreviations (or discursive descriptions) which must subsequently be analyzed or unpacked.[8] *Singular:* because this grasp suffices to encompass the full object, and to distinguish it from any other actual or possible object. And speaking **semantically**, Leibniz tells us that deduction from Caesar's complete concept is the condition for an idea to *correspond* to Caesar himself, and thus the condition for the truth of judgments about Caesar.[9]

---

[8] '... when everything which enters into a definition or distinct knowledge is known distinctly, down to the primitive concepts, I call such knowledge *adequate*. And when my mind grasps all the primitive ingredients of a concept at once and distinctly, it possesses an *intuitive* knowledge. This is very rare, since for the most part human knowledge is merely either confused or *suppositive*'. Leibniz (1686a), §24.

'In this way all adequate definitions contain primitive truths of reason and consequently intuitive knowledge. It can be said in general that all primitive truths of reason are immediate with respect to an immediateness of ideas'. Leibniz (1704), IV, ii, 1.

[9] 'Let us be content with looking for truth in the correspondence between the propositions which are in the mind and the things which they are about', *ibid.*, IV, v, iii.

'It would be better to assign truth to the relationship amongst the objects of the ideas by virtue of which one idea is or is not included in the other', *ibid.*

There is a confluence in this Leibnizian picture of cognition, ontology and semantics. For, God's cognition, His intuitive grasp of Caesar, delivers the completeness and unity that make Caesar a legitimate object, and His grasp is the basis of truth and correspondence.

But there is a problem too in this neat pristine package. It patently denigrates human knowledge and empirical objects. Cognitively, this package of ideas—God's-eye intuition, objects and truth—belittles *human* perception. A glance at the pen I am holding in my hand is momentary and incomplete. It tells me nothing about the pen's interior, about its past, or about its future. Metaphysically, the Leibnizian picture reduces extended bodies like the pen to the status of mere aggregates. And, semantically, it denies that judgments based on perception can correspond to any metaphysically significant reality. For, the empirical concepts out of which these judgments are built do not themselves reflect the true nature of things.

Neither Leibniz nor his scientific and philosophical inheritors were prepared to embrace this downgrading of the human and the empirical. Indeed, he and a generation of followers (including the young Kant) struggled to reconcile this tension between pristine metaphysics, on the one hand, and human knowledge of the empirical world on the other. But they did so, says the mature Kant, without success. In his eyes, only his radical critical philosophy successfully bridged this gap.

2. Kant's solution: empirical intuitions

And how did it do that? How does Kant's critical philosophy reconcile the pristine Leibnizian metaphysics with the possibility of human knowledge? Well, in fact, the critical Kant sharpens the problem, and only then solves it.

He sharpens the problem first by accepting the Leibnizian conditions for objects and intuitions. True objects are for Kant, as they were for Leibniz, predicatively complete:

> But every *thing*, as regards its possibility, is likewise subject to the principle of *complete* determination, according to which if *all the possible* predicates of *things* be taken together with their contradictory opposites, then one of each pair of contradictory opposites must belong to it. (A571–2/B599–600)

Carl Posy

And an intuitive grasp (an intuition) is immediate; it is singular,[10] which means it is the arbiter of identity and distinction from other objects; and it is the vehicle of reference to its object.[11]

But then he turns the tables and declares that these objects, of which he is speaking, are empirical objects—the pen, for instance, and other extended things—and these intuitions are none other than our human perceptions, fleeting and partial as they may be. Indeed, he goes further and says that these intuitions differ in kind and not merely in degree of clarity or completeness from conceptual descriptions. No concept, says Kant, can ever be singular or immediate or referential; perceptions alone have to carry those burdens.

And then he relieves the tension between these conflicting demands by redefining and adapting the Leibnizian criteria. Thus, on the **ontological** side, he relaxes the notion of unity. Empirical objects are organized by *sortal concepts* ('pen', for instance) which dictate what the relevant parts of the object must be and how they are to be organized. These provide the necessary *unity* for their objects, that is a phenomenal unity—and Kant readily speaks of phenomenal objects—but, says Kant, it is unity enough.[12]

On the **cognitive** side, our perceptual intuitions must deliver that unity, and must be singular, immediate and referential. Now in Leibniz there was no point to distinguish cognitive unity from singularity; both are straightforward consequences of the immediate grasp of a complete concept, an *infima species*. But, Kant denies that we

---

[10] '...an objective cognition is *knowledge* (*cognitio*). This is either *intuition* or *concept* (*intuitus vel conceptus*). The former relates immediately to the object and is singular, the latter refers to it mediately by means of a feature which several things may have in common'. (A320/B376–7). Translation by CP.

[11] 'In whatever manner and by whatever means a mode of knowledge may relate to objects, *intuition* is that through which it is in immediate relation to them, and to which all thought as a means is directed'. (A19/B33).

[12] This, in turn, is the essence of his Copernican revolution. When he says in that famous passage

> 'If intuition must conform to the constitution of the objects, I do not see how we could know anything of the latter *a priori*; but if the object (as object of the senses) must conform to the constitution of our faculty of intuition, I have no difficulty in conceiving such a possibility' (Bxvii).

Kant is saying that our human intuitions play the ontological role of Leibnizian complete concepts: they tell all there is about their objects. Thus, Kant has fashioned a 'humanized' version of Leibniz's notion of *haecceity*.

humans have any such grasp.[13] So Kant must distinguish these factors. Regarding *unity*, one of the pillars of Kant's theory of synthesis is that perceptual intuitions carry with them the appropriate sortal organization. For Kant, seeing is always 'seeing as'.[14]

As for *singularity*, for Kant, as it was for Leibniz, this comes from considerations of identity and completeness. My perceptions do pick out individual objects and underlie judgments of *identity* and difference. Thus, for instance, my pen-intuition alone will suffice to distinguish this pen from any other actual or possible pen. He insists that no conceptual description will ever suffice to do this.[15] And regarding *completeness*: true, my fleeting perceptual grasp of the pen leaves out a great deal of information (for instance, it does not tell me how much ink remains in the pen and nor about future or even past states of the pen). Nevertheless, having the perception—seeing the pen—tells me that I *can get* this information, if I want to. I need only look further and deeper at what I already have in view. And that guarantee of eventual access to all the parts and determination of all the potential predicates is enough, according to Kant, to say that the perception delivers the object's completeness. And as for *immediacy*, this now means that my perception presents its object in a way that goes beyond any particular conceptual description.

[13]   'But there is no lowest concept (*conceptus infimus*) or lowest species in the series of species and genera under which not yet another would be contained, because it is impossible to determine such a concept. .... In respect to the determination of the concepts of genera and species, the following general law is valid: *There is a genus that can no longer be a species; but there is no species that can no longer be a genus*', 'Lectures on Logic', I, 1, fn. 11, in Hartman and Schwarz (1974).

[14]   See Posy (2000) for an elaboration of this point.

[15]   Famously, Kant argues in the Amphiboly that just seeing the spatial distance between a pair of objects suffices to tell them apart. This is his refutation of the identity of indiscernibles:

'Thus in the case of two drops of water we can abstract altogether from all internal difference (of quality and of quantity), and the mere fact that they have been intuited simultaneously in different spatial positions is sufficient justification for holding them to be numerically different. ... **For one part of space, although completely similar and equal to another part is still outside the other,** and for this very reason is a different part, which when added to it constitutes with it a greater space. **The same must be true of all things which exist simultaneously in the different spatial positions, however similar and equal they may otherwise be'** (A264/B320), emphases added.

Carl Posy

Finally, coming to the **semantic** side and the Kantian parallel to the Leibnizian notion of correspondence, Kant tells us that when we contemplate objects, only intuition (perceptual intuition for humans) can actually *give* the objects,[16] and 'give' here really means 'refer to'. Indeed, when Kant speaks of truth, he quite explicitly defines it as correspondence to (or 'agreement with') the object.[17] And, like Leibniz, Kant too uses intuition to underwrite that correspondence by presenting the object in all its aspects.

But, even more than that, for Kant my pen-intuition (my perception of the pen) actually serves to establish the pen's *existence*. That is because in presenting the pen to me, my pen-intuition is actually allowing the pen to act upon me, and thus is demonstrating that pen's existence.[18] But it is important to add that as he did with completeness, here too Kant takes a wide view: any perception that is somehow causally linked to an object serves to establish that object's existence.[19] Once again, Kant will insist, no concept alone can play that role. [20]

Here, we see one of those more current issues that I promised: Kant's referential notion of truth is based upon a forerunner to the modern causal theory of reference—championed in the 1970s by Saul Kripke and Hilary Putnam—according to which we successfully refer to something in the world by virtue of our causal contact with the thing or stuff in question.[21] On the other hand, in this regard,

[16] 'But all thought must, directly or indirectly, by way of certain characters, relate ultimately to intuitions, and therefore, with us, to sensibility, because in no other way can an object be given to us' (A19/B33).

[17] See A58/B82 and A191/B236.

[18] 'In whatever manner and by whatever means a mode of knowledge may relate to objects, *intuition* is that through which it is in immediate relation to them, and to which all thought as a means is directed. But intuition takes place only in so far as the object is given to us. This again is only possible, to man at least, in so far as the mind is affected in a certain way. The capacity (receptivity) for receiving representations through the mode in which we are affected by objects, is entitled *sensibility*' (A19/B33).

[19] 'The postulate bearing on the knowledge of things as *actual* does not, indeed, demand immediate *perception* (and, therefore, sensation of which we are conscious) of the object whose existence is to be known. What we do, however, require is the connection of the object with some actual perception, in accordance with the analogies of experience, which define all real connection in an experience in general' (A225/B272).

[20] 'In the *mere concept* of a thing no mark of its existence is to be found', *ibid*.

[21] See Kripke (1972), and Putnam (1975). Famously, this theory allows us to refer successfully to someone or something even though we might have an incomplete or even incorrect concept of the object of reference. And Kant

Leibniz's theory of reference—based, as it is, on the relation of concepts—foreshadows the so-called 'descriptivist' theory of reference that Kripke and Putnam strived to refute.[22]

This then is Kant's updated philosophical package: a four-faceted perceptual intuition, full-fledged empirical objects and a proto-causal theory of reference and truth. And with this humanized package he confronts the challenge of infinity.

3. The un-intuitability of the infinitely large

Kant, as I said, denies that there any infinite empirical objects; he denies that there are infinitely large objects—in particular, he denies that there is an infinitely large physical universe—as well as denying that there are infinitely small physical points. I will first explain his attitude towards the infinitely large, and then about the infinitely small.

A. Far Away Regions

So what is wrong with an infinitely large physical universe (i.e., an infinite expanse inhabited by physical objects)? Why can we not intuit such a thing? It cannot be simply because we are unable to apprehend it in a single perceptual glance. For, after all, we now

---

correctly sees that the causal notion of empirical reference, which he now champions, does allow for fallibility and revisability:

> (...) an *empirical* concept cannot be defined at all, but only *made explicit*. For since we find in it only a few characteristics of a certain species of sensible object, it is never certain that we are not using the word, in denoting one and the same object, sometimes so as to stand for more, and sometimes so as to stand for fewer characteristics. (...) We make use of certain characteristics only so long as they are adequate for the purpose of making distinctions; new observations remove some properties and add others, and the limits of the concept are never assured (A727−8/B755−6).

[22] 'And indeed what useful purpose could be served by defining an empirical concept, such, for instance, as that of water? When we speak of water and its properties, we do not stop short as what is thought in the word, water, but proceed to experiments. The word, with the few characteristics which we attach to it, is more properly to be regarded as merely a designation than as a concept of the thing, the so-called definition is nothing more than a determining of the word', *ibid*.

see that according to Kant, not only my pen, but also the table near which I am sitting, and this room are legitimate intuitable objects. So too is all of London, all of the UK, Europe, the earth, our solar system, our galaxy. None of these latter can be taken in at a single glance, yet each of them is intuitively graspable. So, what is wrong with the sum of the whole increasing series itself, the possibly infinite universe? Why does Kant insist, as we saw at the start, that we can have no intuition of that sum? Here is Kant's official reason:

> We cannot therefore say anything at all in regard to the magnitude of the world, not even that there is in it a regress *ad infinitum*. All that we can do is to seek for the concept of its magnitude according to the rule which determines the empirical regress in it. This rule says no more than that however far we may have attained in the series of empirical conditions, we should never assume an absolute limit, but should subordinate every appearance, as conditioned, to another as its condition, and that we must advance to this condition. (A520–21/B548–49)

Kant is concerned here with the sequential progress of our knowledge about the size of the universe. And here is where I will do some textual exegesis to play out this Kantian train of thought.

Suppose that we have succeeded in finding physically inhabited regions, i.e., a sequence of 1, 2, 3, . . . , n objects, each further from here than its predecessor by at least a fixed minimal distance.[23] This, I say, is as far as we have gone so far; and now we face the question 'is there a yet further inhabited region (call it an $n + 1^{st}$–region)?' So, we form a scientific task-force to answer this question, and we check back with them regularly, say once a month, starting tomorrow. Speaking now, we know that there are two possible answers we can get tomorrow: **yes** (*we have found a further region housing as it were the $n + 1^{st}$ object*) or **no** (*we have not yet succeeded in finding such a region*). Of course, if the answer is yes, then the search for an $n + 1^{st}$ region is done. If the answer is no, then that does not mean that there is no such region, but only that the search will continue. Indeed, that means that after the inquiry tomorrow, we are in the same situation we are in now but with respect to the subsequent check (a month from tomorrow). And so in fact—regarding that $n + 1^{st}$ region—we *currently* envisage a situation that looks like Fig. 1:

---

[23] I stressed the minimal distance here because in the Antinomy Kant is concerned with the sequential progress of our knowledge. Thus, the question as to whether an infinite sequence of regions might converge to a finite limit is simply not to the point.

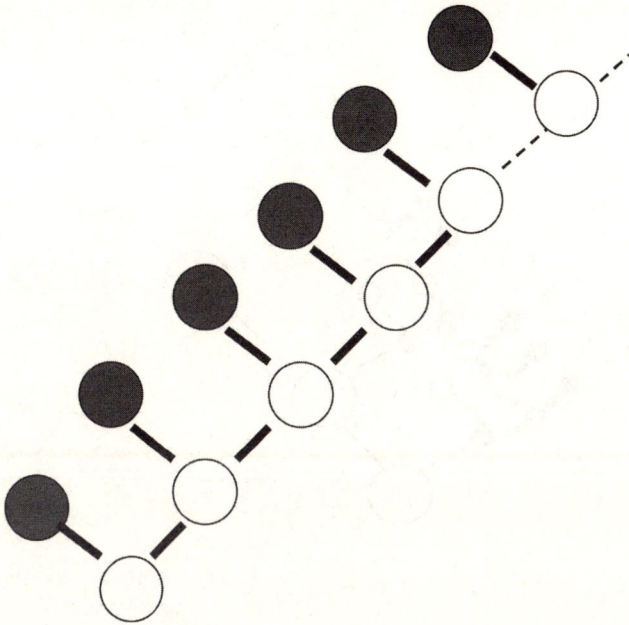

Figure 1.

So long as we do not find such a region, the search continues; if we do, it stops. Speaking right now, we do not know how that will play out. We do not know whether the search will terminate or will go on forever.

Now, should we ever find an $n + 1^{st}$ inhabited region, then, of course, we would send off our crew to find an $n + 2^{nd}$ region, and so on. So in fact what we currently envisage is a more complex situation which looks schematically like this big tree in Fig. 2.

Each dark circle stands for a situation in which we have found a new region and thus embark upon a fresh start. To say that the inhabited (physical) universe is infinite is to say that for each k-region that is found, there will be a $k + 1^{st}$ region that will also be found (i.e., this is to say that our actual path will contain an infinite string of dark circles). This is a *dynamic* notion—a large seek-and-find process—and at no check point in this process can we ever prove that the universe actually is infinite in this sense. For, at each check, there is always the possibility that we will not ever proceed any further; the possibility, that is, of an infinite sequences of light circles. Quite similarly, at no point can we prove that the world is finite, i.e., that the actual path will be all empty from that point on.

Carl Posy

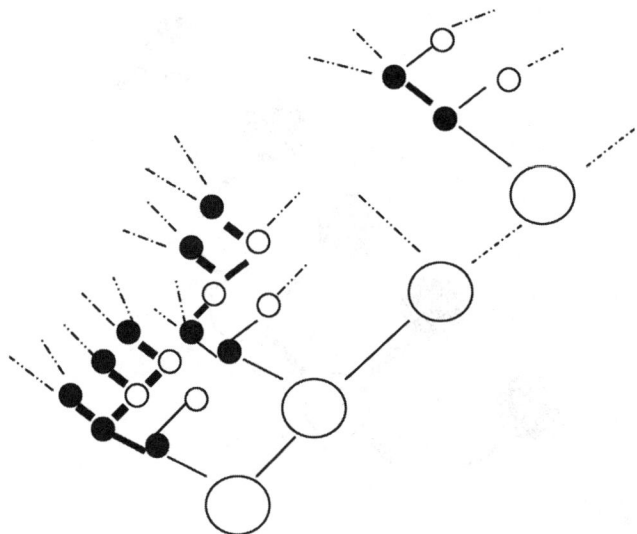

Figure 2.

For, at each dark circle there is always the possibility of a next dark circle.

B. *A second modern parallel*

As I said, this sketches Kant's reasoning at A520–1/B548–9; but let me at this point mention yet another modern twist. When speaking of the universe as a whole, Kant says not merely that we cannot say that it is finite. He says outright that it *not finite*.[24] Now, only the modern 'assertability theory of truth' would allow him to move from impossibility of knowledge to actual falsity. This is the theory—in our own time, championed most prominently by Michael Dummett—which equates truth with warranted assertability for human beings. Dummett has striven hard to show that this is the appropriate underlying semantics for ordinary discourse and for scientific discourse in various fields.[25] And the best way to understand Kant's claims here is to assume that he is indeed a proto-assertabilist.

---

[24] 'Thus the first and negative answer to the cosmological problem regarding the magnitude of the world is that the world has no (...) outermost limit in space' (A520/B548).
[25] See for instance Dummett (1978), (1991).

There is good historical ground for this assumption. Leibniz was himself a proto-assertabilist,[26] and that is something that Kant would naturally have inherited. But, of course, for Leibniz it is God's knowledge that underlies the assertability theory of truth, while Kant's assertabilism would rest truth on the human knowledge and *empirical* evidence. In particular, Kant would adapt the idea that I described above, namely that a guaranteed grasp is as good as a psychologically actual grasp. And in this regard Kant's view would be a forerunner of what I call a 'mild assertabilism'.[27] This is a theory that allows us to assert $\exists xFx$ even without having in hand an object, a, satisfying Fa, so long as we know that we can eventually come to find an x such that Fx holds. And that is indeed Kant's position, at A225/B273:

> the perception which supplies the content to the concept is the sole mark of actuality. We can also, however, know the existence of the thing prior to its perception (...) if only it be bound up with certain perceptions, in accordance with the principles of their empirical connection (the analogies).

He is speaking here about the fact that we can infer the presence of a magnet simply from the observation of the movement of iron filings. But in fact this position underlies his view that we can have intuitive evidence for very large, very small, and very distant objects as well, objects that fall outside our perceptual thresholds.

To be sure, Kant combines his assertability theory together with the correspondence theory of truth that I described above. That indeed is a semantic rendition of his Copernican Revolution: our empirical judgments are true in virtue of meeting the conditions for warranted assertability, and the objects in the world are such that these judgments truly describe them. This in fact puts him very close to Hilary Putnam's modern 'internal realism'.[28]

C. The non-intuitability of the infinitely large
But all of this—internal realism, mild assertabilism, and a tolerance for very large objects—leads us to expect that Kant *will* allow us an

---

[26] Indications of an underlying proto-assertabilism are scattered throughout Leibniz's work. One of the most explicit texts is the 'General Inquiries about the Analysis of Concepts and Truths' (1686b) where in §130 he says: 'That is true, therefore, which can be proved, i.e. of which a reason can be given by analysis...', English translation by Parkinson (1966). I explore this point more fully in Posy (2003).

[27] See Posy (1992).

[28] See Putnam (1981). See also Posy (2000), (2003).

intuitive grasp of the universe as a whole, and will accept the universe as a legitimate object.

So what is missing? *What is missing is the singularity of our grasp; or more specifically the predicative completeness that underlies singularity.* For, there is a pair of opposed predicates—finite magnitude/infinite magnitude—which, come what may, will never be decided. Or, put in terms of identity, were we to contemplate a universe that is actually infinite—i.e., whose map contains an infinite sequence of dark circles—then our current grasp (or the grasp at any node along the way in the sequences of explorations) could not determine whether our actual universe is equal to or different from this contemplated infinite one.[29] So, failing the test of intuition, our grasp, as Kant says, is just a conceptual description ('the collection of inhabited regions') not an intuition; and the thing grasped is a collection but not an object.

Let me add two brief points here. First, let me point out that this indeterminacy—which denies to our grasp of the universe the status of being a legitimate intuition—comes from what Kant calls the 'receptivity' of intuition. At each check point our scientists must wait for additional information to tell them the outcome of the next check point. They are motivated by the hope that they will get the further information, but that wait could be eternal. That is the fate of empirical science in general. Our inbuilt receptivity entails that such science contains endless conjectures and uncertainty.[30] For, as Kant says, the key to this knowledge does not lie in us. In this case it means that we can never establish that we are on a path through this tree that will determine that the world is infinite nor one that will show it to be finite.

Secondly, notice that this receptivity and its attendant indeterminacy serve to *split* the standard distinction between infinite and finite. For here we have a set—the set of occupied regions—which is neither. Actually, the split is even more subtle. Speaking of the expanding series of inhabited regions Kant says:

> This is the *regressus in indefinitum*, which as it determines no magnitude in the object, is clearly enough distinguishable from the *regressus in infinitum* (A520/B548)

---

[29] Similarly, at each checkpoint, k, with positive outcome, our grasp cannot determine whether the actual universe is identical to a contemplated one in which there are exactly k occupied region.

[30] 'In natural science, (...) there is endless conjectures, and certainty is not to be counted upon' (A480/B508).

And that contrasting *regressus in infinitum* concerns Kant's view of the infinitely small (the result of infinite divisibility). This notion of the infinitely small brings different considerations and a different diagram, so let us look at it briefly.

4. The non-intuitability of the infinitely small

Here too there is a process; it is a process of dividing material things into smaller parts and discovering their natures. And once again the question is whether or not that process must stop at some finite point. If so, then there are physical atoms. And here too, Kant will deny us the ability to say either yes or no.

But there is a subtle difference here: for, in this case, Kant is absolutely certain that the process of division does go on forever. As I said, he speaks of it as continuing *ad infinitum*. The reason is that the material stuff for the smaller and smaller parts is clearly available. We in fact get the following picture regarding the smaller and smaller inhabited special regions (Figure 3).

Each bar represents another level of fine-tuned micro-structure. We know that we can get to any given level, but nevertheless, Kant still says that we have no intuition of the whole ultimate chain. He is denying that we intuitively grasp this infinite converging sequence of physical regions. As he puts it, we have no intuition of an object which is 'organized all the way down'.[31]

This is a subtle, almost paradoxical position: The division continues *ad infinitum* but will not give a manifold with infinitely many smaller and smaller parts. The reason, once again, is receptivity, or more precisely, ignorance due to receptivity. We simply cannot know in advance what the next organizing concept will be; we shall have to see how science plays itself out.[32] We do not know what the micro-structure of the smaller particles will be like.[33] So our grasp of each stage fails the criterion of conceptual unity, while our grasp

[31] 'We cannot assume that every part of an organized whole is itself again so organized that, in the analysis of the parts to infinity, still other organized parts are always to be met with; in a word, that whole is organized to infinity. This is not a thinkable hypothesis' (A526/B554).

[32] Moreover, there is no causal link to the 'next organizing concept', so we cannot allow ourselves to claim the existence of the $k + 1^{st}$ division already at the kth checkpoint.

[33] We might ask, for instance, whether there will ever be a conceptual system with exactly 12 fundamental quantities.

Carl Posy

Figure 3.

of the whole sequence once again fails the criterion of determinate identity and hence singularity.

The bottom line of the above discussion is then the following: in each of these cases, the infinitely large and the infinitely small, because our knowledge is receptive, we can have no intuitive grasp of the alleged infinite sequence. And, as I said, there is yet a finer division of the ways in which a collection can be non-infinite.

II. Mathematical intuition and mathematical infinity

5. Regulative grasp and the transcendental project

Before turning to Kant's treatment of mathematical intuition and its grasp of infinity, I need first to say a word about what he calls 'transcendental philosophy' and its special 'regulative' treatment of infinity. Actually, the diagrams that I have been using already give us a glimpse of it. For, in each of them *I already do define and grasp* an infinite path! I spoke in exactly this way when I described what it would mean for the universe to be in fact infinitely large or finite in extent. So, while the diagrams serve to undermine any grasp of an empirical infinite series, they themselves clearly do presuppose a grasp of infinite series of their own.

Why is this legitimate? Because I was talking here at the level of *modeling* scientific inquiry; and I was not engaged in scientific inquiry itself. The formal level at which I was talking defines the project that Kant calls 'transcendental philosophy'. In this project, I abstract away the 'receptivity' of ordinary empirical intuition. Thus, for instance, I do not care what object our crew actually announces at a check point, I merely think about what will happen, if there is or is not a new discovery.

Now at this level of abstraction, Kant says, there is no issue of receptivity. I am addressing questions which I have all the resources to solve. They are questions about my own abilities and limitations. And so, Kant will say, there is now no indeterminacy, and no impediment to defining infinite sequences (just as I did above). Drawing these diagrams, and designating the possible paths within them, this is a crucial project. It gives science its direction and goals. This is what Kant calls the *regulative* force of reason. It tells us about our search, and enjoins us to continue.

Because of this regulative effect on science, this project has what Kant calls *objective validity*. It is a legitimate scientific enterprise. Objective validity, yes; but scientific knowledge, no! The transcendental project gives only guidance. It formulates objects: objects like an infinite path of light circles in Figure 2 (an object which bespeaks a finite universe) or like a path with infinitely many dark circles (corresponding to a universe that is spatially infinite). But it can never prove that either exists. It is 'regulative' but not 'constitutive', in Kant's terms. This means that the transcendental project cannot establish the existence of anything in the world. Indeed, there is no actual intuition here at all. Transcendental philosophy sets goals for our epistemic reach; but it cannot provide the requisite material (not the parts of the universe, and certainly not the entire universe itself) to satisfy our intuitive grasp. Any of these infinite paths can be thought about, but none can ever be known to exist.

In our scientific and philosophical lives we may jump back and forth between the empirical and transcendental projects. The jump is like a Wittgensteinian duck/rabbit. For, we must always remember that the two projects are absolutely separate: they have different subject matters, different rules, and indeed incompatible attitudes towards those infinite paths.

181

Carl Posy

6. The grasp of abstract mathematical space

Coming to mathematics, it too abstracts from the receptive, empirical content of experience. If we use my pen to exemplify a cylinder, then we will abstract from its color and tapering. Similarly, we will imagine this room without its people and its furniture, if we want to exemplify a pure mathematical spatial region. We will also ignore its actual size and volume. But, in so doing, we are not thinking merely of an empty empirical region, we are speaking of pure mathematical space. We can imaginatively expand it, contract it, and translate it at will. When we move to this sort of discourse, once again, there should be no indeterminacy here. And indeed Kant quite explicitly says that:

> It is not so extraordinary as at first seems the case, that a science should be in a position to demand and expect none but assured answers to all the questions within its domain (*quastiones domesticate*), although up to the present they have perhaps not been found. In addition to transcendental philosophy, there are two pure rational sciences, (...) namely, pure mathematics and pure ethics. Has it ever been suggested that, because of our necessary ignorance of the conditions, it must remain uncertain what exact relation, in rational or irrational numbers, a diameter bears to a circle? (A480/B508)

I call Kant 'an epistemic optimist' in mathematics. He holds that all mathematical problems are ultimately solvable. And he believes that because they are *domestic*, they pose no need to wait (receptively) for information to come in from the 'outside'. Thus they pose no threat of an infinite wait.

If we compare this to the empirical situation, then in principle the level of abstraction should once again allow us to grasp an infinite sequence—the expanding sequence of mathematical spatial regions, for instance—for it removes the impediment of 'receptivity'. And, as we saw at the outset, Kant does indeed tell us that we do grasp infinite mathematical space. This resolves the first part of our opening apparent contradiction: the receptivity of empirical knowledge blocks any grasp of empirical infinity, and thus there is no infinite empirical object. Mathematics, like transcendental philosophy, removes that block; and so we do grasp, and there indeed is, mathematical infinity.

But recall that in the Aesthetic Kant goes a step further. In mathematics, he says, unlike transcendental philosophy, our grasp is a legitimate intuition. That was a second contrast with empirical grasp. And, so presently, I will show you that Kant does indeed provide our grasp of mathematical space with all four marks of a legitimate intuition: unity, singularity, immediacy and reference. Having done so, it will be natural to say that mathematics provides us with more than a merely regulative pull; it provides us with an actual infinite object. It is natural to say this, but it will be only partially true. Mathematics will indeed act constitutively, but only 'internally' so. It will not give us an 'actual' infinite object, and we will have yet one more subtle Kantian distinction to make.

7. The grasp of mathematical space: unity and singularity

In the case of mathematical space, we are concerned about the process of extending our grasp from region to region: extending a line, if you like, in three-dimensional space.[34]

A) *Unity*: The unity of space means now that the parts of the space so delivered are related to one another in a graspable organized fashion, and that each part is itself similarly organized. This aspect is codified in the axiomatization of geometry. Each axiom may itself be a synthetic claim,[35] but in codifying the axioms, in forming the axiomatization, geometers revealed the underlying unity of our grasp of space.

B) *Singularity*: Clearly this step by step process itself looks again something like Figure 3 above. In this case each balloon represents a stage in our sequence of extensions, and the bars stand for the regions that have been described.

But while this may be a good schematic model of the 'regulative push' of Reason, it is not the right model of our grasp of mathematical space itself. In this case we already know exactly what we will reach at each stage. We already know now all of the relevant properties of each and every region that we will, or can reach through this process. There are no 'wait and see' imponderables.

Using what I called a mild assertabilism, we can say that even future indicated regions already exist. The situation we have is actually Figure 4.

---

[34] This is clear in the first edition version of the Aesthetic where in speaking of the infinity of mathematical space, Kant says 'If there were no limitlessness in the progression of intuition, no concept of relations could yield a principle of their infinitude' (A25).
[35] See in particular B16–18, B40–41.

Carl Posy

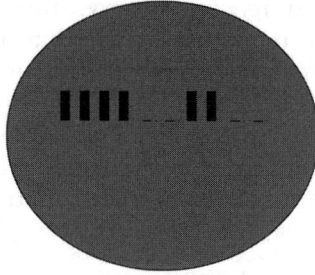

Figure 4.

So we do have a grasp of mathematical space which delivers all its parts, and decides all the relevant predicates. The regulative force does act constitutively here. This tells us that indeed we do have a grasp of a fully infinite space. And it also tells us that our grasp does pass the test of singularity: it delivers predicative completeness, and it thus distinguishes its object from any other object.

We are thus on the way to validating Kant's claim that the grasp is an intuition. What about immediacy? And what about the reference-granting (and existence-granting) tie to actual perception?

8. The grasp of mathematical space: immediacy

Here, I suggest, we should look at Kant's treatment of the continuity of space, which he rests on the visual image of flowing motion. Imagine, for instance, the smooth motion of a hand before your eyes.

In our time (and in Kant's as well) it is natural to turn to an algebraic or analytical expression to depict that motion. It is now, and was then, standard to use equations to study motion in general. Kant knew this, but nonetheless he resorted to the visual description of motion,[36] and the metaphor of flowing[37] to characterize motion. Why?

In one sense Kant is following Aristotle here. He is proposing what I call a 'viscous' conception of continuity: a continuum is viscous

---

[36] 'We cannot think a line without *drawing* it in thought, or a circle without *describing* it' (B155).

[37] 'Space and time are *quanta continua*, because no part of them can be given save as enclosed between limits (points or instants), and therefore only in such fashion that this part is itself again a space or a time. (. . .) Such magnitudes may also be called *flowing*, since the synthesis of productive imagination involved in their production is a progression in time, and the continuity of time is ordinarily designated by the term flowing or flowing away' (A169–70/B211–12).

because its parts stick together, and it is impossible to divide it sharply. Try to cut it, and some part or other will always stick to the knife. Traditionally, the image of a flowing liquid exemplifies this property.

But still mathematics had progressed since Aristotle, and in using visual images here Kant is making an active choice. He is following Euler in a dispute between Euler and D'Alembert about kinematics and mathematics. It is a dispute that came to a head in a disagreement between these two mathematicians about the theory of a vibrating string. D'Alembert, who provided a means to describe the motion of a vibrating string, restricted his treatment to cases in which the initial position of the string was described by an equation. Euler objected that D'Alembert's description was too narrow. He insisted that any general solution to the problem of tracking a vibrating string must be able to consider arbitrary initial conditions, in particular initial conditions which are described by visualizable motion.[38]

I should mention that this disagreement was part of a larger dispute about the role of physical intuition in science and mathematics, a dispute whose roots lay in the Leibnizian tension that I mentioned above. But Euler's position in the specific case of the vibrating string stems from his view that the collection of analytically defined functions does not suffice to give all the ways in which we can pick out points in space. The notion of 'analytically defined function' is an avatar of what I above called 'conceptual grasp'. Euler is effectively saying that conceptual grasp is not enough for the grasp of space. This is, of course, the Kantian version of the condition of immediacy! So Kant sides with Euler and adopts his imagery, because Euler is advocating that the grasp of space must be immediate in Kant's own sense.

So, our grasp of space satisfies the tests of unity, singularity and immediacy. There remains now only the question of reference.

9. The grasp of mathematical space: reference

Here is where the situation is a bit more subtle. On the one hand, clearly Kant believes that mathematical space is 'given'. That is his precise language in the Aesthetic. 'Given' is indeed the code word for reference.

Kant is here exploiting the Leibnizian confluence: the grasp of space meets the criteria of unity, singularity, and immediacy. And therefore

---

[38] 'The various similar parts of the curve are therefore not connected with each other by any law of continuity, and it is only by the description that they are joined together. For this reason it is impossible that all of this curve should be included in any equation', Euler (1755) in Stüssi and Favre (eds.) (1947).

in so far as it satisfies these conditions, the grasp will be referential too. Hence, within our mathematical practice, we readily do refer to space. And in mathematics we allow it along with other mathematical objects to exist. So, speaking in purely mathematical terms, we do have the fourth component, reference, and a full-fledged intuition of infinite mathematical space. The Aesthetic's claim is justified.

But, on the other hand, something is missing here: the causal connection to empirical objects is missing. Yes, inside mathematics there are perfectly good existence claims. But, for Kant, the mark of empirical existence is, as we saw, a *causal* connection to a perceivable object. And that is missing. The same abstraction which gives inner reference in mathematics blocks *empirical* reference. There is none, we have abstracted too far.

To be sure, mathematics is linked to empirical objects as their form. That relation indeed is the ground for mathematics' 'objective validity'.[39] However, mathematical terms do not refer directly to actual empirical objects, but only indirectly, as the forms of such objects. And, from an empirical point of view, mathematical objects in general, and space in particular, have no ontological status:

> Space is merely the form of outer intuition (formal intuition). It is not a real object which can be outwardly intuited. Space, as prior to all things which determine (occupy or limit) it, or rather which give an empirical intuition in accordance with its form, is, under the name of absolute space, nothing but the mere possibility of outer appearances (B457 fn.).

Nor do they exist:

> But in mathematical problems there is no question of (...) existence at all, but only of the properties of the objects in themselves, solely in so far as these properties are connected with the concept of the objects (A719/B747).

---

[39] 'Therefore all concepts, and with them all principles, even such as are possible a priori, relate to empirical intuitions, that is, to the data for a possible experience. Apart from this relation they have no objective validity, and in respect of their representations are a mere play of imagination or of understanding. (...) The mathematician meets this demand by the construction of a figure, which, although produced a priori is an appearance present to the senses. (...) The concept itself is always a priori in origin, and so likewise are the synthetic principles or formulas derived from such concepts; but their employment and their relation to their professed objects can in the end be sought nowhere but in experience, of whose possibility they contain the formal conditions' (A239–40/B298–9).

From an empirical point of view, space is a specter, a nexus of possibilities, but no more than that. In this respect, mathematics, like transcendental philosophy is a separate discourse, a separate project. Like transcendental philosophy, mathematics too is concerned with formal possibilities of empirical experience, rather than with the experience itself. Mathematics gives the 'form' of perceptions. So like transcendental philosophy, mathematics has its own rules, and its own infinity. We have here the same duck/rabbit as in transcendental philosophy. And like transcendental philosophy, mathematics gets its objective validity only in virtue of the fact that it affects empirical objects by giving them their form.

So, this is the Kantian story that I have put before you: on the one hand, receptive empirical intuition of concrete empirical objects, with its endless conjecture, and its splitting of infinity-related concepts; on the other hand, mathematical intuition with optimism, true infinity, but merely spectral objects.

III. Hilbert and Brouwer

Now the pieces are in place to show you how these themes play out in the twentieth century 'foundational debate' between Brouwer and Hilbert. As I said at the start, both of these thinkers were motivated by philosophical as well as mathematical interests, and both wanted to anchor mathematics in human intuition while still accommodating mathematics' need for infinite objects.

10. Brouwer

I shall start with Brouwer. There is a striking difference between Brouwer and Kant on the question of mathematical intuition. For Brouwer, mathematical intuitions give full blooded objects; mathematical objects, to be sure, but objects that exist with no restriction. Thus, for Brouwer, mathematical intuition is fully and directly referential. Moreover, Brouwer's notion of mathematical intuition is not Kantian mathematical intuition, with its built-in epistemic optimism. On the contrary, Brouwer rejects any claim that every mathematical problem is solvable.[40] Brouwer's version of mathematical intuition is, ultimately, a variation on Kant's empirical package.

---

[40] This is a constant theme in Brouwer's thought. See in particular Brouwer (1928).

Carl Posy

Intuition for Brouwer is, as I said, referential; it is also immediate in a very Kantian sense of the term. Brouwer staunchly rejects all attempts to exhaust a mathematical theory by means of formalization or axiomatization. These are the modern versions of D'Alembert's equations and Kant's own 'conceptual grasps'; and for Brouwer they will never play a constitutive role in mathematics.[41] And Brouwer, just like Kant, satisfies the criterion of unity by restricting attention to objects of particular sorts: natural numbers, rationals, real numbers, functions and sequences.

Semantically, Brouwerian mathematical intuition, like Kant's empirical intuition, lies at the base of an assertabilist conception of truth. Indeed Brouwer's philosophy is one of the main inspirations for modern assertabilism.[42] And, like Kant's, Brouwer's is a mild assertabilism: in order to support an existence claim Brouwer does not require an all encompassing grasp that determines all elementary predicates, he is satisfied with a grasp that guarantees that opposing pairs of predicates can be eventually decided. Brouwer's is indeed the modern paradigm of mild assertabilism.

His famous theory of choice sequences highlights this point. A choice sequence is a sequence α of mathematical objects (rational numbers, for instance) which is thought of as growing in time. The determination of its elements might be based upon some algorithm, but it might just as well be dependent upon some non-algorithmic process, even a process of free choice.

Here is a formal definition:

A choice sequence α is given by setting out some preset finite initial segment $<\alpha(1), \alpha(2), \ldots, \alpha(n)>$ together with a growth rule which, given $<\alpha(0), \alpha(1), \ldots, \alpha(n), \ldots, \alpha(k)>$ determines the range of possible choices for $\alpha(k + 1)$.

The important point here is that for Brouwer such a sequence is perfectly intuitable, even though you may well have to wait to determine what occurs at any given stage. Moreover, if you assume the process is eternally continuable, then the sequence is a legitimately infinite object.

---

[41] See *op. cit.*

[42] Brouwer's student, Arend Heyting, gave one of the initial formulations of inductively defined truth conditions for assertabilism. And he did this as part of an attempt to formalize the reasoning that underlay Brouwer's intuitionistic mathematics. Dummett's book on intuitionism (1977) centers on this aspect of Brouwer's thought.

Consider for instance the real number r defined as follows:

r = 0.499...n... such that at some point onward we freely choose the digits in that decimal expansion, or throw a 10 sided die.

For Brouwer this is a perfectly good real number. Although we do not have all the parts (i.e., digits) in hand, we know that we can get each and every one of them. And that is enough to say of each and every one of them that it exists, and thus, of the sequence, that it proceeds to infinity.

Even more striking is the fact that in his most mature work Brouwer actually introduces an explicit mathematical parallel to the receptive side of Kant's empirical discourse. He does this with his notion of sequences generated by the solving of mathematical problems. As an example, let us suppose that we track the progress of a mathematical crew working on Goldbach's conjecture. You might, if you like, think of the entire mathematical community, or some idealized mathematician who has no finite limit to his active research life. The main thing is that we get a progress report once a month. Now let the number $r^{\#}$ be defined as follows:

$r^{\#} = 0.4\ d_2 d_3 \ldots d_n \ldots$, where the $d_n = 9$ if by the nth month, neither a proof nor a refutation has yet been found for Goldbach's conjecture. If the conjecture is decided during month k, then for all $j \geq k$, $d_j = 0$.

Instead of the astronomical crew that we imagined in the Kantian case we now imagine a mathematical research crew which reports back regularly on its efforts to prove or refute Goldbach's conjecture (of course, any other unsolved mathematical problem will do). The Kantian parallel is quite striking: we need to wait at each stage of research to hear the outcome at that stage. And, indeed, we have the same issue of a possible eternal wait. As I said, Brouwer is quite persuaded that we cannot assume every mathematical problem is solvable. But if the problem is not solvable—if the conjecture is neither provable nor refutable—then, of course, we might go on forever not knowing that, and like Uncle Patros in the novel,[43] hoping that the solution is just over the horizon.[44]

---

[43] Doxiadis (2000).

[44] A note for *aficionados*: those Kantian paths in Figures 1 and 2 can represent Brouwerian choice sequences. In earlier work, I have used diagrams such as these to represent Kripke models, and then have used the intuitionistic reading of the logical particles to provide a precise account of some

Carl Posy

The real numbers r and $r^{\#}$ show us that Brouwer—again like the empirical Kant—admits a degree of indeterminacy into his discourse. Thus, we know that the number r is in the interval [0, 1] and that r is not greater than $1/2$; but we do not know, and perhaps may never know whether $r = 1/2$, (which would happen if the digit 9 is chosen for ever) or whether $r < 1/2$ (which would happen if some other digit is ever chosen).

And, because of this, Brouwer too will have a 'splitting of concepts': for r and $r^{\#}$ are not greater than $1/2$; but neither can we say that they are less than $1/2$ or equal to it. So we have a new finer-grained notion of 'not greater than'.[45]

Here is one place where Brouwer deviates from Kant's empirical picture of intuition. Notice that it is identity that is undecidable here. Our intuitive grasp of neither r nor $r^{\#}$ suffices to distinguish between the number grasped and $1/2$. By the same token, these intuitions cannot assure predicative completeness. So, this is indeed a *variant* of Kant's empirical theory. Brouwer's version dispenses with the Kantian notion of singularity.

But notwithstanding this deviation, it is important to observe that all of this is in service of a mathematical but still deeply Kantian position, i.e. the viscous continuum. Early in his career, Brouwer adopted quite the Kantian description of this viscosity and its intuitive basis:

> Having recognized that the intuition of 'fluidity' is as primitive as that of several things conceived as forming a unit together, the latter being at the basis of every mathematical construction, we are able to state properties of the continuum as a 'matrix of points to be thought of as a whole'. (. . .) However, the *continuum as a whole* was given to us by intuition; a construction for it, an

---

Kantian arguments and concepts. In particular, with an appropriate interpretation of the predicate B, Figure 1 will validate the formula $\forall x \sim \sim \exists y\, B(x, y)$, (i.e., given any x, you cannot deny that there will be a y such that $B(x, y)$ holds) while Figure 4 will validate $\forall x \exists y\, B(x, y)$ (i.e., given any x, you can affirmatively assert that there will be a y such that $B(x, y)$ holds). The difference between these two formulae (read intuitionistically) nicely summarizes the difference between regulative force, on the one hand, and constitutive claims, on the other. See for instance Posy (1992). Figure 1 here gives a more fine tuned account of Kant's reasoning than the diagrams I used in this and some other papers.

[45]   Indeed we can say definitely that $r^{\#} \neq 1/2$, though still we are not entitled to say $r^{\#} < 1/2$. Brouwer (1925) actually has an elaborate analysis of the 'splitting of mathematical concepts'.

action that would create from the mathematical intuition 'all' its points as individuals, is inconceivable and impossible' Brouwer (1907).

But within ten years of the Dissertation, Brouwer found a way to express this viscosity, and exploited his theory of choice sequences to prove it without appealing to a special intuition of flowing. Here is a precise expression of this viscous continuum:

There are no disjoint non-empty A and B such that $\Re = A \cup B$.

As for proving that it characterizes the continuum: suppose that the continuum could be split at (say) $1/2$. If it could, then we could form the two disjoint non-empty sets $A = \{x|x < 1/2\}$ and $B = \{x|x \geq 1/2\}$ and we would indeed have $\Re = A \cup B$. But our two indeterminate numbers r and $r^{\#}$ show that this is not possible. For we have seen that they cannot be put into either one of these sets.

Indeed, Brouwer's notorious continuity theorem is simply a general proof of this overall viscosity. For, if the continuum could be split at $1/2$, then we could define a discontinuous total function f, such that

$$f(x) = 1 \quad \text{for} \{x|x < 1/2\}$$

$$f(x) = 2 \quad \text{for} \{x|x \geq 1/2\}.$$

In this case, our two numbers r and $r^{\#}$, give us points at which such a function cannot be defined. And so the function cannot be total. Brouwer's proof of the theorem in general terms shows that the continuum cannot be split anywhere. It is the mathematically most sophisticated statement of viscosity.

So Brouwer's deviant mathematics is not just a crotchety constructivism about existence claims. Even with its deviation on singularity, it is a deeply Kantian view about the interplay of intuitive grasp, receptivity, and infinity (keeping in mind that it is Kant's theory of empirical intuitive grasp that provides the analogy here).

11. Hilbert

Now we can see that, by contrast, the heart of Hilbert's position is Kant's model of mathematical intuition. Quite explicitly Hilbert adopts Kant's epistemic optimism within mathematics, declaring famously: '[T]here is no *ignorabimus* in mathematics'.[46] Indeed,

---

[46]   Hilbert (1926).

Carl Posy

Hilbert's epistemic optimism was one of the central bones of contention in the debate with Brouwer, and Brouwer sometimes made it seem as though this was for Hilbert a baseless article of faith. But, in fact, Hilbert adopts this view for precisely Kantian reasons. The full quotation is:

> There is the problem, find the answer; you can find it just by thinking, for there is no *ignorabimus* in mathematics (*ibid.*)

You are assured that you can in principle solve the problem, because it is only a matter of thinking about it. There is no receptivity to block finding the solution.

Moreover, Hilbert follows very closely Kant's picture of the relation of pure mathematics to the empirical realm. Hilbert wants mathematics to proceed internally on its own, even beyond the bounds of empirical intuition. But he insists that those transcendental elements of mathematics are 'ideal' (what I called 'spectral') objects, with no causal connection to the physical world.

> We have established that the universe is finite in two respects, i.e., as regards to the infinitely small and the infinitely large. . . . (*ibid.*)

> [S]imilarly, to preserve the simple formal rules of ordinary Aristotelian logic, we must supplement the finitary statements with ideal statements (*ibid.*).

And he wants ideal mathematics to gain 'objective validity' by anchoring it in empirical intuition. Formally, that anchoring is by axiomatization in a formal system. But it is important to note that Hilbert strives to show that this anchoring rests on a grasp that meets the needs of a true intuition. And here he adopts two of Kant's conditions of sensory empirical intuition: immediacy and singularity which, in turn, he says, give a grasp of the whole. Indeed, his picture of the empirical component is Kantian even to the point of using surveyability in place of the 'on the spot' grasp:

> [A]s a condition for the use of logical inference and the performance of logical operations, something must already be given to our faculty of representation, certain extra-logical concrete objects that are intuitively present as immediate experience prior to all thought. If logical inference is to be reliable, it must be possible to survey these objects completely in all their parts, and the fact that they occur, that they differ from one another, and that they follow each other, or are concatenated, is immediately given intuitively, together with the object, as something that can neither be reduced to anything else nor requires

reduction. This is the basic philosophical position that I consider requisite for mathematics, and in general for all scientific thinking, understanding and communication (*ibid.*)

Most of all, Hilbert's notorious ε-symbol (sometimes called a choice operator) represents the ideal objects. In particular, εxFx picks out an x such that Fx holds, if there is one, and gives nothing, if there is not. Now suppose that F represents one of the infinite sequences about which I have been speaking, and which, in an empirical context, defines a regulative pull. This can be a sequence which might lead to an eternal wait. It could also be a sequence based upon the solution of an as yet unsolved mathematical problem. Then Hilbert's ε-Axiom

$$F(\varepsilon xFx) \leftrightarrow \exists xFx$$

simply translates quite precisely the Kantian principle that in mathematics the regulative does act constitutively.

So there is no mean spirited taunting here. There is a sophisticated rendition of a deep Kantian principle, right where it should be!

12. Echoes

There is much more to be said both in setting out the Kantian picture and in refining the points of contact with (and of deviation from) the twentieth-century applications. But, for now, let me add just one important *caveat*.

My subheading speaks of 'echoes', and not of 'influences'. I do not want to claim, or even to hint, that either Brouwer or Hilbert was influenced by reading Kant directly (and indeed reading him in the way that I do) and then applied his insights to their own philosophical penchants. There is substantial historical work to be done about that.

My point here, rather, is that the parallels are interesting even without establishing an historical link. They stem from the issue itself: how can a finite intuitive grasp confront inherently infinitary mathematical thought? The cross-generational comparison that I have sketched teaches us that when we formulate this question in terms of infinite series, then both the question and its potential answers have internal structures that remain stable across the generations.[47]

[47] I owe special thanks to Michela Massimi for her support and patience.

References

Please note that works are identified by the original date of publication, followed by the publication date of the edition used. When a different translation or edition of the same text has been used by contributors, to respect their intellectual choice, this has been left unaltered, and indicated in the text as appropriate.

Immanuel Kant's works cited in this volume

Kant, I. (1766) *Träume eines Geistersehers, erläutert durch Träume der Metaphysik*. In *Kants gesammelte Schriften* (Berlin: de Gruyter); Ak 2: 315–73. English translation (1992) 'Dreams of a spirit-seer elucidated by dreams of metaphysics', in D. Walford and R. Meerbote (eds.) *Theoretical Philosophy 1755–1770*, The Cambridge Edition of the Works of Immanuel Kant (Cambridge: Cambridge University Press), 301–360.

Kant, I. (1781/1787) *Kritik der reinen Vernunft* (Riga: Johann Hartknoch). In *Kants gesammelte Schriften* (Berlin: de Gruyter); Ak 4: 1–252; 2nd edition Ak 3: 1–552. English translation (1997) *Critique of Pure Reason*, by P. Guyer and A. W. Wood, The Cambridge Edition of the Works of Immanuel Kant (Cambridge: Cambridge University Press).

Kant, I. (1786) *Metaphysische Anfangsgründe der Naturwissenschaft* (Riga: Johann Hartknoch). In *Kants gesammelte Schriften* (Berlin: de Gruyter); Ak 4: 465–565. English translation (2004) *Metaphysical Foundations of Natural Science*, by M. Friedman (Cambridge: Cambridge University Press).

Kant, I. (1790) *Kritik der Urteilskraft* (Berlin: Lagarde). In *Kants gesammelte Schriften* (Berlin: de Gruyter); Ak 5:165–485. English translation (2000) *Critique of the Power of Judgment*, by P. Guyer and E. Matthews, The Cambridge Edition of the Works of Immanuel Kant (Cambridge: Cambridge University Press).

Kant, I. (1793/1804) *Welches sind die wirklichen Fortschritte, die die Metaphysik seit Leibnitzens und Wolf's Zeiten in Deutschland gemacht hat?*. In *Kants gesammelte Schriften* (Berlin: de Gruyter); Ak 20: 259–351. English translation (2002) 'What Real Progress Has Metaphysics Made in Germany since the Time of Leibniz and Wolff?', in H. Allison and P. Heath (eds.) *Theoretical Philosophy after 1781*, The Cambridge Edition of the Works of Immanuel Kant (Cambridge: Cambridge University Press), 337–424.

Kant, I. (1936, 1938) *Opus postumum*. In *Kants gesammelte Schriften* (Berlin: de Gruyter); Ak 21, 22. English translation (1993) *Opus postumum*, by E. Förster and M. Rosen, The Cambridge Edition of the Works of Immanuel Kant (Cambridge: Cambridge University Press).

doi:10.1017/S1358246108000106   © The Royal Institute of Philosophy and the contributors 2008

References

Other sources

Adelung, J. C. (1793) *Grammatisch-kritisches Wörterbuch der Hochdeutschen Mundart*, (Leipzig: Breitkopf).

Alexander, H. G. (ed.) (1956) *The Leibniz–Clarke Correspondence*, (Manchester: Manchester University Press).

Allison, H. E. (2004) *Kant's Transcendental Idealism: An Interpretation and Defense*, revised edition, (New Haven and London: Yale University Press).

Anderson, P. (1972) 'More is Different', *Science* **177**, 393–96.

Bangu, S. (2008) 'Reifying mathematics? Prediction and symmetry classification', *Studies in History and Philosophy of Modern Physics* **39**, 239–258.

Beck, L. W. (1968) 'The Kantianism of Lewis', in Schilpp (1968), 271–285.

Bergson, H. (1907) *L'évolution créatrice*, (Paris: F. Alcan). English translation (1911) *Creative Evolution*, by A. Mitchell (London: Macmillan).

Bertoloni Meli, D. (in press) 'The axiomatic tradition in 17th century mechanics', in M. Domski and M. Dickson (eds.) *Discourse on a new method: reinvigorating the marriage of history and philosophy of science* (Open Court).

Bogen, J. and Woodward, J. (1988) 'Saving the Phenomena', *Philosophical Review* **97**, 303–352.

Brading, K. and Castellani, E. (eds.) (2003) *Symmetries in Physics*, (Cambridge: Cambridge University Press).

Brading, K. and Brown, H. (2003) 'Symmetries and Noether's Theorems', in K. Brading and E. Castellani (eds.) *Symmetries in Physics: Philosophical Reflections*, (Cambridge: Cambridge University Press).

Brading, K. and Ryckman, T. (2008) 'Hilbert's "Foundations of Physics": Gravitation and Electromagnetism within the Axiomatic Method', *Studies in History and Philosophy of Modern Physics* **39**, 102–153.

Brouwer, L. E. J. (1907) *Over de Grondslagen der Wiskunde*, Dissertation, University of Amsterdam.

Brouwer, L. E. J. (1925) 'Zur Intuitionistiche Zerlegung mathematischer Grundbegriffe', *Jahresbericht deutsch. Math. Ver.*, **33**, 251–256. Reprinted in A. Heyting (ed.) (1975) *Collected Works*, vol. I, (Amsterdam: North-Holland), 295–297.

Brouwer, L. E. J. (1928) 'Intuitionistische Betrachtungen über den Formalissmus', *Proc. Akad. Amsterdam* **31**, 374–9.

Buchdahl, G. (1992) *Kant and the Dynamics of Reason*, (London: Blackwell Publishing).

Carlson, T. (1997) 'James and the Kantian Tradition', in R. A. Putnam (ed.) *The Cambridge Companion to William James*, (Cambridge: Cambridge University Press), 363–383.

References

Carrier, M. (2001) 'Kant's Mechanical Determination of Matter in the *Metaphysical Foundations of Natural Science*', in E. Watkins (ed.) *Kant and the Sciences*, (Oxford: Oxford University Press), 117–135.

Caygill, H. (2005) 'The force of Kant's *Opus postumum*. Kepler and Newton in the XIth fascicle', *Angelaki* **10**, 33–42.

Chang, H. (2001) 'How to Take Realism Beyond Foot-Stamping', *Philosophy* **76**, 5–30.

Chang, H. (in press) 'Ontological Principles and the Intelligibility of Epistemic Activities', in H. de Regt, S. Leonelli and K. Eigner (eds.) *Philosophical Perspectives on Scientific Understanding*, (Pittsburgh: University of Pittsburgh Press).

Corry, L., Renn, J. and Stachel, J. (1997) 'Belated Decision in the Hilbert–Einstein Priority Dispute', *Science* **278**, 1270–3.

Debs, T. and Redhead, M. (2007) *Objectivity, Invariance and Convention: Symmetry in Physical Science*, (Cambridge, MA: Harvard University Press).

De Regt, H. and Dieks, D. (2005) 'A Contextual Approach to Scientific Understanding', *Synthese* **144**, 137–170.

DiSalle, R. (1988) *Space, Time, and Inertia in the Foundations of Newtonian Physics*, Doctoral Dissertation: University of Chicago.

DiSalle, R. (1991) 'Conventionalism and the Origins of the Inertial Frame Concept', *Philosophy of Science Association 1990*, vol. 2, 139–147.

DiSalle, R. (2002) 'Reconsidering Ernst Mach on Space, Time, and Motion', in D. Malament (ed.) *Reading Natural Philosophy: Essays in the History and Philosophy of Science and Mathematics*, (Chicago: Open Court), 167–191.

DiSalle, R. (2006) *Understanding Space-Time: The Philosophical Development of Physics from Newton to Einstein*, (Cambridge: Cambridge University Press).

Doxiadis, A. (2000) *Uncle Patros and Goldbach's Conjecture*, (Faber and Faber).

Duhem, P. (1906) *La Théorie Physique: Son Object, Sa Structure* (Paris: Marcel Rivière). English translation (1962) *The Aim and Structure of Physical Theory*, by P. P. Wiener, (New York: Atheneum).

Duhem, P. (1908) 'ΣΩZEIN TA ΦAINOMENA: Essay sur la notion de théorie physique de Platon à Galilée', *Annales de philosophie chrétienne* 79/156, 113–38. English translation (1969) *To Save the Phenomena. An essay on the idea of physical theory from Plato to Galileo*, (Chicago: University of Chicago Press).

Dummett, M. (1977) *Elements of Intuitionism*, (Oxford: Clarendon Press).

Dummett, M. (1978) *Truth and Other Enigmas*, (Cambridge, MA: Harvard University Press).

Dummett, M. (1991) *The Logical Basis of Metaphysics*, (Cambridge, MA: Harvard University Press).

Dupré, J. (1993) *The Disorder of Things*, (Cambridge, MA: Harvard University Press).

References

Earman, J. *et al.* (eds.) (1993) *Philosophical Problems of the Internal and External World: Essays on the Philosophy of Adolf Grünbaum*, (Pittsburgh: University of Pittsburgh Press).

Eberhard, J. A. (1819) *Versuch einer allgemeinen deutschen Synonymik in einem kritisch-philosophischen Wörterbuche der sinnverwandten Wörter der hochdeutschen Mundart*, (Halle und Leipzig: Ruffschen Buchhandlung).

Einstein, A. (1905) 'Zur Elektrodynamik bewegter Körper', *Annalen der Physik* **17**, 891–921. English translation (1923) 'On the Electrodynamics of Moving Bodies', in H. A. Lorentz (*et al.*) *The Principle of Relativity: A Collection of Original Memoirs on the Special and General Theories of Relativity*, (London: Methuen).

Einstein, A. (1921) *Geometrie und Erfahrung. Erweiterte Fassung des Festvortrages gehalten an der Preussischen Akademie der Wissenschaft zu Berlin am 27. Januar 1921*, (Berlin: Springer). English translation (1923) 'Geometry and Experience', in G. Jeffrey and W. Perrett (eds.) *Sidelights on Relativity*, (London: Methuen).

Einstein, A. (1925) 'Nichteuklidische Geometrie und Physik', *Die neue Rundschau* **36**, 16–20.

Einstein, A. (1979) *Mein Weltbild*, (Frankfurt a.M.: Ullstein).

Euler, L. (1755) *Remarques sur les mémoires précédens de M. Bernoulli*, in F. Stüssi and H. Favre (eds.) (1947) *Opera Omnia*, Series secunda, vol. 10 (Birkhäuser).

Falkenburg, B. (1988) 'The Unifying Role of Symmetry Principles in Particle Physics' *Ratio* **1**, 113–134.

Feyerabend, P. (1975) *Against Method: Outline of an Anarchist Theory of Knowledge*, (London: New Left Books).

Folina, J. (1992) *Poincaré and the Philosophy of Mathematics*, (New York: Macmillan).

Förster, E. (2000) *Kant's Final Synthesis. An essay on the Opus postumum*, (Cambridge, MA.: Harvard University Press).

Frank, P. (1949) *Modern Science and Its Philosophy*, (Cambridge, MA.: Harvard University Press).

Frege, G. (1884) *Die Grundlagen der Arithmetik*, (Breslau: Wilhelm Koebner). English translation (1950) *The Foundations of Arithmetic*, by J. L. Austin (Evanston, IL.: Northwestern University Press).

Friedman, M. (1991) 'Regulative and constitutive', *The Southern Journal of Philosophy* **30**, Suppl., 73–102.

Friedman, M. (1992a) *Kant and the Exact Sciences*, (Cambridge, MA.: Harvard University Press).

Friedman, M. (1992b) 'Causal laws and the foundations of natural science', in P. Guyer (ed.) *The Cambridge Companion to Kant*, (Cambridge: Cambridge University Press), 161–99.

Friedman, M. (1997) 'Helmholtz's *Zeichentheorie* and Schlick's *Allgemeine Erkenntnislehre*: Early Logical Empiricism and its Nineteenth-Century Background', *Philosophical Topics* **25**, 19–50.

References

Friedman, M. (1999) *Reconsidering Logical Positivism*, (Cambridge: Cambridge University Press).

Friedman, M. (2000) 'Geometry, Construction, and Intuition in Kant and his Successors', in G. Scher and R. Tieszen (eds.) *Between Logic and Intuition: Essays in Honor of Charles Parsons*, (Cambridge: Cambridge University Press).

Friedman, M. (2001a) *Dynamics of Reason. The 1999 Kant Lectures at Stanford University*, (Stanford: CSLI Publications).

Friedman, M. (2001b) 'Matter and Motion in the Metaphysical Foundations and the First Critique', in E. Watkins (ed.) *Kant and the Sciences*, (Oxford: Oxford University Press), 53–69.

Friedman, M. (2002) 'Geometry as a Branch of Physics: Background and Context for Einstein's "Geometry and Experience"', in D. Malament (ed.) *Reading Natural Philosophy: Essays in the History and Philosophy of Science and Mathematics*, (Chicago: Open Court), 193–229.

Galilei, G. (1638) *Discorsi e Dimostrazioni Matematiche intorno a due nuove scienze*, in A. Favaro (ed.) (1890–1909) *Opere di Galileo Galilei*, vol. VIII, (Firenze: Barbera Editrice). English translation (1914) *Discourses and Mathematical Demonstrations concerning Two New Sciences*, by H. Crew and A. de Salvio, (New York: Dover Publications).

George, A. (ed.) (1994) *Mathematics and Mind*, (New York: Oxford University Press).

Goodman, N. (1978) *Ways of worldmaking*, (Indianapolis: Hackett Publishing Company).

Gray, J. (2000) *The Hilbert Challenge. A perspective on twentieth century mathematics*, (New York: Oxford University Press).

Grene, M. (1974) *The Knower and the Known*, (Berkeley and Los Angeles: University of California Press).

Gross, D. (1995) 'Symmetry in Physics: Wigner's Legacy', *Physics Today* **50**, 46–50.

Guyer, P. (1990) 'Reason and Reflective Judgement: Kant on the Significance of Systematicity', *Nous* **24**, 17–43.

Hartman, R. and Schwarz, W. (eds.) (1974) *Immanuel Kant: Logic*, (Indianapolis: Bobbs-Merrill).

Hatfield, G. (1990) *The Natural and the Normative: Theories of Spatial Perception from Kant to Helmholtz*, (Cambridge, MA.: MIT Press).

Hilbert, D. (1915a) 'Die Grundlagen der Physik (Erste Mitteilung)', annotated *'Erste Korrektur meiner erste Note'*, printer's stamp date '6 Dez. 1915'. Göttingen, SUB Cod. Ms. 634. English translation (2007) as 'The Foundations of Physics (First Communication), First Proof of my First Note', in J. Renn (ed.), *The Genesis of General Relativity*, vol. 4, *Gravitation in the Twilight of Classical Physics: The Promise of Mathematics*, (Dordrecht: Springer), 989–1001.

Hilbert, D. (1915b) 'Die Grundlagen der Physik (Erste Mitteilung)', *Nachrichten Königliche Gesellschaft der Wissenschaften zu Göttingen. Mathematische-Phyikalische Klasse*, 395–407. English translation (2007)

References

as 'The Foundations of Physics (First Communication)', in J. Renn (ed.), *The Genesis of General Relativity*, vol. 4, *Gravitation in the Twilight of Classical Physics: The Promise of Mathematics*, (Dordrecht: Springer), 1003–1015.

Hilbert, D. (1917) 'Die Grundlagen der Physik (Zweite Mitteilung)', *Nachrichten Königliche Gesellschaft der Wissenschaften zu Göttingen. Mathematische-Phyikalische Klasse*, 53–76.

Hilbert, D. (1918) 'Axiomatisches Denken', *Mathematische Annalen* **78**, 405–15.

Hilbert, D. (1922) 'Neubegründung der Mathematik', *Abhandlungen aus dem mathematischen Seminar der Hamburgischen Universität* **1**, 157–77.

Hilbert, D. (1926) 'Über das Unendliche', *Mathematische Annalen* **95**, 161–90.

Hilbert, D. (1930) 'Naturerkennen und Logik', *Die Naturwissenschften* **17**, 959–63. Reprinted in Hilbert (1935), 378–87.

Hilbert, D. (1935) *Gesammelte Abhandlungen*. Bd. III (Berlin: J. Springer).

Hilbert, D. (1992) *Natur und mathematische Erkennen. Vorlesungen, gehalten 1919–20 in Göttingen. Nach der Ausarbeitung von Paul Bernays*, edited by D. Rowe (Basel–Boston–Berlin: Birkhäuser).

Hooper, W. (1998) 'Inertial problems in Galileo's preinertial framework', in Machamer P. (ed.) *The Cambridge Companion to Galileo*, (Cambridge: Cambridge University Press), 146–174.

Jevons, S. (1874) *The Principles of Science*, (London: MacMillan and Co.).

Kellert, S. H., Longino, H. E. and Waters, C. K. (eds.) (2006) *Scientific Pluralism*, Minnesota Studies in the Philosophy of Science, vol. 19, (Minneapolis: University of Minnesota Press).

Kitcher, P. (1983) 'Kant's Philosophy of Science', Midwest Studies in Philosophy, Volume VIII (Minneapolis: University of Minnesota Press), 387–407.

Kitcher, P. (1986) 'Projecting the Order of Nature', in R. Butts (ed.) *Kant's Philosophy of Physical Science*, Western Ontario Series in the Philosophy of Science (Dordrecht: Reidel), 201–238.

Klein, F. (1917) 'Zu Hilberts erster Note über die Grundlagen der Physik', *Nachrichten Königliche Gesellschaft der Wissenschaften zu Göttingen. Mathematische-Phyikalische Klasse*, 469–82. Reprinted, with additions, in Klein (1921), 553–67.

Klein, F. (1921) *Gesammelte Abhandlungen*, Bd.I, (Berlin: J. Springer).

Klein, J. (1968) *Greek Mathematical Thought and the Origin of Algebra*, (New York: Dover).

Kockelmans, J. J. (ed.) (1968) *Philosophy of Science: The Historical Background*, (New York: The Free Press).

Koyré, A. (1939) *Etudes Galiléennes*, (Paris: Hermann). English translation (1978) *Galileo Studies*, by J. Mepham, (NJ: Humanities Press).

Kripke, S. (1972) *Naming and Necessity*, in G. Harman and D. Davidson (eds.) *Semantics of Natural Language*, (Dordrecht: Reidel). Paperback edition 1981, (Oxford: Blackwell Publishers).

References

Kuehn, M. (2001) *Kant: A Biography*, (Cambridge: Cambridge University Press).

Laughlin, R. and Pines, D. (2000) 'The Theory of Everything', *Proceedings of the National Academy of Science* **97**, 28–31.

Leibniz, G. W. (1686a) *Discourse on Metaphysics*, in L. E. Loemker (ed.) (1969) *Gottfried Wilhelm Leibniz: Philosophical Papers and Letters*, Second Edition, (Dordrecht: Reidel).

Leibniz, G. (1686b) 'General Inquiries about the Analysis of Concepts and Truths', in G.H.R. Parkinson (ed.) (1966) *Leibniz: Logical Papers*, (Oxford: Oxford University Press).

Leibniz, G. W. (1704) *New Essays on Human Understanding*, translated and edited by P. Remnant and J. Bennett (1981), (Cambridge: Cambridge University Press).

Lewis, C. I. (1929) *Mind and the World Order: Outline of a Theory of Knowledge*, (New York: Dover).

Lipschitz, R. (1877) *Lehrbuch der Analysis*, (Bonn: Max Cohen & Sohn).

Longuenesse, B. (1998) *Kant and the Capacity to Judge: sensibility and discursivity in the Transcendental Analytic of the Critique of Pure Reason*, (Princeton NJ: Princeton University Press).

Mainzer, K. (1996) *Symmetries of Nature*, (Berlin: de Gruyter).

Majer, U. (1993a) 'Hilberts Methode der Idealen Elemente und Kants regulativer Gebrauch der Ideen', *Kant-Studien* **84**, 51–77.

Majer, U. (1993b) 'Different Forms of Finitism', in Johannes Czermak (ed.) *Philosophie der Mathematik: Akten des 15. Internationalen Wittgenstein Symposiums*, (Wien: Verlag Hölder-Pichler-Tempsky), 185–94.

Majer, U. (1995) 'Geometry, Intuition and Experience: From Kant to Husserl', *Erkenntnis* **42**, 261–85.

Massimi, M. (2007) 'Saving unobservable phenomena', *British Journal for the Philosophy of Science* **58**, 235–262.

Morrison, M. (1989) 'Methodological Rules in Kant's Philosophy of Science', *Kant-Studien* **80**, 155–172.

Morrison, M. (2000) *Unifying Scientific Theories: Physical Concepts and Mathematical Structures*, (Cambridge: Cambridge University Press).

Murphey, M. (2005) *C. I. Lewis: The Last Great Pragmatist*, (Albany, N.Y.: SUNY Press).

Norman, J. (2006) *After Euclid*, (CSLI Publications. Chicago: Chicago University Press).

Norton, J. (1985) 'What Was Einstein's Principle of Equivalence?', *Studies in History and Philosophy of Science* **16**, 203–246. Reprinted in D. Howard and J. Stachel (eds.) (1989) *Einstein and the History of General Relativity*, (Boston: Birkhäuser).

Parsons, C. (1984) 'Arithmetic and the Categories', *Topoi* **3**, 109–121.

Paton, H. J. (1936) *Kant's Metaphysic of Experience: A Commentary on the First Half of the* Kritik der reinen Vernunft, 2 volumes, (London: Allen & Unwin).

References

Pauli, W. (1921) 'Relativitätstheorie', in *Encyklopädie der mathematischen Wissenschaften*, vol. 19, (Leipzig: B.G. Teubner). English translation (1958) *The Theory of Relativity*, (Oxford and New York: Pergamon Press).

Pecere, P. (2006) 'Space, aether and the possibility of physics in Kant's late thought. From the *Metaphysische Anfangsgründe der Naturwissenschaft* to the *Opus postumum*', in C. Cellucci and P. Pecere (eds.) *Demonstrative and non-demonstrative reasoning in mathematics and natural science*, (Edizioni dell'Università degli Studi di Cassino), 237–306.

Plaass, P. (1965) *Kants Theorie der Naturwissenschaft*, (Gottingen: Vandenhoeck and Ruprecht). English translation (1994) *Kant's Theory of Natural Science*, (Dordrecht: Kluwer).

Poincaré, H. (1902) *La Science et l'Hypothèse*, (Paris: Flammarion). Translated as *Science and Hypothesis* in Poincaré (1913b).

Poincaré, H. (1912) 'Pourquoi l'espace a trois dimensions', *Revue de Métaphysique et de Morale* **20**, 483–504. Reprinted in Poincaré (1913a).

Poincaré, H. (1913a) *Dernières Pensées*, (Paris: Flammarion). Translated by J. Buldoc (1963) as *Mathematics and Science: Last Essays*, (New York: Dover).

Poincaré, H. (1913b) *The Foundations of Science*, translated and edited by G. Halstead, (Lancaster: Science Press).

Posy, C. (1992) 'Kant's Mathematical Realism', in C. Posy (ed.) *Kant's Philosophy of Mathematics: Modern Essays* (Kluwer).

Posy, C. (2000) 'Immediacy and the Birth of Reference in Kant: The Case for Space', in G. Sher and R. Tieszen (eds.) *Between Logic and Intuition: Essays in Honour of Charles Parsons*, (Cambridge: Cambridge University Press).

Posy, C. (2003) 'Between Leibniz and Mill: Kant's Logic and the Rhetoric of Psychologism', in D. Jacquette (ed.) *Philosophy, Psychology and Psychologism* (Kluwer).

Putnam, H. (1975) 'The Meaning of "Meaning"', in *Mind, Language and Reality: Philosophical Papers*, vol. 2, (Cambridge: Cambridge University Press).

Putnam, H. (1981) *Reason, Truth and History*, (Cambridge: Cambridge University Press).

Putnam, H. (1982) 'Why there is not a ready-made world', *Synthese* **51**, 141–67.

Reich, K. (1932) *Die Vollständigkeit der kantischen Urteilstafel*, (Berlin: Schoetz).

Reichenbach, H. (1920) *Relativitätstheorie und Erkenntnis Apriori*, (Berlin: Springer). English translation (1965) *The Theory of Relativity and A Priori Knowledge*, by M. Reichenbach, (Berkeley and Los Angeles: University of California Press).

Reichenbach, H. (1935) *Wahrschenlichkeitslehre*, (Leiden: Sijthoff). English translation (1971) *The Theory of Probability*, by E. H. Hutten and M. Reichenbach, second edition, (Berkeley: University of California Press).

References

Renn, J. and Stachel, J. (1999) *Hilbert's Foundation of Physics: From a Theory of Everything to a Constituent of General Relativity*, (Berlin: Max-Planck-Institut für Wissenschaftsgeschichte, Preprint 118). Reprinted in J. Renn (ed.) (2007) *The Genesis of General Relativity*, vol. 4, *Gravitation in the Twilight of Classical Physics: The Promise of Mathematics*, (Dordrecht: Springer), 857–973.

Riemann, B. (1867) 'Über die Hypothesen, welche der Geometrie zugrunde liegen', *Göttinger Abhandlungen* **13**, 133–152.

Rosenthal, S. B. (1976) *The Pragmatic A Priori: A Study in the Epistemology of C. I. Lewis*, (St. Louis, Missouri: Warren H. Green, Inc.).

Rosenthal, S. B. (2007) *C. I. Lewis in Focus: The Pulse of Pragmatism*, (Bloomington: Indiana University Press).

Ryckman, T. A. (2005) *The Reign of Relativity: Philosophy in Physics 1915–1925*, (Oxford: Oxford University Press).

Salmon, W. C. (1988) 'Rational Prediction', in A. Grünbaum and W. C. Salmon (eds.) *The Limitations of Deductivism*, (Berkeley and Los Angeles: University of California Press), 47–60.

Schilpp, P. A. (ed.) (1968) *The Philosophy of C. I. Lewis*, The Library of Living Philosophers, vol. 13, (La Salle, Illinois: Open Court).

Schröder, E. (1873) *Lehrbuch der Arithmetik und Algebra*, (Leipzig: Teubner).

Schultz, J. (1784) *Erläuterungen über des herrn Professor Kant 'Critik der reinen Vernunft'* (Königsberg: Hartungschen Buchhandlung). The 1791 edition is reprinted in Schultz J. (1968) *Aetas Kantiana* (Bruxelles: Culture et Civilisation). English translation (1995) *Exposition of Kant's 'Critique of Pure Reason'*, by J. C. Morrison, (Ottawa: University of Ottawa Press).

Schultz, J. (1789) *Prüfung der Kantischen Critik der reinen Vernunft*, (Königsberg: G. L. Hartung).

Scriven, M. (1962) 'Explanations, Predictions, and Laws', in H. Feigl and G. Maxwell (eds.) *Scientific Explanation, Space, and Time*, (Minneapolis: University of Minnesota Press), 170–230.

Stachel, J. (1980) 'Einstein and the Rigidly Rotating Disk', in A. Held (ed.) *General Relativity and Gravitation*, (New York: Plenum). Reprinted as 'The Rigidly Rotating Disk as the 'Missing Link' in the History of General Relativity', in D. Howard and J. Stachel (eds.) (1989) *Einstein and the History of General Relativity*, (Boston: Birkhäuser).

Stein, H. (1977) 'Some philosophical prehistory of General Relativity', in John Earman *et al.* (eds.) *Foundations of Space-Time Theories*, (Minneapolis: University of Minnesota Press), 3–49.

Stein, H. (1990) 'Eudoxus and Dedekind: On the Ancient Greek Theory of Ratios and Its Relation to Modern Mathematics', *Synthese* **84**, 163–211.

Stosch, G. J. E. (1772) *Versuch in richtiger Bestimmung einiger gleichbedeutenden Wörter der deutschen Sprache*, (Frankfurt an der Oder: Anton Gottfried Brauns Wittwe).

References

Sutherland, D. (2004) 'Kant's Philosophy of Mathematics and the Greek Mathematical Tradition', *Philosophical Review* **113**, 157–201.

Sutherland, D. (2006) 'Kant on Arithmetic, Algebra, and the Theory of Proportions,' *Journal of the History of Philosophy* **44**, 533–558.

Tait, W. (2005) 'Frege versus Cantor and Dedekind: On the Concept of Number', in W. Tait *The Provenance of Pure Reason. Essays in the Philosophy of Mathematics and its History*, (New York: Oxford University Press), 212–251.

Teller, P. (2001) 'Whither Constructive Empiricism?', *Philosophical Studies* **106**, 123–50.

Thomae, J. (1880/1898) *Elementare Theorie der analytischen Functionen einer complexen Veränderlichen*, (Halle a.S.: Nebert).

Torretti, R. (1990) *Creative Understanding: Philosophical Reflections on Physics*, (Chicago and London: University of Chicago Press).

van Fraassen, B. (1990) *Laws and Symmetry*, (New York: Oxford University Press).

van Fraassen, B. (2001) 'Constructive Empiricism Now', *Philosophical Studies* **106**, 151–70.

van Fraassen, B. (2006) 'Structure: its Shadow and Substance', *British Journal for the Philosophy of Science* **57**, 275–307.

van Fraassen, B. (2008) *Scientific representation: paradoxes of perspective* (Oxford: Oxford University Press).

Weinberg, S. (1993) *Dreams of a Final Theory*, (Cambridge, MA.: Harvard University Press).

Wigner, E. (1967) *Symmetries and Reflections*, (Bloomington: Indiana University Press).

Wigner, E. P. (1995) *Philosophical Reflections and Syntheses*, edited by J. Mehra and A. Wightman, (Berlin–Heidelberg–New York: Springer Verlag).

Wisan, W. L. (1978) 'Galileo's scientific method: a re-examination', in R. Butts and J. Pitt (eds.) *New Perspectives on Galileo*, (Dordrecht: Reidel), 1–58.

Woodward, J. (2003) *Making Things Happen*, (Oxford: Oxford University Press).